They Came Here First

They Came Here First

First

The Epic of the American Indian

D'Arcy McNickle

REVISED EDITION

PERENNIAL LIBRARY
Harper & Row, Publishers
New York, Evanston, San Francisco, London

To JOHN COLLIER,
Who believes in Indians

Reprinted by arrangement with J. B. Lippincott Company

Designed by Eve Kirch Callahan

First PERENNIAL LIBRARY edition published 1975

LIBRARY OF CONGRESS CATALOG CARD NUMBER: 75–981

STANDARD BOOK NUMBER: 06–080247–2

75 76 77 78 79 80   10 9 8 7 6 5 4 3 2 1

CONTENTS

Part 3: Supplanting a People

PREFACE

Trouble had come to one of the Hopi Indian villages. The people had been refusing to dip their sheep. They had even refused to count their sheep. These were matters which expert range managers considered important. Worse than that, since this was wartime, these Hopi Indians had refused to register for Selective Service, and neither would they sign a paper saying that they had religious scruples against taking up arms.

These, the *peaceful* people, as their name signifies, were causing serious trouble. It was necessary to find out why, and to remove, if possible, any causes of just complaint.

The government official drove up the mesa road—perhaps it ought to be explained that the Hopi Indians live in Arizona, in what on most maps is a blank expanse between the arms of the Colorado and the Little Colorado rivers. There are three mesas, like the fingers of a hand, on which the Hopi villages crouch in the sun. The hand itself is the northward running Black Mesa, which breaks into the wild country of the San Juan River.

The government official had to ask why these things were. Perhaps it was a misunderstanding. He was there to make things right. The speaker for the village had come from the fields in work clothes, but he honored the official by slipping a pair of store trousers over his earth-stained dungarees. The afternoon wore to evening while he talked of the things that troubled the villagers. As he talked the troubles which were in his mind settled upon the mind of the government official. And he, who had come to explain away doubt and misunderstanding, found perplexity instead.

The Hopi spokesman was never cantankerous; his voice was not even sharp, but his questions had a terrible urgency. He said: "When the Hopi people came from the underworld, they found people living in this land before them. These people had been living here a long time, and they knew many things about the world and the right way to live. Our Hopi people went to them and said, 'We would like to live here with you.' They replied, 'All right. You can stay here. We have certain rules here, ways of living, and you will have to follow these rules. Then there will be no trouble.' That's how it was. The Hopis did as they were told and they never had trouble. After a while the white men came. They did not ask if they could live with us. They just moved in. They did not ask what our rules were; instead they wrote rules for us to follow. 'Now you just obey these, and you won't get into trouble,' they said. How do you explain that?"

He did not wait for a response. There were too many questions yet to ask.

"Why do you put us in jail?" He was not a large man, but he spoke with such gravity one felt that he was indeed a man of strength and weight.

"In our Hopi life we have had bad people who did not keep the law, who went against the rules of the village. We had our ways of controlling these lawbreakers, without putting them in jail. Now you bring us laws and rules which are not even our own, and then you send us to jail for not obeying them. How do you explain that?"

Still he went on. "Now we have a drought. It has been bad for years and seems to get worse. The rains come less often. The grass is dying everywhere. You tell us we will have to give up our sheep. They are the only food we have. Yet you say we will have to give them up. Is this sensible? The sheep did not stop the rains. It is you who have caused that. You make regulations for us and our children. They must go to school. We must dip our sheep. We must count our sheep. We must write our names on papers we do not understand. You say it is to get sugar or to fight in wars we know nothing about. You have put so many of these regulations on us that we are confused. We are not able to concentrate on the things a Hopi must do, the ceremonies he must keep and the thoughts he must have. That is why it never rains and why the grasses are scarce. Before, we had more sheep than we have now, yet no one suffered. That is what I say."

When the government official came away in the dark, moonless summer night, he thought of all the answers which an intelligent, civilized official must give in defense of his creed and his position. He even wrote them down on paper when he got to a lighted room.

But in the morning, when there was sun again, the written answers did not suffice. Nothing that had been written before by white men would suffice either.

I was present at that conversation on the mesa. I tried to frame answers to the questions. As it turned out, there were hundreds of questions; one led into another and gave the mind no rest.

How did it happen that these Hopi Indians, after four hundred years of sharing their ancient land with invaders from another world, were not crushed? How was it that they could stand off, unhurried, and ask the white man to explain himself?

This was not the vanquished and the vanishing American. Here was a living voice, and a competent voice, asking the white man to justify his works. This was not what one read in the books.

To explain it, I discovered, one had to start way back and explain the Indians. Where did they come from? and when? and how? What was it like when they first came into the land? Where did they make their homes?

Perhaps, if one really tried, one could visualize something of what it was like. One ought to try. It was important.

PREFACE TO REVISED EDITION

Since the first edition of *They Came Here First* appeared in 1949 much has happened to affect Indian life, directly or indirectly. An enormous body of literature has accumulated, ranging from archaeological findings to inquiries into cultural process, and from reexamination of the Indian wars to studies of contemporary tribal government. This published material has helped to change public attitudes and, in a limited way, to modify national policy. The most remarkable development, however, is the manner in which Indian tribes, communities, and individuals have challenged the institutions within the general society, which through the years pursued a course of diminishing the Indian world. Tribes and communities did not disappear, the individual did not disclaim his kinship ties.

The consequence of this development is that the venturing people who were the first to come into the New World and who adapted to its infinite variety may yet adapt to the conditions imposed by the competitive, acquisitive majority. But in adapting, by long experience, they will remain a separate and identifiable tradition, adding color to the fabric of American life.

It seemed appropriate, in revising the text of this early study, to describe something of the process by which Indians have survived and yet remained constant to their own past.

Albuquerque
April 1975

PART 1

Unsealing a Continent

1

A FABULOUS LAND

"There is a new land over there. Somebody has been there and come back. So we hear. They had all the meat they could eat."

The world was full of rumors just then. A marvelous thing had happened. A new land had been discovered, and just when it was needed. The people had wandered for generations, their numbers dwindling, into a country of cold fogs, wild winds, without sheltering trees. Game was uncertain. Nights were long. A pitiful country. The people divided their camps into smaller numbers, each camp going on its own. And soon they were lost to each other, moving somewhere in that chilling fog.

And then, there were these rumors, voices coming out of the fog.

"Beyond over there . . . the land rises again. Wind comes up from the south, a warm wind. It clears away the fog. We came back to tell you."

The older people, sitting in their shelter of brush and skins, their eyes watery from smoke and age, were inclined to shrug it off. They had heard of such wonders before: only a little way ahead, things would be different. The winds would be warm. Their bellies would be filled.

The young ones, though, would not be put off. They would go ahead, if necessary, and find out for themselves. Across many campfires the matter was discussed, until the old ones saw that they had no choice. The camp must stay together. That was the only rule by which they lived. Wolves and the shadows took those who stayed behind.

That was how it started.

Earth and water will not tolerate barrenness. Life forms of all shapes and sizes move into any beckoning zone, however wretched its offering, take hold and multiply. When the nourishing environment can no longer sustain the feeding population, whether plant or animal, the seeds of new generations fly on the wind and footed creatures nudge their way into fresh fields.

"There is new land over there . . . plenty to eat."

Neither by accident nor by design, hunting populations moved northward and eastward, following the grass and the grass-eaters, across land that one day would not be there, swallowed by the waters of ocean. The movement was unhurried, since it had no destination. The trek was life itself, nothing stopped it for long. Here a folk might sojourn for a generation, or later ten generations; no one counted time. When the grass thinned and the game disappeared, young men ventured out in search of fatter land.

For thousands of years, wandering bands of hunters drifted toward the end of one world and entered a new. No one could tell that this was happening. Until the dividing waters came there would be only one world. The people followed where game fattened and where shelter and fresh water invited. They went where the young men scouted. Generations of men, children born, maturing, and dying as old men. The camps stayed together.

It seemed at first that they had moved into an entirely empty land. They saw mountains blocking the horizons, their summits perhaps locked in ice; broad rivers came out to breast the sea; prairies stretched out, a tawny ocean; forests darkened areas greater than the eye could encompass —and in all that emptiness, no living human folk. But wait! Here was an old campfire. Here a cave where smoke had blackened the roof. They paused there, and the land was less empty!

They had no name for the land they left, and no name either for the land they entered. No man knew the earth beyond the reaches of what he or other wanderers might cover in a lifetime. One man and his women folk and the men who married his daughters and all their children, with the goods they carried on their backs—these were the instruments of time and space by which the land was measured. Rivers and mountains and seacoasts were nameless except that a man in his own camp might lend his notion of what the thing looked like to him. In time some of these private-notion words would stick and be passed on as part of common speech.

They moved with their faces to the noontime sun, ever

southward. With a fresh new world to roam in, the old habit of wandering swept them along. The land grew fatter. Wild fruits flowered and bore. Edible roots were savored. Most gratifying of all were the sleek animals feeding in lush prairies, never before hunted and knowing no alarm. This was a land of feasting, just as had been told by a fireside. A fabulous land.

Even in speaking of themselves these moving bands had no common use term by which they recognized that they were one people with a common origin. When strange groups met by the greatest chance and found that they had no common speech, their amazement was mutual. Each had thought that no other such body of folk existed. Each in his own tongue, not understanding the other, would say: "I am Inunaina. . . . I am Tanekshaya. . . . I am Hasinai. . . . I am Diné. . . ." by which they meant, "I am of the people, or the first people, or the real people." It did not sound strange or presumptuous. Then, having identified themselves, no doubt, they hastened away.[1]

One day the bright new land would be called America and the people, by one man's miscalculation, would be called Indians.

So it began.

Before passing from generalizations to particulars, one final generalization is offered. Somewhere in the depths of time and space, which for now can be thought of as the lake country of East Africa, a primate branch turning into man scattered over the continents. The creature-becoming-man was a wanderer from the beginning. He went northward and eastward to the Asiatic mainland and the offshore islands. He spread westward along both shores of the Mediterranean Sea and reached the Atlantic, where he polished his tools and improved his posture. As ice retreated in the north, and forest and grasslands emerged, another human stream flowed northward and eastward out of the European heartland. As hunters in pursuit of their foods, their lives remained uncomplicated, perhaps even reduced in cultural baggage, as the land in which they wandered increased in harshness and allowed no ease. The populations making up this last great trek would climax their lives and build their temples in another place and another age.[2]

So it must have been.

2

ICE TELLS THE TIME

The story of creation told by the Indians of Acoma pueblo in New Mexico opens thus: "In the beginning two female human beings were born. These two children were born underground at a place called Shipapu. . . ." They were in darkness and they had to climb upward to reach the light.

The Tlingit story begins with the birth of Raven, who first had to make the world, then find out how to bring light to it. An old man living on the Nass River (in British Columbia) had the only light in the world, which he kept just for himself. He also had a daughter. The ingenious Raven quickly solved the problem of how to get into the old man's house. He not only contrived to get the girl pregnant, he was also the offspring, and as the grandson playing in the old man's house he managed to release first the stars, then the moon, and finally daylight itself.

The Kiowas of the Plains tell of how in the beginning: "All the creatures had one tongue. There was darkness, no light." They had to steal the sun and bring it to the earth.

The Zuñis, rather more elaborately, begin: "Yes, indeed. In this world there was no one at all. Always the sun came up; always he went in. No one in the morning gave him sacred meal; no one gave him prayer sticks; it was very lonely. He said to his two children: 'You will go into the fourth womb. Your fathers, your mothers . . . you will bring out yonder into the light of your sun father.'

"When they entered the fourth womb it was dark inside. They could not distinguish anything. They said, 'Which way will it be best to go?' They went toward the west, and in good time they gathered together all the things worth having, all the sacred observances, and brought them into the light of the sun father. He has never been lonely since, if sacred meal and prayer sticks could keep him from loneliness."[1]

In all of this myth and story there is no hint of another continent, no memory of a troubled past and a long trek out of the north. Nor should one expect any such tradition or memory. It was too long ago.

Speculation about the origin of man in the New World was as fanciful as the tribal myths and legends. Different theories were advanced, beginning within a few years of Columbus's voyages. Columbus himself did not speculate on the matter, since he assumed he had reached the outer boundaries of Asia. The early writers were constrained by theological concepts which traced man's ancestry to Adam and Eve, through Noah and his offspring. The search for New World origins accordingly was at first confined to biblical interpretation, with embellishments from classical mythology. A tale attributed to Aristotle told of certain Phoenician sailors who sailed westward and disappeared into the Atlantic. The tale was resurrected after Columbus's voyage with the explanation that he had discovered the descendants of the lost mariners. In another account, Plato's fabled continent of Atlantis provided a land bridge over which people crossed to the Americas, where they were isolated when Atlantis was destroyed by earthquake. A favorite theme, one which persisted into the nineteenth century, identified the Indians with the Lost Tribes of Israel, based on a supposed similarity between Hebrew and Aztec words and on certain customs and traditions said to be common to Jews and New World tribal people.

Writers of the sixteenth and seventeenth centuries might recognize the inadequacies of their explanations, but, like men in any age, they were circumscribed by the intellectual concepts of their times. There were exceptions, of course. Such an exception was José de Acosta, who in 1590 in Seville published the first of several volumes in which he argued that man and animals had crossed to the New World over a land bridge, the location of which was either in the South Seas, across from the Strait of Magellan, or off the northwest coast of North America. Acosta also reasoned that the migration of man and beasts was not accomplished as a single mass movement, but occurred over a period of time; and further, that the original migrants were nomadic hunters who in due course developed agriculture and a civil life of their own. He spent seventeen years as a

Jesuit missionary in Peru and Mexico, and hence was familiar with the culture of Middle America and the Andean highlands. In his reasoning he foreshadowed much of what later discoveries would advance as probable fact.[2]

Speculation yielded slowly to rational evidence. Methods for the controlled collecting of data, for analysis and interpretation, for comparative dating all had to be developed before a logic of effects could be surmised. The development of such methods is recent, especially with respect to the measurement of lapsed time, and the story of New World occupation is only now beginning to emerge.

Surveys and excavations carried out in the northwestern reaches of North America and across Siberia project possible migration routes and discover information about the technological level of the migrating populations, if not about the people themselves. Only so much can be inferred from the cultural artifacts a people leave behind.

Because of the close proximity of the Asiatic and American land masses at Bering Strait, and because of the geological history of the region as it becomes known, the northwestern corner of North America can be taken as the main port of entry for the first settlers. Other routes may have been used at later times, but these routes offer difficulties which early migrating man could not have mastered. Studies of the northern region indicate how naturally migration probably occurred.

Bering Strait is a comparatively shallow water passage. A drop in sea level of about forty meters is enough to expose dry land and join the continents. This lowering of sea level happened not once but a number of times during a span of several million years. The early incidents are not of interest here, except that they demonstrate a history of instability of sea level in relation to land masses.[3]

The mechanism accountable for the rise and fall of the sea was glaciation, the periodic conversion of literally mountainous masses of water into continental ice, and its later reversion. The so-called Ice Age, what geologists refer to as the Pleistocene, consisted of four major glacial periods, each divided by an ice-free interval. In North America the four glacial surges are named for the states to which the ice fields reached in their farthest thrust—the Nebraskan, the Kansan, the Illinoisan, and the Wisconsin.

The last of these, with which man's arrival in the New World is associated, is itself divided into several glacial climaxes and intervening ice-free periods. Shoreline studies reveal old beaches lying 135 meters and more below the present sea level, low enough to have exposed the entire Bering Strait basin.

Passage between the two continents depended not only on the presence of dry land, but on the location, extent, and duration of mainland ice. For migration of man, plants, and animals to take place there had to be clement periods when the sea was slowly rising and land routes were not blocked by ice. Such intervals can be roughly estimated, each lasting for several thousand years.

The first of these occurred earlier than 35,000 years ago, and presumably persisted for some time. A second interval occurred between 28,000 and 23,000 years ago. The last such land connection was between 13,000 and 10,000 years ago. During each of these time spans, sea level was 50 meters or more below present levels, and the Asiatic and North American continents constituted one land mass. The connecting bridge was as much as 1,000 miles wide at its maximum development, extending from the Alaskan Peninsula well beyond the Arctic Circle. This land bridge was drowned about 10,000 years ago and has not been reestablished since.

Without dismissing, for lack of a clear record, the possibility of earlier migrations, the five-thousand-year span between 28,000 and 23,000 years ago was an epoch when the Bering Strait was a vast region of tundra and steppe, and travel into the interior of North America was open. After 23,000 years ago the interior was blocked off by ice fields spreading from the Canadian shield all the way to the Rocky Mountains. By 13,000 years ago, the continental interior was again accessible from the north.

In broad lines, then, two time intervals, an early and a late, offered favorable conditions for the spread of populations. Migrations later than 10,000 years ago would have involved crossing open water. Technological advances in toolmaking and boatbuilding after that date would have eased that problem.

The likelihood that a broad land connection existed between the two continents, the duration of which was considerably greater than the entire span of time since the beginning of the Christian era, requires a basic revision in the conception of how the New World was first peopled.

The Bering Sea region, to which the term Beringia is

applied by geologists, was not an inhospitable Arctic desert through which living things hurried toward more inviting climates. Even to describe the movement of people into and across the area as a migration must be questioned. Adaptations were made, as other adaptations would be made elsewhere in the continent. Along the southern coast of the land bridge, part of which today remains as the eastern end of the Aleutian Island chain, a maritime culture flourished. On Umnak Island, midway along the chain, and formerly attached to the Alaska mainland, a village site 8,400 years old was apparently occupied by a population of sea hunters. As shorelines retreated before the advancing sea, the Aleuts withdrew to the island habitats they occupy today.

Inland on the land bridge, a different environment necessitated a different kind of conditioning. A possible reconstruction of the region is suggested by W. S. Laughlin: "There was ample space in the interior for small groups of hunters in bands of 50 or 100 . . . to move about in pursuit of game without intruding upon each other. The interior landscape was evidently a low rolling plain . . . lacking in trees or even many bushes. Grass eating herbivores may have been present in fair numbers. The human adaptation to this region must surely have been that of big game hunters."[4] The ultimate submergence of this far northern plain forced the hunters and the hunted alike to move either westward, back toward the Asiatic mainland, or eastward into a continent waiting to be explored and settled.

3

FLINT AND FIRE

If one spotted on a map of North America all the sites at which evidence of man has been found, usually associated with animals which long ago died out of the American landscape, animals such as the mammoth, the mastodon, the camel, archaic species of the horse and the bison, and others, practically every such site occurs south of the line attained by the latest glaciation. This may not prove anything, but it at least hints that some of the first settlers had reached well into the heart of the continent prior to 10,000 years ago. Campsites within the glacial area, with few exceptions, were obliterated.

Another peculiarity about these sites: usually they occur along the banks of the great streams which rise in the mountains. They make a pattern of the headwater drainages of such streams as the North and South Platte, the Arkansas, the Canadian, the Cimarron, the Red, the Brazos —nameless streams then, but offering sheltering thickets of willow and cottonwood. A route of travel it would seem, holding the mountains in view, moved southward from stream to stream. If all the early sites were known and spotted, the pattern might lead into Canada, down the Mackenzie to the Arctic coast or westward through the passes of Alaska.

A second route of travel lay along the high plateau, called the Great Basin, which lies to the west between the Rockies and the Cascade ranges. This region is actually a continuation of the wide corridor which leads from the Fraser River southward across the Columbia Plateau and merges finally with the Colorado Plateau. Today it is arid and not an inviting travel route to a people on foot, but until ten thousand years ago great lakes occupied valleys where today dust storms blow up and obscure the sky. The glacial period was a period of excessive moisture, and great rains fell in the regions where ice did not form. On the shores of these lakes, in today's eastern Oregon, western Nevada, central Utah, and southeastern California, in caves carved out by wave action, men came to lodge. Their fires smudged the walls and ceilings of their cave shelters, and scattered among the ashes have been found the bones of the animals they slaughtered and roasted.

A pattern of a different sort also emerges. These early hunters had a certain way of chipping flint, which is immediately recognizable, whether the specimens are unearthed east of the Rockies, in Saskatchewan or Texas. The first specimens of this distinctive flint work were found in Union County, New Mexico, almost at the headwaters of the Cimarron River, near a town named Folsom. A wandering cowboy, with no cattle on his mind at the moment, is said to have spotted some unfamiliar-looking bones protruding from the bank of a recently cut wash, many feet below the valley floor. The bones were those of an extinct bison, but what interested the scientists who came to investigate the find in 1926 was the fact that a spear point was embedded in one of these bones. They had never seen a spear or lance point like it anywhere. Since one of the tasks of scientists is to give names to things, they called these points "Folsom points."

Characteristically, the edges of a Folsom point are expertly, even delicately chipped. On each side, from base to apex, a broad channel is gouged out. Seen in cross section, it has the appearance approximately of a miniature football, partly deflated, and pushed in from opposite sides: a double concave with sharpened edges.

With the Folsom points are found a great variety of stone and bone weapons and tools, and they are associated with the bones of extinct animals, usually those of the wide-horned bison. They have never been found among the remains of any known historic tribe.

This 1926 discovery was followed within a few years by a number of other discoveries, which together gave the first clear evidence of early settlement in the New World. Still later, as more precise methods were developed for measuring the age of materials recovered from the earth, it became possible to estimate dates for man's presence in the Americas.[1]

The Folsom point, it is now known, was but one of

several projectile types fashioned by a race of skilled flint workers. A slightly cruder and evidently earlier specimen is the Clovis point, named after the Clovis, New Mexico, site where it was first discovered. This lance-shaped blade, like the Folsom point, is also channeled on both faces, but the channeling extends only part way up from the base and the edges are not as finely chipped as are the Folsom specimens. At a period somewhat later than the Folsom tradition a great proliferation of flint working occurred, resulting in a variety of shapes, sizes, and technical refinements. To these later forms the general term Plano is applied. Taken together, these three stone-culture technologies are associated with a period variously termed Big Game Hunting or Paleo-Indian. They refer to a time when the ancestors of the historic Indians were perhaps exclusively hunters, and the tools and weapons they left behind were those used for killing and butchering game animals. Only much later would tools for seed grinding, gardening, woodworking, and other domestic uses be found. The animals hunted in that early period are now extinct.

By radiocarbon dating, a measuring device based on the analysis of the radioactive carbon content of organic materials, it has been possible to determine the age of many of the campsites of this early race of hunters. In some locations where occupation occurred at separate intervals in time, the older or bottom level was occupied by men who fashioned Clovis (also called Llano) points. The Folsom material is found at higher or later levels, and in a few instances the remains of historic Indians are found on or near the surface. Such a stratification occurs, for example, at Ventana Cave on the Papago reservation in southern Arizona.

The range in time of this Big Game Hunting or Paleo-Indian phase is within the span of 15,000 to 7,000 years ago, with the greatest number of established dates clustered around 11,500 to 7,000 years before the present.[2]

While the first discoveries of early occupation were made in the High Plains, along the foothills and the drainages cutting through the plains, later investigations revealed that hunters fashioning the Clovis-type armory, within the time span indicated above, spread all the way to the Atlantic coast, northward to the retreating ice fields, and southward into Mexico and beyond. The Strait of Magellan was reached by at least 7000 B.C. The whole of North America and much of South America was occupied, with a variety of local adaptations, within a remarkably short time for travelers on foot unaided by burden-bearing beasts.

These established dates do not exhaust the possibilities of man in the New World. Throughout both continents, in sheltering caves and in open sites, remains have been found of an older and cruder style of existence. Instead of the skillfully fashioned spearpoints and knife edges of the Clovis-Folsom-Plano occupation, the tools and weaponry are heavier, blunter, suggesting a simpler order of technical skill. The implements commonly found at these locations are those used for pounding, crude cutting or chopping, and scraping. The people lived by hunting (at one location more than thirty different animal species were identified), but the method of taking game probably involved the use of wooden spears and clubs.

Archaeologists have been reluctant to accept the time depths suggested for this apparently older occupation. Where dates have been proposed based on radiocarbon findings, some contaminating circumstance injects elements of uncertainty that leaves the findings in doubt. At Lewisville, Texas, for example, organic material dated at more than 38,000 years is questioned because of the presence of an intrusive artifact belonging to a much later age. By what accident this might have occurred cannot be explained, and therefore the evidence is rejected, at least until corroborating findings can be accepted.[3]

These difficulties aside, there is a growing volume of evidence favoring the view that the first settlers in the Americas preceded by several thousand years the Big Game Hunters whose presence has been established by dated findings. The possibility of occupation occurring 35,000 or 40,000 years ago is not beyond reason. A certain logic supports the possibility, since the delicately fluted and edged projectile points of the Clovis-Folsom-Plano traditions were developed in the New World. Their counterparts have not been found, if they ever existed, on the Asiatic side of Bering Strait. Highly efficient flint workmanship is found along the route of travel out of Asia, but it occurs at a much later time.

The existence of a land bridge at a time prior to 35,000 years ago, as already noted, further supports the possibility of the earlier migration. Other factors pointing to that possibility will be discussed further along.

For reasons not yet clarified, a major ecological crisis was encountered by the Big Game Hunters in the centuries immediately preceding 10,000 years ago. By that time man had occupied the northern continent from coast to coast and had penetrated well into South America. The last glacial advance had receded and a warmer and drier climate brought about the recession of many of the great bodies of water that formerly lay trapped in mountain valleys.

As a contemporary occurrence of these gross environmental changes, the game animals upon which the hunters subsisted began to disappear and were never replaced by species of like size and habits. The last mammoth was killed by hunters in Arizona some 11,000 years ago. The mastodon, another form of elephant, may have survived until later in the Great Lakes region. Altogether some thirty or more genera of major animals, most of them grass-eaters but including predators like the saber-tooth cats who hunted them, disappeared before 10,000 years ago.

The view is no longer maintained that these biological losses were a direct result of climatic changes coming at the end of the glacial period.[4] The ancestors of the same species had survived previous postglacial transformations, which occurred at irregular intervals all through the so-called Ice Age. Plants and animals are not permanently fixed in place, but are capable of moving away from unfavorable conditions and making new adaptations. One element had been added, however, which had not been present during previous glacier-free epochs. This was the human hunter armed with greatly improved equipment, with projectile points that with the aid of a spear thrower could be hurled with great force. The bow and arrow may not have been in this early arsenal, but a four-inch spearpoint of finely edged flint mounted on a shaft delivered a lethal thrust. The frequency with which Clovis and Folsom points are found in association with the fossilized bones of extinct animals of late glacial times raises a distinct possibility that man contributed more than casually to the disappearance of these beasts. The later developed and more varied Plano points are associated with the hunters of later times, who pursued the modern bison and lesser animals of the grasslands. By that time, also, life in the Americas was undergoing a gradual adaptation to other subsistence modes.

4

FLESH AND BONE

Other factors, less substantial than shaped flint, have their place in time reckonings.

The long reach of the hemisphere from the Arctic to the Strait of Magellan is marked by at least eight major climatic zones, each of which presented challenges to human settlement. The mastering of these challenges occupied some thousands of years and brought about the widest variation in life-styles, economies, and efficiency in ecological adjustment. It was an experience calculated to develop a venturing, adaptable people, deeply attached to a responsive earth. Such a people, understandably, came to have a reverence for the land that subsisted and sheltered them.

While migrating groups moved about and settled in, another kind of clock measured off their days. The languages they spoke bore some internal relatedness, within broad divisions, but with a single exception they bore no relationship to other languages in the world, a consequence of long separation from other language families. The exception is the Eskimo-Aleut group, whose speech shows some affinity with the speech of eastern Siberian tribes, but the resemblance is more theoretical than confirmed.

This Eskaleut group, while related, constitutes a system in the process of separating into fragments—again a function of time lapse. Since Aleut occupation dates appear to be older than known early Eskimo sites, it is assumed that Eskimo speech diverged from Aleut. Linguists have a formula by which they can approximate the rate at which word forms and meanings change through time. The Aleut and Eskimo speakers evidently began going their separate ways some 4,500 years ago. A lesser division within the Eskimo language itself developed about 1,500 years ago. The divergence has progressed to a point where Arctic coast Eskimos and the Eskimos in Greenland can no longer communicate with the Eskimos of the Kuskokwim region.[1]

The factor of language change, and more particularly the slow rate at which such change takes place, is thus an element in reckoning the age of man in the New World. It is unlikely that each of the several hundred separate languages spoken in the two continents represents a separate migrating population. This leaves the alternative probability that a few base languages were involved initially and that then these proliferated over varying time spans to account for the linguistic diversity of native America. This will be discussed again in another context.

What has been said about language can also be said, in a limited way, about physical characteristics—the few gave rise to the many. The first migrating populations represent a relatively uniform biological type—possibly a composite of earlier stocks, but carrying the genetic potential for a great variety of adaptations and modifications.

The Indian constitutes one of the major races of mankind. As used here, race signifies, in its simplest terms, a group of physical characteristics which are passed on from one generation to another. Race has nothing to do with language, types of political, religious, or social organization. Racial traits, moreover, are not easily affected by changes in environment. Also they appear to be a mass of related features. Individuals within a racial group may vary considerably, yet if all the individuals are measured and described and an average computed for all the extremes, it will be found that no individual differs so widely as to fall entirely outside the group.[2]

The Indian racial type has this variability within a broad homogeneity. The Indian, typically, is pictured as possessed of a strong eagle beak of a nose, but actually the nose is one of the most variable of all the features in the composite picture.

The traits which remain fairly constant have to do with such features as color and texture of the hair, which is black, straight, and coarse; eye color, ranging from medium to dark brown; and skin color, which has a wide range, from light yellow brown to a dark red brown. The blood type of the pure Indian is also a constant. Types A and B are almost universally lacking, leaving type O to dominate. Because of this consistency, serologists place Indians in an American-Pacific blood class, including pure-blood Filipinos.

The range of variation reaches the widest extremes in such factors as head form, from long and narrow to broad or round; nasal index, as mentioned; and body length.

The profile view of the composite Indian type shows a face that is rather large for the mass of the head. The line of the face runs straight up and down, or it may bulge slightly where the teeth come together. The chin projects moderately, the cheekbones are usually heavy and prominent, and the brow may have a slight backward slope.

For convenience in describing and classifying the human species, physical anthropologists have attached certain names to head and facial forms. It is more convenient to measure and describe a skull than an entire skeleton, but no other significance attaches to the measurements or the terms used. Granted the soundness of the theory that racial characteristics are passed on by inheritance and tend to persist, it should be possible to identify the race of a thousand- or a ten-thousand-year-old skull.

Physical anthropologists, working separately from the geologists and the archaeologists, have sketched out a pattern of migration into the New World, which agrees in many respects with material dredged up by the other workers. And this in spite of the fact that skeletal remains are missing from the earliest deposits of fabricated weapons and tools.

The very earliest skulls are strikingly similar in one detail: they are all long-headed. Further, these long-headed skulls have all been found southward from the farthest reach of glaciation, a distribution which would appear to support other evidence that the first waves of migration may have preceded the final ice stage. If the settlers had come after the ice had cleared away, long-headed skulls would have been found north of the glacial line.

The change of head shape, from long to broad or round-headedness, was not a sudden occurrence, such as might result from an invading population supplanting an earlier people. The shift was gradual and proceeded unevenly over the two continents. The probability favors a long process of interbreeding between mingling population groups, although it has also been suggested that the genetic change reflects an ongoing evolutionary process, a development not limited to New World populations.

5

AND STRANGE TONGUES

It has been remarked that the diversity of languages—the number of separate languages spoken—in the New World was greater than in all the rest of the world combined. In North America alone it has been estimated that at least 500, perhaps as many as 1,000 languages, were spoken in pre-Columbian times; while for the entire Western Hemisphere the number may have been as high as 2,200. Each language, moreover, was usually a cluster of related forms or dialects, some close and mutually intelligible, others only remotely related. Rarely was a language represented by a single population group.

Contrary to what was once believed, Indian languages were not "primitive" in the sense of having limited vocabularies or of lacking in grammatical structure. Any language reflects the environment in which the speakers function, but, again as with any linguistic system, Indian languages were capable of incorporating new elements and expanding the range of understanding and meaning. It has even been suggested that Kant's *Critique of Pure Reason* could be translated more readily into the Achomawi language of northern California than into English, because the Indian tongue handled abstract thought with greater ease.

The process by which this amazing diversity of speech came about is only imperfectly understood. At one time it was assumed that New World settlement did not extend far enough back in time to allow for any considerable language growth. But this assumption gained currency at a time when first settlement was expressed in terms of a few thousand years.

Franz Boas held the view that a multiplicity of languages characterizes the early history of man everywhere in the world, and that the tendency was for certain of these languages to disappear either by falling out of use or by coalescing with others.[1]

Later writers, Morris Swadesh among them, see a reverse process operating through time. They look for nuclear languages or stocks, "mother" tongues, to which other languages can be related in varying degrees of affinity. In connection with this search modern linguists developed a system for comparing languages by which degrees of relatedness can be established. By working first with historical languages having a written form, it was discovered that basic vocabularies change at a fairly constant rate. Over a period of 1,000 years, an average of about 20 percent of the words in a standard word list will change from their original form. This makes it possible to compare word lists in two related languages and compute in approximate terms the elapsed time since the languages separated. The theoretical assumption is that language speakers spread out from original homelands and develop local speech habits, which become more pronounced with the passage of time and the loss of association with the parent group. By such a process the languages first carried into the New World broke into segments to form separate variants of the mother tongue, and in time to pass beyond the range of mutual communication. Given a time span of from 15,000 to 30,000 years for the beginning of settlement, linguistic shifts, including the disappearance of older forms of speech as well as new growths, could easily account for the bewildering variety of languages in native America.[2]

The first attempt to classify the languages of the American Indians was made by J. W. Powell, of the Bureau of American Ethnology, in 1891. He also adopted a system of nomenclature still in use, by which tribal proper names are given the suffix -*an* to denote groups of related languages Thus, the Sioux-speaking people are classified as Siouan, Shoshone as Shoshonean, and so on.

Powell compiled for the region north of Mexico a list of fifty-six language stocks, each of which contained at least one language, while some contained forty or more sister languages. Altogether, the fifty-six stocks contained about five hundred separate languages and dialects within languages, some of which were extinct long before Powell wrote. He based his classification principally on an examination of vocabularies. He took no account of structural peculiarities or phonetics, largely because he lacked material to work with.

Others who followed Powell, notably Boas and Sapir, aided by investigations in language form which they and others carried out, were able to establish relationships where none had appeared to exist before. Sapir was particularly brilliant in identifying connectives and suggesting new combinations. Although he died while still relatively young, he had already succeeded in regrouping Powell's fifty-six language stocks into six basic types. Some modifications have since been adopted, but essentially his types have been accepted. The scheme given here is intended only to indicate how the plan of classification works out.[3]

The Pacific coast from California to the northern boundary of Oregon was a region of astonishing language diversity. Dozens of small groups lived side-by-side, speaking in tongues that were incomprehensible outside of the groups that spoke them, yet never apparently influencing each other's languages. Other linguistic groups included large populations. Kroeber estimated that more than 70 percent of the population north of Mexico was comprised in eight language groups or families. These were: Algonquian, with 192,000; Eskimo-Aleut, 89,700; Siouan, 88,500; Iroquoian, 71,700; Muskogean, 66,500; Uto-Aztecan, 63,100; Athabascan, 60,500; and Salishan, 57,900. Eighteen other language groups had populations ranging from 27,000 down to 6,000; and thirty had a range of from 5,000 to 500. These are estimates as of the time of Columbus.

The number and distribution of related languages, or units within a language family, can be useful in estimating time intervals, particularly in determining the relative age of contrasting linguistic groups. By using such factors, C. F. Voegelin has suggested a possible order of migration into the New World.[4]

Examining the six language types of Sapir's classification, he notes that the Hokan-Siouan type contains the greatest number of separate linguistic families, which in turn are divided into the greatest number of individual languages. Also, these various divisions and subdivisions had the widest geographical distribution, from the Gulf of St. Lawrence (Iroquois) to the California coast (Karok, etc.), and from the Canadian border (Assiniboine) to the Gulf of Mexico (Chitimacha, etc.). All of this vast territory was not continu-

Table 5-1. LANGUAGES NORTH OF MEXICO

TYPE	FAMILY	COMPONENTS
I. Eskimo-Aleut	1. Eskimo	two languages
	2. Aleut	possibly two languages
II. Algonquian-Wakashan	1. Algonquian	thirteen languages
	2. Wiyot and Yurok	one language
	3. Kutenai	one language
	4. Quileute	one language
	5. Wakashan	six languages
	6. Salishan	fifteen languages
III. Nadene	1. Athabascan	nineteen languages
	2. Eyak	one language
	3. Thlingit	one language
	4. Haida	one language
IV. Aztec-Tanoan	1. Uto-Aztecan	ten languages
	2. Tanoan	four languages
	3. Kiowa	one language
	4. Zuñi	one language
V. Penutian	1. Yokutan	three languages
	2. Maiduan	four languages
	3. Miwokan	two languages
	4. Wintuan	two languages
	5. Klamath-Modoc	one language
	6. Molala	one language
	7. Sahaptin	two languages
	8. Takelma	one language
	9. Lower Umpqua-Siuslaw	one language
	10. Alsea	one language
	11. Coos	one language
	12. Kalapuyan	two languages
	13. Chinookan	two languages
	14. Tsimshian	one language
VI. Hokan-Siouan	1. Washo	one language
	2. Pomo	four languages
	3. Yukian	three languages
	4. Shasta-Achomawian	three languages
	5. Karok	one language
	6. Yuman	four languages
	7. Iroquoian	six languages
	8. Siouan	eight languages
	9. Caddoan	four languages
	10. Keresan	one language
	11. Muskogean	four languages
	12. Tunica	one language
	13. Natchez	one language
	14. Chitimacha	one language
	15. Yuchi	one language
	16. Tonkawa	one language

ously occupied, but rather it was broken into numerous areas of various sizes, suggesting that segmentation had taken place repeatedly, that later invading peoples had split the territory apart. All these factors, together with the assumption that at least the major language blocks came intact from the Asiatic side, lead to the conclusion that the Hokan-Siouan peoples must have been the first to enter the strange land. Only the passage of incalculable time lapses could account for this pattern of wide speech diversity and extensive territorial distribution.

The contrasting group is, of course, the Eskimo-Aleut, which occupied a continuous territory around the northern rim of Asia and North America and within which there was a minimum of speech deviation. The archaeological record, moreover, makes almost certain the conclusion that the Eskimo-Aleut peoples were the latest to arrive.

The arrangement of the four remaining groups requires some arbitrary judgments, but a plausible order of precedence would place the Algonquian-Wakashan group next in succession following the Hokan-Siouan, the Aztec-Tanoan next, followed by the Penutian, and the Nadene.

This division into language groups is a convenience of classification; it provides no information about the people who spoke the languages.

Before describing some of these societies of pre-Columbian America, it will help to have in mind how the Indian population was distributed in the area north of Mexico and where its principal concentrations occurred. And it ought to be recalled that discovery extended over a period of more than four hundred years, from Columbus to the final exploration of the western United States. Hence, it has been exceedingly difficult to arrive at a satisfactory population estimate.

The first explorers often had only the vaguest notion of population counts in the tribes they encountered, or they gave exaggerated accounts. Tribes jarred out of place by the first settlements were thrown into competition with outlying tribes, competition which not only produced wars of extermination, but brought on food shortages and starvation. Deadliest of all were the European diseases, which started with tribes in contact with white men and scourged tribes a thousand miles away whose existence was not even suspected by the white settlements on the littoral.

It has been suggested that aboriginal America was relatively free of disease. As the early populations passed through the Arctic north infectious bacteria were destroyed by freezing temperatures. The north served as a decontaminating station. This, of course, is conjecture, but for whatever reason the Indian population was exceedingly vulnerable to disease imported from Europe. The physical anthropologist Ales Hrdlicka noted, "The condition of the skeletal remains, the testimony of early observers, and the present state of some of the tribes in this regard, warrant the conclusion that on the whole the Indian race was a comparatively healthy one."[5]

Population figures for aboriginal America obviously cannot be cited as of a given date. What we have is a composite taken from widely separated points of time, often from overlapping and conflicting original sources.

The first compilation of this sort was made by James Mooney of the Smithsonian Institution. He died before his task was completed and Swanton took it over, adding considerable material of his own.[6]

The total population for the area north of Mexico, according to this Mooney-Swanton estimate, was 1,153,000. Geographically, the distribution was as follows: for that area within the present boundaries of continental United States, 849,000; for Canada and all the area in the Far North, 221,000; for Alaska, 73,000; and for Greenland, 10,000.

Kroeber made an independent investigation and arrived at a slightly lesser figure, 1,000,880, for the same total area. He arranged his material in eight territorial divisions, as follows:

Table 5–2. POPULATION NORTH OF MEXICO

AREA	POPULATION	DENSITY
California	84,000	43.30 per 100 km.
Northwest coast	129,200	28.30
Southwest	103,000	10.70
Columbia-Fraser	47,650	7.15
Eastern	426,400	6.95
Arctic coast	89,700	4.02
Great Basin	26,700	2.47
Northern	94,230	1.35
Total: 1,000,880		Average: 5.35

This arrangement brings out a rather interesting impression. While generally it is assumed that agriculture permits and indeed encourages the greatest concentration of population, this apparently was not the experience of aboriginal America. The Pacific coast, from California northward through the Columbia-Fraser region and up the Northwest coast to Bering Strait, was almost exclusively a fishing economy, but apparently it was also the area of greatest population density, having a combined average of 25.2 per 100 km. The primary agricultural area, stretching from the Southwest eastward to the Atlantic, had a population density of 10.1 per 100 km.

Mooney made an incidental listing of the various epidemics referred to in the early records. In the Plains region alone he found: in 1691 an epidemic of unknown character struck east Texas and adjacent Louisiana and 3,000 members of the Caddo tribe perished; in 1778 smallpox ravaged the same territory and nearly obliterated several tribes not specified; in 1781–82 smallpox spread over the entire country of the upper Missouri River and northward as far as Great Slave Lake and the fur trade was paralyzed for two years; in 1801 smallpox swept the region from the Gulf to the Dakotas; 1837–38, a smallpox epidemic spreading from the Red River of the North to the Saskatchewan practically wiped out the Mandan tribe; 1849, cholera moved into the central plains area and killed about one-fourth of the Pawnee tribe; 1870–71, still another smallpox epidemic swept the northern plains, striking the Assiniboine, Blackfeet, and Cree Indians.

California provides in stark detail the record of Indian decline following white settlement. In 1853, four years after the great gold rush, the Indians in the state have been estimated at 100,000; by 1856 the number was reduced to 48,000; in 1864 it was not over 30,000; and in 1906 it fell to 19,014.

Population studies of aboriginal America in recent years suggest the possibility of a sharp upward revision of previous estimates. Dobyns finds that earlier studies often gave little credence to population counts reported by early missionaries or military men, without adequately defending their skepticism, while a more serious defect was the failure to take account of population losses resulting from epidemic disease following contact with Europeans. By applying a "standard" depopulation ratio to account for losses due to disease or other factors introduced by European settlement, Dobyns proposes a population estimate for North America including Greenland of between 9,800,000 and 12,250,000. The proposal is tentative and will be subjected to rigorous examination.[7]

6

NEW WORLD PERSPECTIVES

By such means and at such times as those roughly suggested, the first comers, whom we call Indians, crossed over into the New World and settled the land. They were not all one people; each tribe or band was probably a self-contained unit, with its own language, its own tools, its own customs.

Where these tribes and bands came to rest, there they lived, in torrid heat and parched plain, along green forests, and in tundra wastes. Along with the sustenance which they drew from the earth and the sun, they also drew visions and a sense of their everlasting place in the universe.

The adjustments which the people made were at least as varied as the land was broad and diverse. The longer they lived in the environment the richer and more subtle became the adjustments, as their lives flowed together and as the generations reached deeper into the wells of experience.

Kroeber suggested a basic pattern of Indian economy, which can be taken as a useful starting place. He designated two broad areas in which farming dominated: the first one running from the Valley of Mexico in a narrow strip up the west coast of Mexico and fanning out somewhat to include the eastern half of Arizona and the western half of New Mexico and ending in Utah, Nevada, and Colorado; the second, a larger area, going northward from the Gulf of Mexico along the one hundredth meridian to the Canadian border and including the entire eastern country to the Atlantic.[1]

The western farming area evidently acquired its food habits from Mexico. Corn was ground on a stone slab, or metate, and the meal was made up into a thin dough and fried on a hot stone, making a tortilla. In the eastern area, by contrast, the corn was pulverized in a wooden mortar, then boiled plain or with meat or converted into hominy. These food-processing habits appear to derive from the West Indies, though it is difficult to demonstrate a method or a time of contact.

Generalizations about the Indian race are to be approached cautiously, or they disappear in verbiage. In describing native America it is customary to divide the population into type groups, using a variety of defining characteristics. A favorite model is the culture area, in which all of North America is segmented into some eight or nine geographical regions, each characterized by its special life-style. According to the culture-area concept, a hunting region was occupied by hunters, and it was possible to generalize about the camps in which they lived, the kinds of tools and weapons they used, the makeup of their families, the beliefs they sustained or were sustained by, their relationship to the land, and any number of other attributes that identify the people as hunters. That was what they were by definition. That was their destiny. Or if they were seed gatherers of the Great Basin, fish eaters of the Northwest Coast, or corn growers of the Southwest, they could not be anything else without doing violence to the concept. The generalizations were true, within limits, but they obscured the individual, the hunter who was first of all a man, and maybe the kind of hunter who tripped over his own feet in the woods.

What is most lacking in the culture-area concept, as first adopted by Clark Wissler as a device for classifying museum specimens, is any reference to sequential change or growth. Populations are seen as locked in time and space, like the figures in a still photograph. The concept made for convenience in classifying a mass of artifactual information, but it perpetuated an old habit of presenting Indians in the language of stereotype.

Native America was not a static world, but was rather a theater of action, of movement, of climactic growth, of decline and rebirth. In the Ohio and Mississippi river valleys great burial mounds, representing vast communal efforts, were already abandoned and overgrown when first observed by white men early in the nineteenth century. In the Southwest, masonry houses comparable in size to modern apartment blocks had fallen into ruins before Coronado entered the area in 1540. A tribe of hunting people traveled out of the far north, from somewhere in the Alaskan interior or the Northwest Territories of Canada, and came to rest alongside the village-dwelling Pueblos. One of these tribes, the Navajos of today, adopted many practices, including farming, from their Pueblo neighbors, and thereby demonstrated that a hunting people could make over its way of life. Their kinsmen, the Apache tribes, incidentally, remained closer to their traditions as huntsmen. Still another northern group, presumably hunters whose original homeland has not been determined, blustered their way into the Valley of Mexico where they learned new skills and ideologies, out of which they fashioned the Aztec empire.

Tribal movements are only dimly discernible in the ages before first contact with the explorers, traders, and missionaries who preceded the first waves of European settlers. But enough has been learned from archaeological recovery to suggest the major thrusts of a radiating population. Out of the Mississippi River valley, beginning about A.D. 1, agricultural people moved westward, following tributary streams, planting gardens of corn, beans, and squash in river bottoms, and building permanent villages. Historic tribes, such as the Mandan, Arikara, Pawnee, Wichita, and others, are the likely descendants of these early Plainsmen. Some of these agriculturists, as a consequence of their acquisition of the horse, abandoned their plantings and became the restless Dakotas and Cheyennes, living off the thundering buffalo herds. In the Canadian north, Algonquian-speaking bands emerged from the coniferous forests north of the Great Lakes and spread westward until they reached the Rocky Mountains. These were the Ojibwa, the Saulteaux, the Crees, who ran the trap lines and manned the canoes of the northern fur industry.

The impression of mobility, of people moving on to the land and blending with it, is reinforced by plotting out trade routes along which the feathers of exotic tropical birds and little copper bells were carried out of Mexico into the southwestern United States; Rocky Mountain obsidian reached the Ohio River valley; pipestone and copper, mined in the Great Lakes region, was transported east and west; iridescent seashells went from both oceans deep into the interior to appear as ear pendants and breast plaques. Even the stories recited by grandfathers to eager young listeners told of travels to far places, fabled or otherwise, encounters with strangers, gift exchanges. The young were encouraged to strike out on their own and learn about the world around them. In the accounts of early explorers and traders frequent mention is made of finding Indians from distant tribes visiting the host tribe. Tribes knew their own boundaries, and they knew and respected the boundaries of their neighbors, but there were no walls in native America.

It is true, nevertheless, that adaptations were made to the different environmental opportunities and limitations, and in this sense it is possible to describe the land and the people in terms of a museum classification system.

WHERE MANY TRAILS CROSSED
The East

The vast region between the High Plains and the Atlantic shoreline, consisting of a variety of habitats, climates, and natural resources, can be thought of as sharing some elements of a common development and giving rise to a wide range of adaptations and sequential change. The greater Southwest suggests a similar area-wide uniformity of experience, more limited in physical expanse and with a narrower range of adaptation and change, a factor of a less generous environment.[2]

After the disappearance of the early animal species already mentioned, hunters adapted to a more varied subsistence base. Game animals continued to be hunted, but these were the modern species of deer, elk, antelope, and bison. In the areas where game was abundant, as in the grasslands of the High Plains and in the timbered north, hunting still provided the main source of foodstuffs, shelter, and clothing. But to an increasing extent, where the climate was mild and plant life flourished, people learned to supplement their meat diet with the proteins and starches of wild plants. It is entirely likely, of course, that the big-game hunters of earlier times made use of vegetable foods where these were available. What was different in this later period was an increase in knowledge about useful plants, and also a remarkable growth in the number and variety of tools and techniques for gathering, processing, storing, and cooking vegetable foods, and for preparing vegetable fibers for weaving domestic goods.

The transition took place about 9,000 years ago. This is not a precise date and it was not everywhere the same, but at approximately that time throughout the eastern half of the continent the first stone slabs for milling or grinding seeds came into use. As will be discussed at another place, this seed-grinding equipment had an earlier development in the desert country west of the Rocky Mountains.

The adaptation that eventually spread across the eastern region was varied, reflecting available natural resources, but within this diversity a basic similarity of life-style prevailed. The physical environment was explored for its life-supporting potential. Extensive shell mounds, the accumulation of generations of occupation along shoreline and inland waters, suggest the possibility of permanent villages. In deciduous forest areas acorns modified to make breadstuffs, together with other wild fruits and nuts, supplemented by small game, supported settlements equally enduring.

Over a 5,000-year period, between 7000–2000 B.C., exploitation of the natural environment became so efficient in terms of subsistence and population growth that when domesticated maize reached the eastern region, presumably from Middle America, it had no immediate effect in altering or increasing the food supply. Corn was a minor addition to an already ample diet.

Preoccupation with death became a major emphasis after about 1000 B.C. This gave rise to literally thousands of earthen mounds, often of spectacular shape and size, representing massive public-works efforts. The earliest of these mounds, identified as Adena, are found in central Ohio, and from there the practice spread into Indiana, Kentucky, West Virginia, and Pennsylvania. A later and somewhat more elaborate cultural involvement with death, called Hopewell, had an even wider distribution. From what was probably its place of beginning on the lower Illinois River, the Hopewell influence reached to Iowa, Kansas, Missouri, Wisconsin, Minnesota, Michigan, eastward to Pennsylvania and New York, as far south as Florida and Louisiana. These burial structures, giving rise to the term Mound Builders, were a source of much speculation and erroneous assumptions in the early years of exploration by Europeans.

When the English astronomer-traveler Francis Baily accompanied a party of settlers down the Ohio River in 1796, he investigated a number of mounds at Grave Creek and found that they had already been opened up and human bones and other materials had been removed. Visitors had even carved their names in the bark of a tree growing at the top of the highest mound. He commented that the mounds were obviously "built by a race of people more enlightened than the present Indians, and at some period of time far distant; for the present Indians know nothing about their use, nor have they any traditions concerning them."

The mortuary practices of the Adena and Hopewell periods are not properly descriptive of the culture of the people but represent an intrusive cult, probably religious, with associated art forms, symbols, and ideologies. The source of at least some of the symbolism if not the burial practices as well can be traced to the Valley of Mexico. There is no indication of a migrating or invading population from the south, but rather a possible migration of ideas carried along trade routes. The influences from Middle America became more pronounced at a later date, but up until the end of the Hopewell period, about A.D. 250, the people of the midcontinent experienced few basic changes in their way of life. They had long ago achieved a balanced economy based on skillful exploitation of their environment. The Hopewell style persisted long after the characteristic burial mounds ceased to be built. In places far removed from the Ohio River, where the Hopewell culture flourished most vividly, its effects were registered in pottery designs, decorative symbolism, ceremonial practices, and possibly in social structure.

After centuries of increasing regional specialization and diversity, a trend toward a kind of mass culture set in at about A.D. 500. From its nurturing center along a stretch of the Mississippi River between St. Louis, Missouri, and Natchez, Mississippi, a new and vigorous life-style spread to all corners of the eastern half-continent. The initiating force was probably a newly acquired and higher yielding variety of maize, introduced from Mexico; and it is also likely that people from elsewhere moved into the nuclear area bringing new crops and a new social order with them. Older populations were not disturbed in their prior settlements, but new centers grew up all around them. Villages of thatched-roof houses increased in size, many of them occupying up to twenty acres in area, and there was a general population growth.

What is most characteristic of the new order, now called Mississippian, are the ceremonial centers, dominated by one or more massive platform mounds. These were earthworks, built in the form of a truncated pyramid, on the flat surface of which were erected temples or other public structures. A leveled plaza surrounded the mound and presumably accommodated crowds of performers and onlookers.

Largest of these was the Cahokia Mound in the river bottom near St. Louis. This stands one hundred feet high, after centuries of settling and erosion, and measures 700 by 1,080 feet at the base. The entire complex occupied sixteen acres. The central mound has been estimated to contain 22 million cubic feet of earth, all of which was carried probably in baskets on human backs. A lesser but still impressive structure is the Etowah Mound in northern Georgia.

The centers were not occupied by a secular population but were used for religious and possibly political purposes. The supporting population lived in and farmed the surrounding countryside—a pattern of settlement that duplicates more or less similar centers in Middle America. The building and functioning of such centers suggests some form of social hierarchy, with farmers and laborers occupying a status distinct from artisans, priests, and a ruling class of functionaries.

This expanding Mississippian culture, with its productive agriculture, ceremonial complexes, and highly sophisticated pottery reached northward to the Great Lakes, eastward along the Ohio River, southeasterly along the Tennessee River and across the Appalachians into Georgia and Florida, and southward to the Gulf. Some of the great centers were still occupied or had only recently been abandoned when Europeans first came ashore in the Southeast. It was a vigorous growth that by A.D. 1400 had refashioned the life of much of what is now the United States east of the desert West.

The country rolling westward from the Mississippi to the foothills of the Rocky Mountains experienced the same growth cycles described here, but the rate of growth was slower and the evolving forms were less spectacular. Burial mounds reminiscent of the Hopewell structures spread westward up the Missouri River and northward into what is now southern Manitoba and southern Saskatchewan, but the largest of these were not over ninety feet in diameter and twelve feet high. Good pottery was fashioned by these prairie mound builders, but it lacked the variety of form, design, and embellishment of the eastern woodland production. The massive platform mounds with superposed temples of the Mississippian period were not erected west of the river, perhaps a consequence of more limited resources and a thinner population.

After about A.D. 700 the established centers such as Cahokia generated a movement of people westward along the rivers and branch streams flowing through the High Plains. Permanent multifamily houses were built in fixed villages, where previously scattered communities of a hunting-gathering people existed. Apparently the incoming population succeeded in developing hardy varieties of maize, beans, and squash capable of surviving in the dry, wind-swept Plains climate. The great numbers of storage pits within the village enclosures suggest that food production was ample. Game was hunted in the river bottoms and on the surrounding uplands, but hoe agriculture provided the main subsistence base.

Some of these Plains villages survived the coming of the horse and the greater mobility that resulted and were still occupied when white men first ventured into the oceans of grass. Such were the villages of round lodges thatched with grass occupied by the Wichita Indians whom Coronado encountered along the Arkansas River in central Kansas in 1541. And such were the earth-lodge villages of the Mandan Indians on the Missouri River visited by La Verendrye in the winter of 1738. At the time of La Verendrye's visit the Mandans occupied nine villages located on both sides of the river, near the mouth of Heart River, but when the Lewis and Clark expedition wintered with the tribe in 1804–1805 only two villages were inhabited. A smallpox epidemic in 1780–81 inflicted heavy losses, while a second epidemic in 1837 almost destroyed the tribe.

The Plains tribes obtained horses at the beginning of the eighteenth century, soon after the Pueblo Rebellion of 1680, when the Spanish were driven out of New Mexico. The advent of the horse (the primitive three-toed horse which once roamed the Plains became extinct, along with the primitive camel and elephant) profoundly affected life in the midcontinent. Some change had occurred even before the Spanish reached the Southwest. At least villages on the upper reaches of such streams as the Republican and Loup rivers had moved downstream and were concentrated in larger settlements. Also the new settlements were located on river bluffs and were enclosed within palisaded walls and dry moats—obvious defensive measures. Presumably new tribes were moving into the area and competing for living space. This change gathered momentum with the coming of the horse. Tribes living on the margins of the Plains, some of them former agriculturists, the Cheyennes and Sioux among them, now became mounted huntsmen. Others who had been forest and mountain hunters came out of the north and the west, and they, too, became horse Indians. Such were the Comanches, the Kiowas, the Assiniboines, Blackfeet, and the Arapahoes.

So the tribes which usually are thought of as typifying Plains culture were, in part, renegades of an earlier, settled society and in part they were boisterous newcomers in a wide new world. They needed only the addition of the European gun to transform them into the nineteenth-century stereotype of the red Indian—a man depicted in the early literature as devoid of tradition, or purpose, or redeeming virtue. So long as that stereotype prevailed, the Plains Indians, and by extension all Indians, lived as social outcasts in the land they had made their own.

BASKETS AND HOUSES
The Southwest

The underlying cultural adaptation of the southwestern region was that of a gathering and foraging people. Big game animals of the elephant (mammoth) order occurred only in peripheral areas, suggesting that from very early times, at least by some nine to ten thousand years ago, the population spreading into the region obtained at least part of its subsistence from wild plant foods. They were people of the so-called Desert Culture, the western version of the transition from hunting to food planting.

Maize cultivation entered the region from the south, evidently from Mexico, as early as 2000 B.C., but it had no immediate effect on the food habits of the region. For almost two thousand years the only food growers were those above the headwaters of the Gila River in southwestern New Mexico, where maize was first introduced. How the idea reached that location will be discussed later.[3]

By 300 B.C. a people called Mogollon, from the name of one of the first sites excavated, were living in small villages scattered throughout the upper Gila River drainage. Their houses were partly underground with wooden posts supporting a dirt roof. They planted crops of corn, squash, and beans but still relied on wild foods and small game. They wove a variety of textiles out of vegetable fibers and strips of fur. They made pottery, which, over the centuries, developed into a variety of delicately shaped and decorated forms. The Mimbres ware, a late development, is famous for its painted designs of animals, insects, and human forms. After A.D. 1400 the distinctly Mogollon culture blended into the cultures of neighboring areas, while the people disappeared as a distinctive group, or, as has been suggested, they may be ancestral to the historic Zuñi tribe.

An almost parallel development occurred farther downstream on the Gila River. This was desert country lying below the high plateaus of the north. Here, too, the earliest inhabitants were foragers, making use of wild plant food and small game. By 100 B.C. small villages were being built, the houses partly underground as in the Mogollon country to the east and north. In an important detail these desert people, called Hohokam (a Pima word meaning "they who went before"), differed from their Mogollon neighbors. Their pottery was fashioned by hollowing out a solid lump of damp clay and gradually thinning the walls by scraping and shaping. Mogollon pottery was built up by successive coils blended into a solid wall. Hohokam pottery shapes and styles of decoration also differed, suggesting that the potters in the two areas derived their art from separate traditions, both of which probably originated in Mexico.

The Hohokam people differed in another major respect, in that at a very early time they began to divert water from the Gila River and tributary streams to irrigate their fields. By A.D. 800 an elaborate canal system had been constructed, but the first ditches were much earlier, since farming in the area can only succeed by bringing water to the land. The major canals extended for many miles away from the river and were as much as twelve feet deep and eighteen feet across.

The historic Pima Indians and their near kinsmen, the Papagos, were living in the territory of the prehistoric Hohokam when the first Europeans came upon them. The Pimas were practicing ditch irrigation while the Papagos, who lived farther away from the Gila or other permanent streams, planted crops in low areas watered by winter rains. The Pima-Papago tribesmen are probably the lineal descendants of the Hohokam people, but possessed of a less elaborate life-style.

Somewhat later in time people inhabiting the northern sector of the southwest region began a course of development that carried through to historic times. These people, the Anasazi (the Navajo word for "ancient ones"), followed the foraging small-game-hunting economy that characterized the Desert West until about the beginning of the Christian era of the European calendar, when a gradual shift to corn growing began. The first corn was evidently introduced by agriculturists moving out of the Mississippi Valley and settling along streams flowing eastward out of the Rocky Mountains. This can be surmised from the fact that the first corn grown in the Anasazi country differed from that grown by the Mogollon people to the south. As in the Mogollon area, however, agriculture did not result in any sudden transformation of living habits or increase of population. The earliest known of these northern corn growers lived along the headwaters of the San Juan River in northern New Mexico, in scattered individual houses of poles, brush and mud erected over shallow pits. Pottery had not yet reached these first settlements, but the people wove a variety of baskets, bags, sandals, nets, and cord out of vegetable fiber. The dry southwestern climate preserved much of this woven material, a fact that led to the designation Basket Makers.

After some 500 years the population had spread northward into Utah and southward, where contact was made with the Mogollon people, from whom the art of pottery making was acquired. Beans and an advanced type of corn made for a more secure food supply, and this in turn brought about more settled habits and the establishment of the first villages. In some locations as many as 100 houses were grouped together in irregular patterns, while individual houses ranged in size from nine to twenty-five feet. The pit house was transformed into a surface structure and in each village after a time one or more structures served as ceremonial chambers. In floor plan these structures anticipated the arrangement peculiar to the kiva, in which Pueblo religious activities were centered in later times.

By about A.D. 700 the trend in house architecture was

toward the construction of single-story multiroom buildings with masonry walls, a characterizing feature of the Pueblo tradition. The first kivas were built, decorated pottery appeared, cotton was planted and woven into fabrics, and agriculture supplied a greatly increased subsistence base.

The Great Pueblo period that had its beginning about A.D. 1050 saw the maturing of a number of features in the culture. Outstanding was the development of house architecture, which produced the cliff dwellings of the Mesa Verde district and the massive Pueblo Bonito in Chaco Canyon. The latter structure was a community under one roof, consisting of some 800 rooms, rising to a height of four stories. The kiva by this time, as seen at Pueblo Bonito and at other sites, was a dominant feature of the community, some structures measuring sixty feet or more in diameter, built entirely underground. Pottery was highly developed, both in design and workmanship. Glazes of various metallic salts were applied in decoration. Ditch and flood water irrigation was practiced, as circumstances allowed, and food production reached a higher level of efficiency. This allowed for a marked population increase and for such concentrations as those at Mesa Verde and Chaco Canyon, and at hundreds of lesser locations spreading from southern Utah and Colorado into the Chihuahua Basin of northern Mexico.

After A.D. 1300, for reasons not clearly determined, this great Pueblo expansion reversed itself and all of the communities north of the San Juan River, and from the San Juan itself, withdrew southward and eastward to the Rio Grande. The culture itself did not diminish in range of achievement. On the contrary, some of the finest architecture, pottery, weaving, and other crafts were produced in this later prehistoric period. Life-form paintings on kiva walls, for example, marked a new dimension presumably of religious expression.

A possible reason for the withdrawal from outlying settlements was a deterioration of climate, resulting in a prolonged drought during the period A.D. 1276–99. Marginal agriculture could not survive and the retreat was in the direction of perennial streams. It is also possible that the falling back was precipitated by the encroachment of desert tribes, the ancestors of Utes and Paiutes, and somewhat later by the invading Athabascan Navajo and Apache tribes on their way down from the north.

No firm date has been fixed for the arrival of these northern tribesmen in the southwestern region. By the middle of the sixteenth century the Navajo people were in the upper San Juan River country, which by then had already been abandoned by the builders of the cliff dwellings and the great community houses. Some evidence exists, however, to suggest the presence of Apacheans in that area as early as the beginning of the twelfth century, in which case their competition for living space might have contributed to Pueblo withdrawal. Some burned villages suggest further that the competition was not friendly.

The Apache branch of these Athabascan invaders followed the High Plains east of the mountains and eventually occupied territory in what had been the southern extension of Pueblo settlement in southern New Mexico and southeastern Arizona.

The Navajos and Apaches, alike, were influenced by Pueblo culture, the Navajos showing more of this influence by being in closer contact with the village Indians. Both acquired agriculture, for example, but the Navajos developed a greater dependence on planted crops than did their kinsmen. When the Spaniards brought sheep to the Southwest, the Navajos became adept at making away with the herds of Pueblo Indians and Spaniards alike, while the Apaches developed no fondness for herding.

Groups marginal to the southwestern cultural domain were the flood-plain farmers along the lower Colorado River, whose earliest occupation occurs slightly later than the earliest Hokokam settlements in southern Arizona. This riverine tradition is referred to as *Patayan*, or "ancient ones," in the Yuman language. Resemblances to the neighboring Hohokam are seen in such practices as cremation of the dead. The descendants of this peripheral culture are the modern Yuma, Cocopah, Maricopa, Havasupai, Mojave, and Hualapai tribes, all of the Yuman-language stock.

WHERE TIME STOOD STILL
The Great Basin

The arid, sagebrush, and alkali-flat country known as the Great Basin contains some of the oldest remains of human occupation yet found in North America. Considering that this aridity has persisted for ten thousand years or more, and that man has lived in the area through all that time, says something for human endurance. These were the human beings who when first encountered were considered to be an especially low form of humanity. Jedediah Smith, an early explorer in the region, referred to them as "the most miserable objects in creation."

Because of the scarcity of moisture and the low capacity for supporting plant life, the Great Basin did not attract the large land mammals of other regions. Thus the earliest settlers in what is now eastern Oregon, southern California, Nevada, Utah, and parts of adjoining states have no early history as big-game hunters, the tradition that prevailed elsewhere in North America. The absence of game, except for small species, was not a barrier to settlement, however. At Tule Springs, Nevada, human occupation may have occurred as early as 23,800 years ago. That date has not been accepted as yet, but throughout the area the possibility exists of a very old time horizon characterized by crude stone implements and a notable lack of finely edged cutting tools. This contrasts with the equipment of the early hunters on the High Plains, and eastward, who fashioned sophisticated stone tools and weaponry.[4]

A different kind of adaptation was accomplished, which served the purpose of supporting human life. The adaptation, in time, was infinitely varied and made efficient use of a scant resource base. By about 8000 B.C. the people had not only learned enough about the plant life of the region to subsist themselves, but they had devised equipment to utilize wild foods. Great numbers of grinding stones (metates) are found in the caves and rock shelters occupied during that early period. Baskets were woven for seed gathering, winnowing, and storage. Watertight baskets were used for cooking by dropping hot stones into the water. Sandals, cordage, nets, matting, all woven of a variety of vegetable fibers, are suggestive of the extent to which the people coped with a harsh environment. At Danger Cave in western Utah occupied over a period of nine thousand years prior to A.D. 100, the remains of some sixty-five plant species were identified as having been used for food or other domestic purposes. The fact that all of these species are still found in the area indicates that the conditions under which that early people lived have been little changed.

What is remarkable, is that the people were as unchanging as the climate. It is known that within the early centuries A.D., Indians from the Anasazi province to the south had introduced agriculture in what is now southern Utah and southern Nevada, but the Great Basin tribes seemingly made no attempt to adopt the practice for themselves, or to migrate to a kindlier climate where farming could be followed. They had achieved an accommodation to their environment and the tools required for efficient exploitation; hence they found no reason to remake their lives. The yearly round they followed had variety and its own satisfactions.

The historic inheritors of these desert tribes, the Shoshonean-speaking Paiutes, Utes, and Shoshones, stayed within the tradition of their ancestors. The Utes and Shoshones became accomplished horsemen when Spanish horses reached their domain, and the Utes especially turned to raiding their neighbors with spectacular results. The desert hardiness of their inheritance was a quality which early white men passing through their country were unprepared to understand or accept.

NEW WORLD BABEL
California

Approximately one-third of the total number of tribal languages spoken north of Mexico were found in the California-Oregon coastal region. The region was also notable for the relative density of population in pre-Columbian times. While it constituted approximately 1 percent of the landmass north of Mexico, it is estimated that California alone was inhabited by 10 percent of the total Indian population.[5]

It is commonly assumed that concentrations of population become possible only when a people settle down as tillage farmers. The California climate was ideally suited to agriculture and early dwellers along the Colorado River practiced flood-water irrigation, and yet agriculture was never an area-wide adaptation. From earliest times the California tribes lived by hunting small game, gathering wild foods, and fishing the streams and coastal waters. The greatest single food resource were the extensive groves of oak trees scattered throughout the area. By at least as early as A.D. 1, and possibly earlier, the people had developed a technique for leaching the bitter tannic acid from acorns and grinding them into flour. This was then cooked as a soup or stew in watertight baskets. Basketry was one of the earliest arts to be developed and some of the finest baskets in the world were created by California Indians.

The great linguistic diversity of the area probably reflects the manner in which the area was settled. The eastern border of the state is guarded by the rugged Sierra Nevadas and by formidable desert terrain. Access to the fertile central valley of the state was thus limited and the likelihood is that small bands of people, each an offshoot of a larger linguistic body, crossed the mountains or the deserts and were satisfied not to repeat the experience by returning. Professor Kroeber described the aboriginal setting of California as a "fish trap" situation, with in-migrating groups finding themselves effectively, if perhaps pleasantly, prevented from retracing their steps.

How far back in time these first settlements occurred is not established. Material from Santa Rosa Island, for which a date of 30,000 years has been suggested, has not found support. By 7,000 years ago a number of locations were occupied. By that time gathering and grinding seeds as a food staple was practiced, possibly as an extension from the neighboring Great Basin culture. Great shell mounds dating from a slightly later period are evidence that the shore was exploited, notably in the San Francisco Bay area. Later still, by about 2,000 years ago, marine resources were more fully utilized as a true coastal culture developed. Ocean-going boats or dugouts gave access to offshore fishing beds and permitted the taking of sea mammals —seals, sea lions, and sea otters.

Permanent villages were occupied by at least 1000 B.C., along the central valley and coast. By this time also considerable specialization of crafts occurred and a fuller exploitation of resources encouraged population growth. Villages containing as many as 1,400 persons have been identified and their numbers estimated from burial sites.

Typical of the historic groups inhabiting the area were the Pomo, Patwin, and Maidu. They built great boats, elaborately decorated, capable of faring in rough coastal waters. A well-defined caste system developed, with debt slavery a feature of it. Money, taking the form of dentalium shells, obsidian, and woodpecker crests, was widely used, and wealth was a measure of honor and prestige.

A LAND OF BEGINNINGS
The Arctic North

In the Arctic North, as in other areas of North America, human habitation occurred at an early time, perhaps farther back in time than any of the dates now known and accepted. A common notion about the Arctic zone is that migrating people hurried through it looking for a friendlier environment and only the Eskimos, blocked by earlier arrivals on the continent, made the effort to adapt to polar conditions. The notion often carried with it the assumption that Eskimo culture is Asiatic in origin, not an indigenous development. The absence of relatedness between the Eskimo and any other North American culture seemed to affirm the view. Even the Eskimo physical type differs from the Indian, and the language is confined to the circumpolar regions, with a southerly extension to the base of the Aleutian Islands and the Islands themselves.

The history of occupation in the far north, only now being reconstructed, is more complex than was at first surmised. It is now known that the Eskimos were not the first people by several thousand years to settle in the frigid north. Just how much earlier occupation occurred is not documented, but materials recovered from old sites are comparable in style and workmanship with the tools and weapons fashioned by the Big Game Hunters of other regions of North America. One such site (British Mountain) located on the Arctic coast near the eastern boundary of Alaska has been tentatively dated at 10,000 B.C., and other locations approximate the same time horizon.[6]

More certain is the nature of early occupation. The remains are those of inland hunters. Even where the sites are located on or near the coast, the hunters went in pursuit of caribou or other mainland game. It is this characteristic that distinguishes the pioneer settlers from the later emerging Eskimo culture. Eskimo life was basically and primarily an adaptation to the sea and the hunting of sea mammals. In some of the first ancestral Eskimo settlements, whale and walrus hunting was already established—a deduction based on surviving material equipment.

The transformation from land to marine subsistence evidently occurred between about 3000 B.C. and 1800 B.C. By the later period the house form appeared which characterized later Eskimo villages. This was a semisubterranean oblong or rounded structure, with a long entrance tunnel. The tunnel was lower than the house floor and served to trap cold air from the outside. Equipment and weaponry revealed the shift from land to sea hunting, with the emphasis on harpoon heads, spears, and fishing gear. Pottery, with feathers or grass used as a tempering material, was being produced by about 700 B.C. Whale hunting in skin boats in the open sea, requiring skill and a high degree of cooperation among crew members, suggests a tightly knit social fabric. Ceremonies aimed at success in taking the whale probably involved the entire community, as was the later custom. At one site near Point Hope, at the northwest tip of Alaska, a cult of the dead is suggested by elaborate carvings in ivory, including human skulls fitted with ivory eyeballs and jet inserts for pupils, and also ivory covers placed over the eyes and the mouth of the dead.

Between A.D. 700 and A.D. 1300 the full inventory of Eskimo hunting and household equipment had been developed, spreading eastward and from north to south. These developments included the umiak, or open skin boat, and the closed-over kayak; the toboggan, snow goggles carved in one piece out of ivory or bone, the toggle harpoon, the whaling lance and special harpoon, the sinew-backed bow, the bow-driven fire drill, pottery, ground slate tools, ivory carving, basketry and matting woven out of grasses, stone lamps for heating and cooking. Dog traction was a late development.

The Asiatic origin of aspects of Eskimo culture is readily demonstrated from older sites in Siberia. The language itself has remote Asiatic origins, while the Eskimo physical type represents a late movement into northeastern Asia of the fully formed Mongoloid racial stock. Eskimo culture, language, and physical type, however, are distinct. The resemblance to other traditions and inheritances are present, but Eskimo technology and life-style are the product of a long course of assimilation and adaptation that took place in an Arctic environment. The region of the Bering Strait supported an abundance of sea and land animals and bird life, once the methods and equipment were developed for exploiting that environment. The people who would be called Eskimos brought knowledge and skills with them from Asia, but they also borrowed and made over to their use the crafts of an earlier indigenous people. This earlier occupation, known as the Arctic Small Tool tradition, was primarily an inland hunting economy. The fusion of the two adaptations produced an Arctic economy that exploited the resources of land and sea.

Regional variations developed in response to environmental influences as people moved away from the Bering Strait hearth. This out movement produced changes not only in subsistence and living habits but in the common language as well. The main thrusts of the culture spread are reflected in dialect changes. The earlier movement was apparently southward, beginning about 1000 B.C. The other migration was northward to the top of Alaska, then eastward across northern Canada all the way to Greenland. The differentiation became so marked that by A.D. 1000 the Eskimos from Bering Strait to Greenland and Labrador spoke an almost identical language, but mutual communication was lost with their linguistic kinsmen south of Norton Sound.

At an earlier time Eskimos and Aleuts spoke a common language, called Eskaleut by linguists, and still earlier this language was part of a Siberian stock, the Chukotan. Based on comparative studies of these related speech forms, it is estimated that the Eskaleut speakers separated from their Siberian counterparts sometime before 3000 B.C. The Eskaleuts in turn drifted apart as they settled in separate geographical regions, and eventually they no longer shared a mutually understood language. The split within the Eskimo component represented not only a geographical division but contrasting environmental circumstances. The Eskimos who moved south to the Pacific coast left behind much of their Arctic tradition as they came into contact with the Northwest Coast fishing Indians.

The interior of Alaska and the inland country extending eastward across northern Canada to Hudson Bay was occupied as early as 6500 B.C. by hunting tribes. They pursued modern species of elk, moose, caribou, and buffalo, and were skillful flint tool and weapon makers. Some sites were occupied as late as 1000 B.C., but before that date Athabascan-speaking people were already in the area.

The Athabascans adapted to the subarctic environment by utilizing the knowledge and crafts of the older inhabitants, without physical conquest evidently. In similar fashion the Eskimo people took over areas previously mastered by an earlier pioneering group and built a culture of their own.

While the Eskimo race spread across the thousands of miles of shoreline, islands, inlets, bays, and cape headings of the Arctic, the Athabascans were discovering and accommodating themselves to the forests and waterways of the vast interior. One of these Athabascan camp groups, perhaps responding to an old habit of trying out new territory, abandoned the north, and, after wandering southward across the grassy plains for some centuries, found a place to their liking next to some farming Indians in the Southwest. When white men first encountered these displaced northerners, they were already separating themselves dialectically into Navajo and Apache speakers.

What is clear from this brief review of aboriginal America is that European adventurers did not come ashore to an undiscovered world, as they so often proclaimed when they planted banners on a sandy beach or carved a royal name upon a tree trunk. Men had been there before them, perhaps gazing seaward from the same beach or resting in the shade of the same tree. No region had gone unexplored, and wherever life was tenable, there men lived.

It is true, of course, that the Europeans who came ashore were not able to see all of Native America at one time. And they had no vantage point in time from which to mark the changes, the widening knowledge, the growth in technical skills reflected in the lives of the people. For that matter, after almost five hundred years of a common history in the Western Hemisphere, there is little understanding of those who were the first to come into the land.

7

THE NOBLE GRASS

The story of maize, or Indian corn, has yet to be written in full, though generations of naturalists have looked into the matter and have published their speculative findings. Long before white men came upon the scene, Indians were conducting elaborate ceremonies and reciting ritual prayers, rendering thanks for corn, the giver of life, the eternal mother. The coming of corn was a legend, and legends require no exegesis.

From the earliest contact Europeans knew that Indians planted corn and beans and squash, but they did not appreciate with what extraordinary aptitude Indians had modified the plant world to provide themselves with food, clothing, and medicinal substances. The failure to recognize the achievement was not surprising, since only the development of modern botany made possible an understanding of the intricate process of converting a plant from its wild state to one of domestic usefulness, in which its growing habits, its yield of fruit, and its resistance to environmental hazards are brought under control and enlarged upon. The Native Americans achieved this control not just in these three prominent plant species, but literally in scores of cultigens, including white and sweet potatoes, peanuts, long staple cotton, tomatoes, tobacco, chili, manioc, avocado, pumpkin, pineapple, amaranth, sunflower, maguey, quinoa, cacao—to name only the less exotic.

Corn stood above all of these as the most widely distributed and the most reliable as a food staple. The incoming Europeans were quick to discover its virtue, since it saved the lives of settlers in Virginia and Massachusetts. It came to be regarded with a pride which even approached the Indian feeling. Something of this pride of accomplishment was expressed by Dr. J. H. Kempton of the United States

Department of Agriculture: "The key crop of the New World . . . was the noble grass we know as corn. . . . Although the European races have largely displaced the Indian population, corn has retained its place as the principal crop of the New World. It is grown in every state of the Union and is by far the most valued single crop produced in the western hemisphere. It is the only domesticated plant that can be grown over the entire range of climate, soils, and day lengths found in the territory extending from the Canadian border to the Central American tropics to southern Chile, and from sea level to an altitude of 12,000 feet. . . . The crop produces more food value per unit of area than any other grain, though of course less per man hour unit than the Old World cereals such as wheat, which requires no care after planting. In maize the American Indian developed a food plant capable of supporting a family of five on the production of four acres."[1]

What was equally astonishing, quoting Dr. Kempton again, ". . . Since the occupation of the Americas by the Europeans no real change has been made in corn, except to discard the gaudy colors [the Indians kept the colored corn for their own planting]. We have not even modified the Indian's cultural system of growing the plants in hills, though we have adopted his system to our machines."

How the prescientific Indians managed these genetic transformations can only be conjectured. No theoretical assumptions and no laboratory controls were available, but they were good observers and they had an intimate association with the earth and its elements. The effort to reconstruct the process of domestication and in particular to discover where and when maize was brought under control has been an absorbing and frustrating preoccupation shared by many students in field and laboratory.

The key difficulty, perhaps finally resolved, was to identify the original wild plant from which modern corn was derived. In this respect, corn (*Zea mays* in botanical nomenclature) differs from other domestic food plants, whose wild ancestors are known and still flourish in their native habitats. Domestication of corn occurred so far back in time, and the system of reproduction was so altered by human intervention, that its primitive forebearers seem to have disappeared as a species. Pollen of what is thought to be primitive maize has been recovered from sites underlying Mexico City, at depths estimated to be 80,000 years old. If the identification is correct, the wild plant was flourishing at least 50,000 years, or more, before the first migrations of men reached the New World.[2]

Two wild grasses closely related to corn, teosinte and tripsacum, still grow in the highlands of Mexico. Their growing habits were not altered by man and they continued to reproduce themselves in their wild state. The corn plant, however, was so greatly modified by crossbreeding that it lost the power of self-propagation; its seeds cannot detach themselves naturally but must be removed and planted mechanically.

A series of archaeological discoveries added more precise information about the age factor. One of the first early dates was obtained, unexpectedly, at Bat Cave not far from the headwaters of the Gila River in southern New Mexico. The cave was occupied intermittently over a period of several thousand years. At the lowest level, for which radiocarbon dates range between 2000 and 3000 B.C., tiny corncobs were found. These specimens, while primitive, were already the product of crossbreeding, representing an advance beyond wild corn. The Mogollon culture flourished in this area some two thousand years later, but the Mogollon corn was still further advanced in hybridization.[3]

Very soon after the Bat Cave discovery in 1948, corn of about the same age and stage of development was recovered from sites in the Mexican states of Tamaulipas and Chihuahua. These early sites were all located at elevations of about 6,000 feet above sea level.

It had become evident after these discoveries that a route of dispersal led from somewhere farther south, perhaps from the highlands of Mexico, since corn seemed to belong to a highland-grass family. Confirmation of this was dramatically borne out by archaeological excavations conducted by Richard S. MacNeish in the state of Puebla in southern Mexico.[4]

At the Tehuacan Valley beginning in 1960 a number of caves and open sites were explored. Piecing together the information obtained from these sites a record of occupation covering almost 12,000 years was obtained. In one of the caves, at a level 7,000 years old, the excavators found corn specimens more primitive than any previously unearthed. MacNeish described the find: "They were only about twenty millimeters long, no bigger than the filter tip of a cigarette, but under a magnifying lens one could see that they were indeed miniature ears of corn, with sockets that had once contained kernels enclosed in pods."

The reference to "kernels enclosed in pods" alludes to the theoretical assumption that wild corn produced seeds along a spike, with each seed ensheathed separately and detachable upon reaching maturity. By selective crossbreeding with related species, the spike was enlarged to form a cob and the cluster of seeds became enclosed in an encompassing husk, as in modern corn.

The interpretation of the Tehuacan material was proposed by Paul C. Mangelsdorf, who has devoted a professional lifetime to the corn puzzle. Until the Tehuacan discoveries, Mangelsdorf had assumed, as had other botanists, that cultivated corn resulted from a crossing of primitive species and had no primitive form of its own. The Tehuacan specimens gave the first substantial evidence that wild corn actually flourished before man began to modify some of its characteristics. In Mangelsdorf's judgment: "The wild ancestors of cultivated corn was corn and not one of its relatives, teosinte or tripsacum."[5]

The view has not gone unchallenged, which is not surprising, considering the range of speculation and the inconclusiveness of many research findings. One countering view which deserves to be mentioned still questions whether corn ever existed as a wild plant. It suggests instead that the ancestral plant was the genetically related teosinte, which still flourishes in the wild state in parts of Mexico, Guatemala, and Honduras. Modern breeding experiments have indeed produced successful hybrids of corn and teosinte, suggesting that such hybridizations could have occurred naturally, and indicating further that the two species are closely enough related as to allow for the possibility that either parental stock could have given rise to the other.[6]

The Tehuacan Valley presents the longest record of continuous occupation of any area thus far explored in North America. For this reason it has an importance beyond the discoveries relating to the possible ancestry of corn. In successive layers of campsites and later village sites a people's progress is recorded from their beginnings as casual wanderers in the land until they attained a substantial mastery of the environment. In microcosm the people of Tehuacan reflect the growth of native society in all of America.

As MacNeish reconstructed the sequence of development

from his surveys and excavations, first settlement in the valley evidently occurred at a time when the Desert Culture was spreading southward out of the Great Basin. If earlier inhabitants were in the area, their remains have not been found. For sometime prior to 7000 B.C., the people were subsisting on a combined diet of small-game animals and wild-plant foods—an economy characteristic of the Desert West of that period.

The evidence suggests that the domestication of corn was not the first step along the way to planned food production. By 6700 B.C. squash was already a cultivated plant, as was the avocado. When corn came under cultivation at about 5000 B.C. the domestic garden already included additional varieties of beans, also chili peppers and amaranths. The population was thinly scattered and moved with the seasonal cycles of plants and animals. The tools and weapon inventory was simple and easily portable.

Between 6700 B.C. and 5000 B.C. the people occupied themselves less with hunting and more with plant gathering. In this interval basic implements for processing plant foods were developed—the stone grinding slab, or metate, the pestle and mortar, and hollowed out stone cooking vessels. Populations may have increased, but the seasonal cycle still prevailed and permanent settlements had not yet come into existence.

After 5000 B.C. food production assumed an increasing importance. It led to more settled living habits and the establishment of villages at about 3400 B.C. The further hybridizing of corn and the introduction of pottery before 2000 B.C. accentuated trends already discernible.

By 850 B.C. ditch irrigation was in practice, adding greatly to the productivity of the land. Population grew rapidly in response to the expanded food supply, and thereafter the construction of urban centers, temple cities, the beginnings of occupational specialization, trade and commerce, all followed in sequence. The Tehuacan Valley did not become one of the great centers of pre-Columbian New World civilization, but it did support a relatively complex indigenous society.

What was not realized until these Tehuacan discoveries was that the beginnings of New World agriculture were roughly comparable in time and in sequence of change to counterpart developments in the Old World. In both regions, as Professor Braidwood observes, "Human groups

. . . learned to live into their environment to a high degree, achieving an intimate familiarity with every element in it."⁷

Braidwood was writing specifically of the "Fertile Crescent," the foothill country extending from the Persian Gulf northwesterly to the eastern shores of the Mediterranean Sea. Here he found that "around 8000 B.C. the inhabitants of the hills around the Fertile Crescent had come to know their habitat so well that they were beginning to domesticate the plants and animals they had been collecting and hunting."

Excavations in the area indicate that the first permanent villages were occupied between 7000 and 6500 B.C., and by 4000 B.C. agricultural production made possible the rise of urban civilization. These developments all antedate comparable stages in the New World, but the process of growth was remarkably similar.

8

OF LAW SYSTEMS

"Primitive law," in the thinking of some writers on juristic matters, is a contradiction in terms—if it is "primitive," it is not quite law. As one writer, William Seagle, maintains, "the test of law in the strict sense is the same for both primitive and civilized communities: namely, the existence of courts."[1] Law removes the settlement of conflicts beyond the reach of blind chance, something that is not achieved in primitive societies, according to this point of view.

In considering this view the warning given by Franz Boas is recalled: "Forms of thought and action which we are inclined to consider as based on human nature are not . . . generally valid . . . but are characteristic of our specific culture. . . . Not all our standards are categorically determined by our quality as human beings, but may change with changing circumstances."[2]

Inquiry has been made in recent years into the law practices of several Plains Indian tribes, people who are usually classed as among the least organized of the New World's inhabitants.

With respect to the Plains tribes generally, it was often affirmed that formal legal procedures were fragmentary and were in operation only on special occasions. That is, law was in effect only when members of the band were on a raiding or a hunting party and it was necessary to impose discipline in order to insure the safety of the group. When James Mooney studied the Kiowa tribe in the 1890s, he could discover only three instances of tribal law in operation. These were in cases of adultery, violations of camp regulations, and personal grievances. In the latter class of cases, he believed, there was no formal procedure. It was recognized rather that the aggrieved individual or his relatives would take matters into their own hands and obtain satisfaction.

This is not said in criticism of Mooney's capacity for observation. It is doubtful whether his colleagues of the 1890s would have accepted any other interpretation of a Plains people as crude and primitive as the Kiowa tribe was thought to be. Our insight is usually that of the times in which we live.

Forty years after Mooney, in 1935, the law practices of the Kiowa Indians were studied once more. Jane Richardson,[3] who made the study, discovered that when she asked a Kiowa Indian what his law was, he would not have an answer ready unless she could specify the exact situation in which a violation had occurred. He would need to know something about the family, the status of the principals involved (for example their membership in certain societies), and their personal accomplishments. Not that there was one law for the rich and one for the poor; but that with a man's position in society and his achievements went responsibilities (a leader of a band had to be more careful of his language and his behavior than a camp follower), and certain tolerances as well.

While there were formal mechanisms, notably in connection with the celebration of the Sun Dance, for terminating disputes, Dr. Richardson found that Kiowa society was quite resourceful in stopping trouble before it got started. She found that "popular sentiment for peace was probably the keystone which permitted the successful functioning of all legal institutions, and in itself was responsible ultimately for more adjustments than the formal mechanism. This feeling, permeating all social ranks, stopped fights and if not preventing quarrels outright, at least inhibited their development into serious affairs."

Thus when a leader of one of the Kiowa bands learned that a serious quarrel had been settled, he was pleased and his comment was: "That's good. We won't have to be uneasy now. We won't have to be prepared for trouble." Or, when a fight started, women would shout, "Somebody stop it!" A bystander would step between the two contenders and, if necessary, promise gifts to each in order to calm them down. Men were complimented on all sides for refusing to prosecute someone who had done them an injury. Angry men would avoid each other. If one chanced to overhear an angry person vow vengeance on another, he might rush off to inform the intended victim to be on guard and avoid the encounter. In carrying out a legally proclaimed death penalty, the tribal officers were careful to choose an out-of-the-way place, so that the kin of the condemned man might not in anger take things into their own hands. The proper behavior of a guilty person and his kin was passive acceptance, but it was realized that passions sometimes overrode duty.

This is not law, in the opinion of some writers, since it was not characterized by formal procedures and court action. The dominant note in all the cases investigated by Dr. Richardson is the wish to preserve the group, to protect society. Keeping the peace was a sacred duty laid upon every individual conscience. Courts and formalized procedures, though these existed in simple form, were not the means by which Kiowa society achieved solutions to conflict behavior.

Another common assumption about primitive law is that tort or private injury, rather than "crime" or public wrong, dominates, and that the injured individual or his family must obtain satisfaction as best he can. The law practices of the Cheyenne Indians, as explored by Llewellyn and Hoebel, permit an assessment of the accuracy of this generalization.[4]

The Cheyenne Indians before A.D. 1700 had lived in the woodlands in the upper drainage of the Mississippi River, or possibly as far eastward as the Great Lakes. They were a farming people who had come out upon the prairie country of the Dakotas even before the arrival of white men in that region. They took over the hunting habits of the Plains people, their institutions as well as their economy. A more varied procedure, a deeper layer of formal behaving, sets Cheyenne justice apart from that of the Kiowa. But there is the same concern for preserving the group, for keeping the peace.

In part, this greater complexity was revealed in Cheyenne social organization, which functioned at two levels. The Council of Forty-four, which apparently came with the Cheyennes out of their village-dwelling past, resembled the church-state organization of other times and other peoples of the world. Its origins were already so obscure when white men first encountered the Cheyennes that they could only explain it as the gift of a legendary first woman.

This Council was presided over by an inner circle of five priest-chiefs, one representing Sweet Medicine or the center of the world. The Sacred Arrows, symbol of Cheyenne life power, were blessed in the incense of sweet grass. The other four represented the corners of the world. The entire Council of Forty-four met each year, in the summer encampment, to transact the business of the tribe, sacred and secular. Every ten years the Council was renewed. "But each time keep five of the old ones," the first woman had instructed. Membership on the Council was not undertaken lightly. It imposed blameless behavior and unsparing generosity, requirements which sometimes caused a potential candidate to back off when approached.

At the second level of organization were the military or soldier societies, six in number. These were the administrative units which enforced the law of Cheyenne society. They were voluntary organizations, open to men of all ages, and were typical of the social organization of the hunting tribes which emerged upon the buffalo plains after the horse had been acquired. The war chiefs of the tribe were drawn from the soldier societies, being the officers (two headmen and two runners) of each society. In later years, as hunting and fighting came to occupy the tribe to the exclusion of almost every other consideration in the bitter struggle for game and territory, these purely secular societies became the dominant organization.

The last renewal of the chiefs (as the decennial ceremony was called) took place in 1892 and it is believed that the last keeper of the Sweet Medicine bundle buried it rather than pass it on. The future must have seemed too hopeless for even Cheyenne power to endure. The buffalo were gone by then and the tribe was divided into two remnants, one in Montana and the other in Indian Territory.

Llewellyn and Hoebel have been to some pains to collect from the old people in the Montana, or northern, branch of the tribe their accounts of what they did in times of trouble. They did not ask simply what was the law of the Cheyennes, but rather what happened when the law was broken. Law is purposeful; law tries to mold behavior. "But there is more to law than intended and largely effective regulation and prevention. Law has the peculiar job of cleaning up social messes when they have been made. Law thus exists also for the event of breach of law and has a major portion of its essence in the doing something about such a breach."

Much of Cheyenne social history and of the struggle within that history to establish a code of behavior is epitomized in the case of Pawnee, a member of the southern Cheyenne band, as reported by Llewellyn and Hoebel in the words of an informant, Black Wolf. The incident recounted took place sometime around 1830.

Pawnee as a young man had been an awful rascal among the southern Cheyennes. He stole meat from people's racks, took horses for joy rides, and when he got to where he was going, he would turn the horse loose and let it find its way back to its owner, if it could. "He was disrespectful to people and sassed them back. Everyone thought he was a mean boy, and whatever happened in camp he got blamed for it."

Pawnee is quoted as telling his own story: "One day I took [two spotted horses] and headed west. Three days passed and I found myself still safe. Now I was out of trouble's way, so I began to feel pretty good. On the fourth day, as I looked back I saw some people coming up. 'It is nothing,' I thought, 'just some people traveling.' When they overtook me, I saw they were Bowstring Soldiers [one of the soldier societies] out after me.

" 'You have stolen those horses,' they cried as they pulled me from my horse. They threw me on the ground and beat me until I could not stand; they broke up my weapons and ruined my saddle; they cut my blankets, moccasins, and kit to shreds. When they had finished they took all my food and went off with the horses, leaving me alone on the prairie, sore and destitute, too weak and hurt to move."

Pawnee describes how for three days and two nights he wandered afoot, starved and bleeding, and at last crawled to the top of a high hill to die.

His tale continues: "As I gazed steadfastly into the south, a hunter came up the hill from behind me. After three days and two nights in my condition I must have been nearly deaf, for I did not hear him until he spoke from his horse right behind me. I was naked. I fell over in fright when I heard his voice start out in the silence.

"This man dismounted and hugged me. He wept, he felt so bad at seeing my plight. It was High Backed Wolf, a young man, but a chief. He put his blanket about me and took me home. The camp was on the creek below, hidden just around a bend where I had not seen it. His wife gave me food and nourished me."

Others were in the camp and, following the example of High Backed Wolf, they gave him food, first a little soup, then meat, then an outfit of clothes. "Until he is fixed up, I shall ask no questions," said High Backed Wolf.

At last they smoked and then they were ready to talk. Having touched his lips to the pipe, Pawnee was reminded that he must tell the truth about himself. This he did. "I told them the whole story. I told them whose horses they were, and I told them it was the Bowstrings who had punished me.

"High Backed Wolf knew I was a rascal, so he lectured me. 'You are old enough now to know what is right,' he preached. 'You know how we Cheyennes try to live. . . . Be decent from now on! Stop stealing! Stop making fun of people! Use no more bad language in the camp! Lead a good life!' "

Pawnee was too ashamed to go back to his tribesmen in the south, so he stayed with the northern band, where he joined a soldier society and became a model of decorum. He concludes ruefully:

"Though I came to be a chief of the Fox Soldiers among the Northern people, I never amounted to much with the Southern Bands. Those people always remembered me as a no-good."

He would add for the benefit of the young people in his audience: "You boys remember that. You may run away, but your people always remember. You just obey the rules of the camp, and you'll do all right."

How another incident involving the taking of horses resulted in the promulgation of a definite law of property is revealed in another case, that of Wolf Lies Down. The informant is again Black Wolf, and the time is somewhat later, perhaps about 1850.

The account runs: "While Wolf Lies Down was away, a friend took one of his horses to ride to war. This man had brought his bow and arrow and left them in the lodge of the horse's owner. When Wolf Lies Down returned, he knew by this token security who had his horse, so he said nothing.

"A year passed without the horse's return, and then Wolf Lies Down invited the Elk Soldier chiefs to his lodge, because he was in their society. 'There is this thing,' he told them. 'My friend borrowed my horse, leaving his bow and arrow; there they are yet. Now I want to know what to do. I want you to tell me the right thing. Will you go over and ask him his intentions?'

"The borrower was in another camp well distant, yet the chiefs agreed. 'We'll send a man to bring him in, get his word, or receive his presents,' they promised.

"The camp moved while the messenger was gone, but he knew of course where it would be on his return. The soldier returned with the borrower, who was leading two horses, one spotted, one ear-tipped. He called for the four Elk chiefs on his arrival. The chiefs laid before him the story told by Wolf Lies Down.

" 'That is true,' the man assented. 'My friend is right. I left my bow and arrow here. I intended to return his horse, but I was gone longer than I expected. I have had good luck with that horse, though. I have treated it better than my own. However, when I got back to camp I found my folks there. Our camps were far apart and I just could not get away. I was waiting for his camp and mine to come together. Now, I always intended to do the right thing. I have brought two good horses with me. My friend can have his choice. In addition I give his own horse back, and further, I am leaving my bow and arrow.'

"Then up spoke Wolf Lies Down, 'I am glad to hear my friend say these things. Now I feel better. I shall take one of those horses, but I am giving him that one he borrowed to keep. From now on we shall be bosom friends.'

"The chiefs declared, 'Now we have settled this thing. Our man is a bosom friend of this man. Let it be that way among all of us. Our Society and his shall be comrades. Whenever one of us has a present to give, we shall give it to a member of his soldier society.

" 'Now we shall make a new rule. There shall be no more borrowing of horses without asking. If any man takes another's goods without asking, we will go over and get them back for him. More than that, if the taker tries to keep them, we will give him a whipping.' "

We read much about the callous treatment of Indian women by their men, but the women often gave as good as they received. The men submitted, as in the case of Bull Head's domestic misadventure, and thus acknowledged that women's rights were tangible. The narrator of the next account was Calf Woman, an old lady when she talked to Llewellyn and Hoebel in 1935.

"We were going toward the lower Missouri when the men went hunting. Bull Head was along with them. He was coming in with his meat when, looking down from the top of a hill, he saw his wife riding along with the other women, sitting on top of her pack and dragging a travois with their camp goods. He rode down and gave her the meat to pack into camp. While she was transferring the meat from his horse to hers, he sat down to wait. Just when she crossed behind the pack horse, it kicked out and hit her hard. She went down and the horse stampeded. Her child burst out wailing, 'My mother is killed!'

"Bull Head came running, all solicitous. 'Where are you hurt? Where did he kick you?'

" 'Keep away from me,' his wife screamed. 'Don't you dare come near me. You men! You lazy fellows! It is not far to the camp, and yet you make me pack the meat. It is all your fault.'

"But Bull Head did not heed her as he went to help her up. She just took his war spear and broke it over his shoulders, wherewith he went off to look after the runaway horse, while she came hobbling after.

"They found the horse mired in a mudhole. 'There, see what you did,' she yelled. 'You stay away.' Then she tried to get the lead rope, but could not reach it. She ordered her repentant husband into the mudhole to get it himself. He obeyed her, but the horse reared, stepping on his foot. He disappeared from sight under the water, going right under the horse's belly and coming up on the other side— a mess. His wife plucked a handful of mud and hurled it just as Bull Head turned his face. He threw some back— and they were at it.

"In the meantime the horse was drowning. Hawk rode up, and while they were fighting he lassoed the horse and pulled it out. Then he yelled to them to stop ducking each other. When it was over, the meat was ruined."

Bull Head had to eat with the neighbors. "The truth is," the story goes, "that wife of his refused to put up the tipi or cook for him. Her mother tried to soften her, saying, 'Maybe you are wrong.'

"But then she remained stubborn. 'Not until my arm is well will I do a thing for him.'

"Whenever the mother-in-law gave the little girl a bit of food to take to her father, the injured wife seized it and threw it to the dogs.

"Bull Head had to go rustling food from camp to camp. 'I am being punished,' he told the people. 'My wife won't feed me.' "

He was a man with "a good war reputation," a strong man, yet he went from camp to camp, looking sheepish.

It was in the formulation of rules and practices for dealing with homicide that the Cheyennes showed their deep concern for the social good and their penchant for orderliness. Homicide was not a common thing—the northern band could list only sixteen willful killings between the years 1835 and 1879. Murder was abhorrent to the Cheyennes and therefore they usually moved vigorously to control it. "The killing of one Cheyenne by another Cheyenne was a sin which bloodied the Sacred Arrows, endangering thereby the well-being of the people," Llewellyn and Hoebel report. Once murder was committed, the tribe could not be safe; there could be no success in war, game would evade their hunters, until the Arrows were renewed. This required a formidable ceremony occupying four days, which must be attended by every living Cheyenne. The soldier societies scoured the plains far and wide until they were satisfied that everyone had been brought in.

As for the individual murderer, a stigma attached to him, a stench of corruption, which required banishment from the tribe. This banishment ran usually for five years or longer, but even after the offender returned to the tribe he might not be permitted to eat from other men's dishes or touch their pipes to his lips. Grace was regained with difficulty.

Finding a guilty party and punishing him is not by any means the most important end achieved by any legal system. Settling trouble in a manner to end the trouble, in a manner that does not leave sore places and a buried desire for reprisal: that would appear to be the greatest good that law can accomplish. Not *res judicata* as an objective, but working harmony between contesting parties, made Cheyenne justice socially effective.

After reviewing these Cheyenne law cases, Llewellyn and Hoebel conclude: "It is not merely that we find neat juristic work, it is that the generality of the Cheyennes, not alone the 'lawyers' or the 'great lawyers' among them (whom they show no signs of having recognized as such) worked out their nice cases with an intuitive juristic precision which among us marks a judge as good; that the *generality* among them produced indeed a large percentage of work on a level of which our rare and greater jurists could be proud. This is the more notable because explicit law—i.e., law clothed in rules—was exceedingly rare among them. It is the more notable because they did not have many fixed rituals of procedure to guide them, around whose application or whose ceremonial formulae and behavior, concepts of legal correctness so readily came to cluster."

While most of the cases gathered by the authors dealt with incidents of a bygone day, the details were still sharp and the meanings were clear. Some events occurred within the lifetime of the informants, while in other cases, of events which date from the early years of the nineteenth century, the fathers and grandfathers were the participants. The events were fresh, but the pattern was dissolving. The soldier societies tended to take the power away from the Council of Forty-four, only to find in time that their functions were no longer needed. The authors of *The Cheyenne Way* conclude their volume on a note of eloquence:

"Cheyenne law leaped to glory as it set!"

It would be a mistake to assume that the pattern of law and right living has been lost. Recently one of the Pueblos on the Rio Grande decided that it should put down in writing some of the rules by which its members had lived since the days before Coronado.[5] It is a simple statement, aimed at the guidance of a few score men, women, and children. Yet one wonders where at this moment in the world a more profound document on human government might be written.

"It is well for our younger men to know our law," the statement reads. "It is well for our older men and our younger men to agree about our law. It is not good to wait until trouble comes up before our law becomes clear to all. This is our law:

"To hold membership and rights in this Pueblo, the member must do his community duties. The duties are known to everyone. Everyone is responsible for doing them. When the Governor cries in the plaza that there is spring ditch work three weeks or a month beforehand, or the War Captain cries in the plaza that there is plastering of public buildings two days beforehand, it is the duty of every one to know and report. We all know it is coming. We have waited to hear. Ours is a little pueblo; in three minutes any man can walk from any house to any other house.

"In regard to the duties of peace, of not assaulting another member with a stock or a hand or a word, we have been trained, all of us, since we could talk. In regard to the duties of right conduct, of hard work, of respect to the people and respect to our officers, we have been trained since we could talk.

"It is not the practice of our pueblo to put on any offender at any time the full penalty which the law makes possible. But the power is there to do that, when the good of the pueblo makes it necessary. Nineteen times out of twenty, the courts of this pueblo stay far inside the penalty which they have the power to order; half of the time the courts of this pueblo are content to make an offender swear on his knees that he will give up bad things and be a right member of the pueblo.

"But when our courts fail to put the full penalty on an offender, or fail to go after an offender, that does not mean under our customary law that the offense is forgotten or washed out. It means that in the judgment of the court, or of the officers of the year, that there was more hope for the man and for the pueblo if things were made easy that time. Our officers know how to go easy some times; our officers also know how to wait. This often helps bring an offender to right ways.

"These are all right parts of the customary law of our pueblo.

"When a man just seems to forget his duties, it is the custom of this pueblo to warn him and advise him; and if he is within reach, he may be warned and advised several times, when he looks like a man who is likely to be reformed.

"But when a man *refuses* to perform his duties, that tells his intention for all the future. It is then for the officers to decide whether to warn and advise him, and how often to do that. The man knows his duty. To 'forget' too often says 'I won't.'

"It is the law and policy of this pueblo to recognize control and the right of control by parents over children. This is a question not of age, but of birth. Under our law children do not grow up to years in which they are free, without consent of their living parents. A widow of sixty-five, on her death bed, has still the power to say which of her thirty- or forty-year-old sons shall be head of the family and family-trustee of family property.

"The law and policy of this pueblo show how great is the reliance of this pueblo on the right education of future members by the parents of the young. It is the parents who are relied on to raise the young in right ways, in ways of hard-working duty and clean living, in ways of quiet and peace with all of our close-living neighbors, in ways of respect for our constituted officers and institutions. It is a matter of shame if a child who has gotten into trouble requires to be advised not by the parents alone, but by the officers and the Council. Therefore, any conflict between the advice and commands of parents and the ways of this pueblo and the commands of its constituted officers, is a conflict which this pueblo cannot have. Such a conflict cannot be permitted to continue.

"Therefore, again, under the law and policy of this pueblo, if parents either leave the pueblo voluntarily or are expelled, the children must lose membership at the same time and by the same fact. Expulsion never happens quickly. It is a last resort, for peace and good order. Membership, even by birth, cannot continue when the relationship of birth itself produces a conflict in duties which the pueblo cannot have within it.

"But if, when a member with children leaves or is expelled, that member gives up parental rights over children, then the case is different. Such rights can be surrendered to a responsible member of this pueblo in good standing, if the children are young; or, if the child is old enough to have judgment of his own, such rights can be surrendered by the parent to the child, by consent of the parent.

"A child born into this pueblo, but taken out by a parent, remains in the eyes of the pueblo a child to be desired as a member, if that child ever desires to be readmitted. As in any other case of new admission, the Council must be careful . . . It is not the policy of this pueblo to make children suffer for the faults of their parents; but it is the policy to make sure that its members have grown up with the respect and understanding for its officers and its laws and ways which this close community requires for its work together."

There runs through the Indian people, through tribe after tribe, a supreme civic sense, an overriding passion to protect and preserve the group. It shows in their work habits, in which families, land-use groups, bands, or entire tribes simultaneously engage in activities in which the benefits are shared by all. It shows in ceremonial life, in which actors and spectators are felt to be equally responsible for a successful performance. It showed, as we shall see later, in the earnest efforts of many tribes to prevent a division of their community lands into individual parcels or allotments, since such a division threatened dissolution of the group.

An incident in recent Hopi history illustrates the depth and character of this civic sense.[6]

The coming of white men to the Hopi country started stresses and conflicts, which at times amounted to social earthquakes. The stresses are there today and, by the very nature of the contrast between white man and Hopi, must continue until some workable accommodation is achieved.

The bad time was in 1906, but it had been building up for many years. When the Government established an agency among the Hopi Indians in 1870, they had already had a long experience with white men, beginning with the coming of Coronado in 1540. They had joined in the rebellion of 1680 with the Pueblo Indians of the Rio Grande, when the Spaniards were thrown out of New Mexico.

A split developed within the tribe in the 1880s, when the leader of one faction showed friendliness toward the Government and urged his followers to do the same. He agreed to send his children to the Government school, and he invited Christian missions to come among the people. This friendliness was resented and publicly repudiated by the second faction. Feelings ran high. White officials were insulted. When a surveying party was sent out by the Government to run lines for the purpose of dividing Hopi lands into individual allotments, the hostile opposition pulled up the iron stakes. The Army was called in, but fortunately the commanding officer kept his head.

The tension was so great by the late summer of 1906 that it seemed as if only a trial by force could settle it. The rival parties met in night meetings, each debating how it could run the other out of the village. Some talked of violence. Others would shout these down, exhorting one and all "not to hurt anybody." The Hopis had their tradition and it was a tradition of peacefulness. Their very name signified that. No hatred, however deep it might be, could be deeper than tradition. But there might be an explosion which would sweep all this aside. The voices rose and fell all through the night.

On the morning of September 7, 1906, the rival groups

poured out onto the plaza of Oraibi village. For several hours they milled around, shouting insults, haggling. Individual opponents would grapple and each would try to throw the other out of the plaza. As fast as one was overpowered and pushed or dragged out of bounds, he returned to grapple again. No heads were broken, no blood was spilled. But passion rode higher as the sun mounted to the midhour. It seemed to be only a question of time until the explosion came.

Then they hit upon an extraordinary idea. Some older head managed at last to be heard. Perhaps the knowledge which each one must have had, that violence was certainly coming, made them willing to listen at last. A line was drawn across the dust of the plaza. The rival parties agreed to place themselves on opposite sides of the line. At a signal, they would begin to push. The side that got pushed back from the line would have to yield.

The two lines locked, two hundred men to a side, swayed, scuffled. A surge of strength would run through the backs, up to the center of contact, and there find itself absorbed. Then the surge would come from the other line. The leaders bearing these repeated shocks were almost crushed. Sweat poured from their faces. The dust rising from the plaza choked them. No words were uttered now, only breaths exploding. The anger of months and years was slowly spending itself. At last there was a decision. The party which had refused to cooperate with the white man and had resisted the schools and the missionaries was literally pushed out of the village. That decision was never questioned.

The village of Oraibi is said to have existed since sometime before A.D. 1050, and at the time of its "civil war" it was still the largest of the Hopi villages. Today, it is populated by scarcely a hundred men, women, and children, living amid the ruins of decaying stone buildings. The group that was pushed out, taking only bedding, food, and personal belongings, moved seven miles north and founded the village of Hotevilla, where they remain today. As they passed beyond the limits of old Oraibi, they said: "Well, it has to be this way. Now that you have passed me over this line, it is done."

The party of the white man had won, but no love went to the white man as a result of the triumph. The Hopis had settled things in their own way, and had remained Hopis.

9

THE TOOL THAT SHAPES ITSELF

Law has to do with outward forms of behavior; it is concerned with the ways in which people work their way out of trouble.

Language, by contrast, has to do with inward habits of the mind and how people see the world and express their notions about it. It is not only a passive instrument by which thoughts and feelings are uttered; it is an active agent helping to create the very things which are seen and talked about. A language in which there were no words for black and white would be the speech of a people who had never experienced black and white.

The first settlers in the Americas had hundreds of languages, so richly varied as to structure and rules of mutation that it is useless to generalize about them. (Sapir's generalizations and the classification noted in chapter 5 are meaningful chiefly to the professional linguist.) Yet studies of certain of these native tongues explain partially at least the habits of mind of the speakers. They tell something about the people which would not otherwise be disclosed.

The Navajo and Hopi languages, differing markedly from each other, are yet each so strikingly different from European languages as to suggest a different realm of experience. It cannot be assumed that all Indian experience is identical, or even similar, but the evidence offered by these two tribal tongues is interesting in itself.

Writing of the Navajo language, Robert Young and William Morgan remark: "The pattern of thought varies so greatly from our English pattern that we have no small difficulty in learning to think like, and subsequently to express ourselves like the Navaho."[1]

Perhaps the first impression derived from a reading of the descriptive material published by Young and Morgan and by the late Clyde Kluckhohn centers on the role played by the verb in the Navajo language. It seems almost as if the language were reduced to verb forms: forms used with infinite flexibility as to time or tense, mode of operation, direction of movement, duration of action, numbers, and identification of the speaker. To a Navajo Indian, evidently, it is of great importance whether an action takes place in the immediate instant and is done with, whether it occurs repeatedly, or customarily, or irregularly, or conditionally, or hypothetically, among many possible modes and aspects. One must suppose that the mind of the speaker of such a language has accustomed itself to viewing action in multiple phases and the language reflects the habit of thought.

Navajo speech does not make an arbitrary division of past, present, and future of an action, but it is exceedingly precise in stating the relationship between the action and the thing acted upon. Vagueness with respect to persons or qualities is avoided. Expressions like "I see" or "I eat" are not used unless the intention is to stress indefiniteness; ordinarily the object seen or eaten would be stated. So subtle are some of the shades of meaning and intention used by the Navajos in rendering the preciseness of their thought that English translation is difficult and may require extensive optional readings.

For the Navajo speaker, moreover, words have function and power in themselves. As Kluckhohn explains: "Some words attract good; others drive away evil. Certain words are dangerous—they may be uttered only by special persons under specially defined conditions. Hence there are specialized vocabularies known only to those who are trained in a craft or ceremonial skill."[2]

The Navajo language is not word poor. An exact word count would be difficult to compute, in the absence of an agreed-upon definition of what a word is, but the richness of the language is suggested by an extensive plant-list vocabulary. Some 600 plants have been identified from their Navajo equivalents, an extraordinary number, considering the sparse vegetative cover of the arid Navajo country.[3] Every occupation, in fact, has its own special vocabulary. Relatively few English words have been incorporated into the language, which readily coins new words or expressions as they are needed. Since the language abounds in words having a like sound but a contrary meaning, it lends itself to pun making, in which the Navajos love to indulge.

The Hopi language, as analyzed by Dr. B. L. Whorf, is concerned in its own way with the visible world and the experience of living.[4] It is difficult to describe the quality of a language—as if one would pick up a handful of water and describe the quality of wetness. There is, for example, the feeling about time, with which language is constantly concerned.

In English it is proper to say "ten days from now." To the Hopi mind evidently that is as inaccurate as saying "I am ten years long." The Hopi language does not employ cardinal numbers to measure time's duration. Numbers are reserved for the counting of things that occur in segments, as sheep in a band. Time is a continuing. It does not break off into particles labeled days, months, or years. If a Hopi agrees to a meeting at some time in the future, he will not say "Meet me ten days from now," but rather "Meet me on the tenth day." Length of time is a relationship between two points, now and later.

In speaking of substances, likewise, the Hopi prefers preciseness. English has many names for things, which, standing by themselves, have no boundaries or dimensions, no tags by which the mind grasps the meaning. So English adds an extraneous element, sacrificing directness and economy. A "glass" of water, a "box" of matches, a "spool" of thread are not expressions concerned with a glass, a box, or a spool; they are circumlocutions indicating dimensions, quantity, or shape of what otherwise would be a formless or indefinite amount of a given substance. In the Hopi language shape and size of an object are not mentioned unless the thought is concerned with them. A small quantity of water has its specific word and the sense does not require that it be contained in a glass or any other object.

Hopi differs from English also in its use of action words. The employment of past, present, and future time with reference to a happening is an artificial division of consciousness. The essential distinction is between things that have happened and things that may be expected to happen at a future time. The Hopi verb limits itself to this kind of division. Tenses are not employed, but instead verbs are put through various shifts to indicate whether the speaker is stating what has happened (immediately or more remotely), what he expects to happen in the future, or a generality like "Birds fly." If it is necessary to state that one event happened before or after a second, or that the two happened simultaneously, the modulation shows that. The relationship remains between the two events, not between the events and an arbitrary division of time labeled past, present, or future.

Much of the subject matter with which any language deals is abstract, generalized, or imaginary. In order to convey meaning in these realms most European languages deal with the abstract, the generalized, and the imaginary as if it had dimensions, substance, duration in time. A box can be grasped, so an argument or an idea is grasped. The mind vaults to a conclusion, as a rider might vault to the saddle. The English language abounds in such expressions as "torrents of abuse," "boundless joy," "burning zeal," "depths of despair," "sleepless devotion."

The Hopi language employs a simple device to achieve the same purpose of expressing ideas of duration, intensity, sequence, differences of degree, constancy, repetition, and similar shadings. The device consists of a special part of speech called tensors, which have no meaning except as they are attached to a noun to lend intensity, tendency, duration, sequence, or other phases of meaning. By the use of tensors the most concrete noun can be loaded with qualifications and limited-sense meanings.

The Hopis are aware of physical existence expressed as shapes, colors, movements—the things which the senses take in. They are also aware of events and existences which seem to be nonphysical and invisible. Qualities attach to physical substances which cause them to grow, to change, to disappear—to eventuate. Also, each thing of substance follows its own mode of growing, changing, disappearing. And finally, the form in which a substance now manifests itself was determined by an earlier form in which it appeared, and as its present form is determining what it will be like later. This complex notion of reality, which the Hopi language expresses and helps to create in the mind of the Hopi speaker, comes to the surface also in Hopi social organization, in ceremonial observances, in Hopi personality itself.

If nothing else were known about the Hopi people, a knowledge of their language intricacies would illuminate their way of life, making apparent what Kluckhohn has remarked: "What people think and feel, and how they report what they think and feel, is determined, to be sure, by their individual physiological state, by their personal history, and by what actually happens in the outside world. But it is also determined by a factor which is often overlooked; namely, the pattern of linguistic habits which people have acquired as members of a particular society. The events of the 'real' world are never felt or reported as a machine would do it. There is a selection process and an interpretation in the very act of response. Some features of the external situation are highlighted; others are ignored or not fully discriminated.

". . . Since persons are trained from infancy to respond in these ways they take such discriminations for granted, as part of the inescapable stuff of life. But when we see two peoples with different social traditions respond in different ways to what appear to the outsider to be identical stimulus-situations, we realize that experience is much less a 'given,' an absolute, than we thought. Every language has an effect upon what the people who use it see, what they feel, how they think, what they can talk about."

Dorothy Lee in describing the language behavior of the Wintu Indians of northern California gives insight into another tribal world.[5] She finds that the Wintu speaker does not presume that man is the measure of all things—his language is innocent of the terms to foster such a presumption. What the individual expresses is only his limited sense of reality, which exists apart from him in timeless and boundless duration. She remarks: "The Wintu actualizes a given design [of reality] endowing it with temporality and form through his experience. But he neither creates nor changes; the design remains immutable."

The practical effect of his language habits is to implant in the Wintu an "attitude of humility and respect toward reality, toward nature and society." Assertiveness of statement is alien, the source perhaps of embarrassment. The Wintu does not say *this is*, but rather something like *this appears to be*, or *my experience makes this seem so*. Even as he speaks out of unique experience, he is conscious of the limitations of his reach.

As a further effect of his habit of expression, the Wintu refrains from any attempt to control or exploit the natural order of which he is a part. He kills game only when he is in need of food, and then uses every part of the slain animal which yielded itself to him. To do less would be to show lack of respect.

10

THE INNER WORLD

In seeking to transform the New World into a "humanly acceptable landscape" (Linton's phrase), these first settlers explored the land, tried new things, and achieved a peace within themselves. They learned to live wherever they paused in their travels—in forest lands, on the prairies of tall grass, along coastal waters, on dry mesa tops. They tamed wild plants and brought them into use. They worked out rules of conduct which eased the tensions of living together.

In all that they attempted they seemed to be most deeply concerned with the moral quality of their relations with each other. They contrived no abstract ethics; they were not idealists. Rather they were constantly seeking a quality of life which was never at any point at variance with the force which created life. Men who thwarted their fellows or the understood rules were not forced back into line. It was not the practice "to put on any offender at any time the full penalty which the law makes possible." Let the offender come back into line of his own volition, as a flooded stream in time slacks off. Repressive measures were used only when the individual in society could not or would not square himself with the rules; and then the measures taken were designed to localize the trouble and prevent its spreading. So a rampaging meteor burns itself out against the friction of a yielding but containing atmosphere.

The effect of these efforts was a deep-lying unity and integration which have persisted after whole segments of prior existence have disappeared. Indians who are no longer hunters, who no longer even inhabit the hunting ground which was once theirs, still think and talk as their grandfathers thought and talked before them. Theirs is the secret of the twig that emerges ever green from the severed stump.

Some of the clues to this unity and integration are found in Indian art. The word is not right, but no other suggests itself. Art as it is understood in the culture of European peoples suggests creations in stone, on canvas, in formalized sound patterns, and is deeply associated with the names of individual masters.[1]

Indian art is least concerned with individual technical mastery of a material or medium of expression. Virtuosity is not prized, though skill is pursued assiduously. Of late years certain craftsmen have been induced to sign their names or their brands to pottery creations, but this is an innovation of no significance. It satisfies the desire of the collector to buy a name, and possibly the Indian potter gets extra pennies for it.[2]

The variety of ways in which Indians combine skill and imagination to evoke works of art reveals a rich inner life. Typical though not necessarily the greatest of these creations are the engravings on ivory of the Eskimos, the goat-hair and cedar-bark (Chilkat) blankets of the Northwest coast, the sculptured masks of the Iroquois, the stone carving (prehistoric) of the Ohio Valley, the polychrome pottery of the Southwest, the basketry of the desert people, the ceremonial pageantry which existed everywhere. In no instance was the product individualized or disassociated from its functional character.

The weaving of the Chilkat blanket will illustrate this.[3] The blanket served as a family coat of arms, but it was also the symbol of an entire society. Among the Tlingit Indians who created the blanket, family was the pillar of the world. One's membership in a family was blazoned forth on every possible occasion, in fantastic imagery—on house fronts, on interior supports within the house, on the canoe and on the tools and weapons used by the individual, on the least important articles of everyday use. It had its most exuberant expression in this blanket, to obtain wool for which involved a desperate scramble over the most inaccessible heights of rock and ice in pursuit of the Rocky Mountain goat. The woman shredded the inner bark of the red cedar and twisted fine wool around it. The yarn was dyed with a variety of pigments steeped in urine as a mordant. In her designs she annihilated the convention of perspective by placing in one plane the front, side, rear and cross-section views of her subject, with accompanying details of landscape, subsidiary animals, or whatever else belonged.

It was not art alone which the Tlingit woman wove into her blanket, but a statement of belief which she conveyed to and shared with every living member of her tribe. She encompassed everything, as the concept of family encompassed everything. The fasting and abstinence which she practiced in the course of creating the blanket further emphasized the social nature of her act.

A student of the Southwest, Helen H. Roberts, watching Apache women create baskets out of the poverty of the desert, was moved to ask how such apparently unimaginative people could accomplish such acts of beauty.[4] Out of nothing, seemingly, they wove a magic of "clear-cut, beautifully balanced designs," reminding her of "flowers, pinwheels, rose windows . . . magnified snowflakes lying on black velvet."

Carl Lumholtz, pondering the same question many years before while living with the Huichol Indians in Mexico, noted that ornamentation was not the end sought.[5] Decorative design was wholly incidental, yet it was not the result of chance. The magic of creation was always for a purpose. The purpose, he decided, was religious. The Huichol Indians spent a great part of their lives at ceremonies and feasts. From May to August, during the dry season, they prayed for rain. Then when the rains came, they still found it necessary to pause for two- and three-day intervals to visit their shrines. Religion was not an institutional performance which professionally trained initiates could render; it was a personal matter which concerned everyone. Life was full of sacred things, and sacred things habitually were reduced to symbols. And these were woven into the fabric of life.

This again is the essence of what Ruth Underhill found among the Papago Indians of southern Arizona, who call upon the powers of song. As she reports: "People sang in trouble, in danger, to cure the sick, to confound their enemies, and to make the crops grow. They sang, as they fought and as they worked, all together. This was a tiny, close-knit community, where the good of one was the good of all; where, if one person starved or was ill, the whole group suffered loss . . . Song became not only the practical basis of Papago life, but also the most precious possession of the people."[6]

In their study of Indian dance steps, Bessie and May G. Evans concluded that Indians worked hard to perfect their art; they persisted in it even though it might mean inviting official displeasure; and they looked for no applause and no economic returns. In short, the dance was "a channel not only for the outlet of his esthetic nature but for the inflow of spiritual power."[7]

What is overtly expressed, of course, has its hidden origins in attitudes and impulses. Language helps to shape these, and is in turn shaped and developed by them. A similar reciprocating action flows between the outward art creation and the covert mind.

Ruth L. Bunzel has explored these attitudes and impulses —call them motivations—for one tribe, the Zuñi.[8]

She reports that: "To the Zuñi the whole world appears animate. Not only are night and day, wind, clouds, and trees possessed of personality, but even articles of human manufacture, such as houses, pots, and clothing, are alive and sentient. All matter has its inseparable spiritual essence."

And again: "Of this animate universe man is an integral part. The beings about him are neither friendly nor hostile. In so far as all are harmonious parts of the whole, the surrounding forces sustain and preserve humanity in the status quo."

Pushing further, she found: "The sense of conflict as the basic principle of life does not dominate man's relation to the universe any more than it dominates man's relation to man. The Promethean theme—man's tragic and heroic struggle against the gods—has no place in Zuñi philosophic speculation. Nor have any of the other concepts of cosmic conflicts which have always absorbed the interest of Asiatic and European philosophers and mystics, the antithesis between good and evil, or between matter and spirit. There is no Satan in Zuñi ideology, and no Christ.

"The world, then, is as it is, and man's place in it is what it is. Day follows night and the cycle of the years complete themselves. In the spring the corn is planted, and if all goes well the young stalks grow to maturity and fulfill themselves . . . So man, too, has his days and his destined place in life . . . Man dies but mankind remains . . . This is not resignation, the subordination of desire to a stronger force, but the sense of man's oneness with the universe."

Or said in another way: "Man is not lord of the universe. The forests and fields have not been given him to despoil.

He is equal in the world with the rabbit and the deer and the young corn plant...."

The Zuñi Indians pray, but with them "Prayer is never the spontaneous outpouring of the overburdened soul; it is more nearly a repetition of magical formulae ... Prayer frequently forms part of set rituals. Then whether publicly declaimed or muttered so as to be inaudible to profane ears, the efficacy of the prayer depends in no small measure on its correct rendition." And moreover, "In their prayers Zuñis do not humble themselves before the supernatural; they bargain with it."

The flavor of all this is captured everlastingly in Zuñi ritual poetry, or what we prefer perhaps to call prayer, carried over into excellent English by Dr. Bunzel:

My fathers,
Our sun father,
Our mothers,
Dawn
As you arise and come out to your sacred place,
I pass you on your road.
The source of our flesh,
White corn,
Prayer meal,
Shell,
Pollen,
I offer to you.
Our sun father,
To you I offer prayer meal.
To you we offer it.
To you we offer pollen.
According to the words of my prayer
Even so may it be.
There shall be no deviation.
Sincerely
From my heart I send forth my prayers.
To you prayer meal,
Shell I offer,
Pollen I offer.
According to the words of my prayer.

Even so may it be.
Now this day,
My ancestors,
You have attained the far-off place of waters.
This day,

Carrying plume wands,
Plume wands which I have prepared for your use,
I pass you on your roads.
I offer you plume wands.
When you have taken my plume wands,
All your good fortune whereof you are possessed
You will grant to me.
And furthermore
You, my mother,
Verily, in the daylight
With thoughts embracing,
We passed our days.
Now you have attained the far-off place of waters.
I give you plume wands,
Plume wands which I have prepared for your use.
Drawing your plume wands to you,
And sharing my plume wands

.   .   .

All of your good fortune whatsoever
May you grant to us.
Preserving us along a safe road,
May our roads be fulfilled.

At this point we have moved ahead centuries after
Columbus, but Zuñi imagery is so timeless that there might
never have been the discovery by Europeans. It is like the
music of a harp beneath the sea.

The prayer offered when a Zuñi infant is presented to the
sun, eight days after its birth, is today what it was a thousand years ago. Constancy exists in the universe, if man can
find it . . .

Now this is the day.
Our child,
Into the daylight
You will go out standing.
Preparing for your day,
We have passed our days.

.   .   .

Now this day
Our fathers,
Dawn priests,
Have come out standing to their sacred place.
Our sun father
Having come out standing to his sacred place,
Our child,
It is your day

.   .   .

May your road be fulfilled
Reaching to the road of your sun father.
When your road is fulfilled
In your thoughts (may we live)
May we be the ones whom your thoughts will embrace,
For this, on this day,
To our sun father
We offer prayer meal.
To this end:
May you help us all to finish our roads.

PART 2

New World Rediscovered

"*Our world hath of late discovered another . . . so new and infantine, that he is yet to learne his ABC. It is not yet fully fifty yeeres that he knew neither letters, nor waight, nor measures, nor apparell, nor corne, nor vines; but was all naked, simly pure, in Natures lappe . . . It was an unpolluted, harmelesse infant world; yet have we not whipped and submitted the same into our discipline or schooled him by the advantage of our valour or naturall forces; nor have wee instructed him by our justice and integrity, nor subdued by our magnanimity. Most of their answers, and a number of the negotiations we have had with them, witnesse that they were nothing short of us, nor beholding to us for any excellency of naturall wit or perspicuitie concerning pertinency. The wonderfull, or as I may call it, amazement-breeding magnificence of the never-like seene cities of Cusco and Mexico, and amongst infinite such like things, the admirable garden of that king, where all the trees, the fruits, the herbes and plants according to the order and greatnesse they have in a garden, were most artificially framed in gold; as also in his cabinet; all the living creatures that his countrey or his seas produced, were cast in gold; and the exquisite beauty of their works, in precious stones, in feathers, in cotton, and in painting, shew that they yeelded as little unto us in cunning and industrie. But concerning unfained devotion, awefull observance of lawes. unspotted integrity, bounteous liberality, due loyalty and free liberty, it hath greatly availed us that we had not so much as they: by which advantage they have lost, cast-away, sold, undone and betraied themselves.*"

—Montaigne, *Essays*, Third Book,
Chapter Six (Florio Trans.).

11

THE CURTAIN RISES

The stream of people crossing over from one nameless world into another as nameless continued without interruption. It flowed through the river valleys in sight of the mountains, and spread out in time over the wide plains and the high mesas.

Countless lifetimes, millennium upon millennium, until the people were everywhere. They had no name for the whole land, but they knew and gave their words to the parts, the mountains and streams and lakes, the trees and grass that grew upon the land, the beasts that moved in the woods and grazed in the open prairies. They knew and became a part of everything that existed between the shores of the two oceans.

The hardest thing these first settlers would ever have to learn was that the land which was theirs, which they had possessed and had everywhere touched by the reaching of the mind, had to be shared with strangers. If they had foreseen how it would turn out, they might have reacted with forceful decision against the first visitors, though that would have violated the almost universal rule of hospitality. European civilization was materially a more powerful force, yet European civilization would have been the poorer without the riches of the Americas.

The record of discovery and colonization is an old one, many times repeated, but it will be useful to mention the more important times and places. The assault came from many directions, and quickly, blow upon blow.[1]

The cost of discovering America probably did not exceed $100,000. That would be the approximate amount expended in outfitting the three vessels which the Spanish rulers made available to the Genoa-born mariner Christopher

Columbus. It was an investment from which the Spanish crown would derive untold millions in dividends.

The Norsemen who went voyaging into the unknown West some five hundred years earlier made no cash investment and sought no returns. The sagas contain one vague reference to an effort at colonization. We are told that Thorfin Karlsefni, presumably in A.D. 1020, brought cattle in his boat and the bellowing of a bull frightened the natives. The effort was abandoned after two years.[2]

Five journeys are recounted in the sagas, not all of which are equally probable. The very first may not have been the voyage of Leif Ericson in A.D. 1000. There is evidence, disputed by some scholars, that the first European to view the western continent was Bjarni, son of Heriulf, who was blown off the course in attempting to reach Greenland from Iceland in about A.D. 996. Bjarni did not make a landing but coasted along three bodies of land before finally coming safe to port before his father's Greenland homestead.

Leif's voyage followed, and it may be that his motive was to explore the landfall reported by Bjarni. He spent the winter in a country he called Wineland, where wild grapes grew in profusion. On his return voyage he brought samples of everything that grew in the strange country.

Thorfin Karlsefni followed with his vague plans for colonization. He spent two years in the land, traded red cloth for the furs of the natives (skraellings), and eventually had a bloody battle with them. Perhaps this was the first such encounter. It would not be the last.

The last recorded voyage was made by Freydis, daughter of Eric the Red, in A.D. 1024. She seems to have been touched with madness and the expedition came to grief when she slaughtered members of her own party.

What adds probability to these accounts is the fact that they may have been recorded in writing before the close of the century in which they occurred. The man who could have written them down was Ari, called The Learned, who was born in A.D. 1067. His grandfather was Gelli, a cousin and contemporary of Karlsefni. An uncle, Thorkel Gellison, could have made available to Ari information which he had obtained directly in conversations with companions of Eric the Red.

Ari is credited with developing a written form of the Icelandic language, and it can be assumed that he recorded these tales of adventure. No manuscripts prepared by him have been found, but it is believed that later writers had access to such manuscripts.

Students of the Icelandic sagas differ sharply among themselves as to the actual regions visited and explored by these Norsemen. The difficulty arises in attempting to identify the place names used by the explorers. *Helluland*, one of the places mentioned, is probably identical with Labrador or possibly Labrador and a portion of Newfoundland considered as a single country. *Markland*, another place mentioned, may again refer to the two countries confused as one. *Wonder-Strands* may be the southern coast of Labrador. *Streamfirth* is thought to refer to the St. Lawrence River estuary. *Wineland*, about which the greatest difference of opinion prevails, may be New England or possibly Long Island Sound and the Hudson River. There is some evidence that Scandinavian explorers may have traveled inland as far as the Great Lakes area, but this would have been somewhat later and the port of entry would have been through Hudson Strait and Hudson Bay.

Columbus never did get clear in his own mind the nature of the discovery he had made. In four voyages to the New World—the first ending at dawn on October 12, 1492—he continued to think that he had been exploring some portion of the Asiatic world, the Indies. His second voyage was made in 1493, the third in 1498, when the mainland of South America was revealed to him, and the fourth and final in 1502, after which he returned home friendless and out of favor. His original landfall was a small coral island named by him San Salvador, and known today at Watling's Island.

During his first visit Columbus built a small fort on the northern shore of Haiti, which he named Española. The island remained the base of Spanish operations in the New World for many years. He left one hundred colonists behind when he returned home that first time, and brought out 1,500 on his next trip. He also brought colonists on his third voyage, and in 1502 Nicolás de Ovando brought 2,500 colonists. Spain acted quickly in those days, as the movements of her sons show clearly.

By 1513 Puerto Rico had been conquered (1508), Jamaica settled (1509), Cuba circumnavigated (1508), and seventeen towns altogether had been chartered in Española. Throughout all of the sixteenth century an average of from one to two thousand Spaniards migrated to the New World each year. Preference in granting permits for emigration was given to married men, who were urged to take their families out with them. Unmarried Spanish women were discouraged from migrating, and the shortage of women grew so acute that the authorities attempted to remedy the effects of their policy by shipping white female slaves to the islands. Either the supply was short or the male population was not satisfied with the choice of partners offered. At any rate in 1514 the Spanish court recognized and approved what was doubtless already well established in practice: marriage with Indian women.

Exploration was pushed even faster than colonization. The Pacific Ocean was discovered by Balboa in 1513. The year 1519 was momentous. It was the year in which Pineda completed the first map of the Gulf of Mexico, coasting from Florida to Vera Cruz, and back, and discovering the mouth of the Mississippi. Magellan found continent's end in the south and, sailing through the Strait which now bears his name, he crossed the Pacific to the Philippine Islands. Finally, that was the year in which Cortés made the great march on Mexico, which was to reveal something of the staggering wealth of the New World.

By 1525 Spaniards had explored the Atlantic coast from Nova Scotia to the Strait of Magellan. Knowledge of the Pacific side came slower. A shipyard was built at Zacatula on the Pacific in 1522, but twenty years passed before the Spaniards got up the coast as far as Oregon.

The first efforts to penetrate the continent north of Mexico were dismally unsuccessful.[3] The mainland Indians were not as compliant as the islanders. Ponce de León, who had discovered Florida in 1513 and found the natives hostile, went back in 1521 with two hundred colonists; his party was attacked, and he himself was mortally wounded. Between that effort and the establishment of St. Augustine in 1565, no less than six efforts to colonize were launched from the West Indies. One of these ventures, led by Pánfilo de Narváez, started at Tampa Bay, crossed to Tallahassee, and terminated in shipwreck on the Texas coast. This shipwreck is memorable because from among the survivors who were not lost at sea or killed (and, it is said, eaten by cannibalistic Texas Indians), emerged Cabeza de Vaca with three companions, who spent the next six years as involuntary guests of their cannibal hosts and in wandering westward across Texas and New Mexico, then southward to Culiacán, in the Mexican state of Sinaloa, where a Spanish outpost had been established only a short time before.

In this same early effort at colonization on the mainland De Soto landed in Florida with six hundred colonists and allowed himself to be persuaded by one Indian tale after another of fabulous riches, always in the next Indian town, until he had gone from Tampa Bay to Pensacola Bay, across the Savannah River, north into the Carolina Piedmont, south to Mobile Bay, then across the Mississippi near Memphis. Next he trekked westward across Arkansas and followed the Arkansas River to its mouth. Finally he died in May 1542 and was buried by his frightened comrades in the Mississippi.

The stories brought back by Cabeza de Vaca from his wanderings across Texas and New Mexico, and rumors circulated in Mexico of an island inhabited by Amazons and of fabulous riches to be found in the Seven Cities of Cibola, stirred up new efforts. What had happened in Mexico and Peru might again happen, up there in the north. Mountains of gold and silver might reward boldness and devotion to the Holy Faith.

The leader chosen for the new expedition was Francisco Vásquez Coronado, who in March 1539 sent forward an exploratory party led by Friar Marcos and Estevan, the Negro, who had made the dolorous journey with de Vaca. They followed old Indian trails up the west coast of Mexico and reached the Zuñi pueblos in New Mexico, where Estevan was killed. Friar Marcos got back to report that, while he had not seen the cities of Cibola, they were thought to be larger and perhaps richer than Mexico.

Coronado left Compostela on the Pacific coast with an expedition that was intended to provide against any emergency. He had two hundred horsemen, seventy foot soldiers, and one thousand Mexican Indian allies; in addition, he had a thousand head of livestock, including horses and mules, cattle, sheep, goats, and pigs. Starting out in February, he reached the Zuñi pueblos in July and in the same month the Hopi mesas were visited by a lieutenant. Still another aide went on past the Hopi country and found the Grand Canyon of the Colorado.

Coronado wintered on the Rio Grande near the pueblo of Isleta, and in April 1541 he went northeastward into the Plains, searching for Gran Quivira. On this journey he crossed the Pecos River, found roving bands of Apaches on the buffalo plains, crossed the panhandles of Texas and Oklahoma, and probably reached eastern Kansas. There he visited villages of the Wichita or Pawnee Indians.

It was a big country, and in the tongues of the many Indian tribes living in it there were names for the hills and streams and all the familiar things that met the eye. To the Spaniards, looking for plunder, it was simply an empty and worthless terrain. Not for forty years would they return for a second look.

The road which Cabeza de Vaca had stumbled upon in his flight from the unpleasant things that had happened to him on the Texas coast, and which Coronado retraced to the Rio Grande, was an old road, perhaps the oldest in all of North America. It was a trade route, over which turquoise went south from the Pueblo country, in exchange for the plumage of parrots and other birds of tropical lowlands. Buffalo hides, shells, pearls, metals, obsidian, and corn were also exchanged.

Its significance was not limited to trade. Professor Carl Sauer, who has studied the region intensively, observes that "the high native culture of Mexico, proceeding ultimately from Mayan Central America, reached as far north as the valley of the Culiacan River on the west coast. There is reason to surmise that the spread of this culture northward was along the Pacific coast, rather than from interior Mexico to the coast."[4] The rugged Western Sierra would have discouraged the movement of people and their ideas westward out of the valley of Mexico. Not the aggressive Aztecs and their neighbors the Tarascans, but cultures older than these, moving out of Middle America, traveled this coastal road.

Possibly it was over this road that the first corn went northward to the Mogollon and the Hohokam people. Pottery making and weaving with cotton would have followed.

It was scarcely an accident that Cabeza de Vaca and Coronado should have found the road. Any Indian familiar with the area would know about it and would have pointed it out as the logical route for traveling north or south. Professor Sauer writes: "In the New World the routes of the great explorations usually have become historic highways, and thus has been forged a link connecting the distant past with the modern present. For the explorers followed main trails beaten by many generations of Indian travel. There was, in varying degree, intercommunication and exchange of goods between Indian villages or tribes. The resultant trails were as direct as the terrain, the need of food and drink en route, and reasonable security permitted, and were fixed by long experience as the best way of traversing a particular stretch of country. Explorers, being sensible men if their explorations succeeded, used Indian guides, who took them over Indian roads."

The honor of making the official discovery of the New World might as readily have gone to a fellow Genoese, Giovanni Caboto, as to Columbus. Giovanni had gone to London in 1484, after an unrewarding early career in Venice, and presently anglicized his name to John Cabot. He, too, was enthralled by the problem of world geography and tinkered with the construction of a wooden globe with the lands and seas mapped out on it, while he sought financial backing for a westward voyage. In Bristol he found such support. In 1491 and again in 1492 he explored the seas westward from Ireland, where unknown islands were said to exist. He failed to go far enough to the west and soon after his second voyage word came from Spain of Columbus's return from the Indies.

This news stirred great excitement in England and Henry VII personally visited Cabot in Bristol. He immediately issued letters patent authorizing the mariner to explore the West, the North, and the East, requiring, however, that he stay clear of the southern regions where the Spanish monarchs had already laid out their claims. Henry's enthusiasm did not carry him so far as to venture his own money in the enterprise, but he did provide that Cabot might bring merchandise into England duty free. The Crown would be satisfied with a fifth part of any profits.

Even with this royal encouragement Cabot spent a year in obtaining the necessary financing. Not until May 2, 1497, was he able to clear Bristol with a single ship and a crew of eighteen men. He was gone just three months, returning August 6. It is thought that he skirted Cape Breton, Newfoundland, and possibly Labrador, and although he made a landing and picked up fresh water, he saw nothing but untenanted shores, great forests, and abundant fish. King Henry was elated nevertheless and gave John Cabot a present of ten pounds together with a pension of twenty pounds a year.

Cabot made a second Atlantic crossing in May 1498 with two ships. The Bristol merchants had decided to risk a little more. He explored from the icy seas north of Greenland down the North American coast to perhaps as far south as Virginia. This voyage was completely disillusioning, for while Cabot found Indians, they had nothing but fish and furs to barter; no silks, no spices or perfumes. The merchants wrote off their investment to the cost of experience and doubtless made it quite clear that they would not pay for more. John Cabot retired to live obscurely on his twenty pounds a year.

The Portuguese mariner Gaspar Corte-Real also made two voyages into the northern seas, in 1500 and 1501. Not content with obtaining fish and furs, he contrived to capture sixty natives, perhaps Eskimos, on the Labrador coast. This was not the first instance of forceful abduction of New World inhabitants. That dubious distinction probably belongs to Columbus himself. Two of Corte-Real's ships, with their human merchandise, reached Portugal; the third, bearing the mariner himself, disappeared without a trace.

The northern lands of the continent remained unexplored for another century, although the coasts and offshore waters had frequent visitors from across the sea. One of these, John Verrazano, an Italian sailing for Francis I, in 1524 struck the Atlantic coast at about the latitude of the Carolinas and probably went as far north as the mouth of the Hudson River. He, too, took home a trophy, a young boy yielded up by a frightened old grandmother. He had designs on a girl of about eighteen as well, "beautiful and very tall," but she shrieked so loud that the landing party hurried back to the ship before the inhabitants of the nearby village could descend on them.

Explorers seeking glory and Asiatic plunder might not care to traffic with fish, but honest fishermen from Norman and Breton ports apparently learned about the fishbanks of the New World very soon after the voyages of Columbus and others. Catholic Europe was a fish-hungry Europe, and nowhere in the world was fish so abundant as off the Newfoundland Banks. Father Biard in the Jesuit Relation for 1616 states that Breton fishermen were in the vicinity by 1504, and that Captain Jean Denys, of Honfleur, brought back the first fish in 1506. For this he gained less renown than was accorded Thomas Aubert, of Dieppe, who brought back some natives in the year 1508 and exhibited them "to the wonder and applause of France."

Father Biard also comments that "certain tribes are now our implacable enemies, such as the Excominquois [Eskimos], who inhabit the northern coast of the great Gulf of St. Lawrence and do us a great deal of harm. This warfare was begun (as they say) when certain Basques tried to commit a wicked outrage. However, they paid well for their cursed incontinence, but not only they, for on their account both the St. Malo people and many others suffered, and still suffer a great deal each year."

One of these Breton mariners, Jacques Cartier, of St. Malo, came nearest to establishing a permanent colony within that first century after discovery.[5] Evidently he had gone out to the fishing banks, and he may also have been a crew member under Verrazano. At any rate he had knowledge of the waters of the New World, and he persuaded Francis I to sponsor a colonizing effort. In 1534 with two vessels and sixty men he entered the Gulf of St. Lawrence by the Straits of Belle Isle. At the Bay of Chaleur in New Brunswick he was in contact with Micmac Indians, easternmost representatives of the Algonquian family. Afterward, rounding Gaspé Peninsula, he met Iroquois Indians at their summer fishing camps. Cartier had no good opinion of these Iroquois. A few sous, he thought, would pay for everything they owned.

It was not until the following year that Cartier actually sailed up the St. Lawrence, getting his boats as far as the Richelieu Rapids, then marching on foot to the Indian village of Hochelaga, on the site of present-day Montreal. He thought he was reaching the city of the great Khan, so firm was the belief in the minds of Europeans that they were in Asiatic lands when they reached the New World. What Cartier found was a village surrounded by timber palisades and long bark-roofed houses—the Longhouse of the Iroquois.

He spent the winter at an Indian village lower down the river, the Quebec of today. It was a bitter experience. Not knowing how to approach the Indians and having contempt for any man who could not claim France as his home, Cartier quickly got himself and his men into a stage of siege. They needed help from the Indians if they were to survive, but they were afraid to trust them. They would not permit the Indians to enter the fort which they hastily built, and the Indians retaliated by demanding exorbitant prices in trade goods for the game which they brought. When scurvy broke out and twenty-five of the best sailors succumbed, they were buried under the snow out of sight of the Indians. The Indians, however, knew the ailment and they had a remedy for it: a tea brewed from the needles of an evergreen tree. It brought the plague under control. Cartier never reveals whether his opinion of his barbarian hosts improved after they had saved his company.

Events in Europe held up the colonizing enterprise until 1541, when Cartier and Sieur de Roberval again were at the Indian village of Stadacona (Quebec) with several hundred colonists recruited from French prisons. After two winters the effort was abandoned entirely, and seventy years would pass before France would again attempt to establish permanent settlements.

The far northwestern corner of the New World, principal port of entry for the earliest of all the settlers, was the last to become known to Europeans. The Russian admiral Vitus Bering sailed first in 1725 to establish the fact that Asia and America were sundered by water. It was not until 1741, however, that he discovered the Alaska mainland, and he did not survive to carry the report home. Actually, it was his lieutenant, Chirikof, who first sighted the mainland and who survived to make the report.[6]

12

THE GOLDEN MYTH

Not often in man's history has anything so astonishing occurred as the discovery of an entirely new and unpredicted world, peopled by an unknown race. The Europeans who made the discovery saw in the event, and in the people encountered, reflections of their own experience and history. They compared the scenery, the climate, and the fruits of the land to the things they knew at home. They ascribed to the people the customs, beliefs, and institutions with which they were familiar. Headmen they called kings and princes. They found evidences of their own type of religious practices, and evidences as well of practices which they considered irreligious. They complained of breaches of their own marriage laws or moral codes.

These hasty conclusions and failures of understanding offered a poor basis on which to build relations for the future.

In the beginning, Columbus was charmed.

"We saw houses and people on the spot, and the country around was very beautiful and as fresh and green as the gardens of Valencia in the month of March," he wrote after his first voyage.[1]

"Villages were seen near the seacoast, but as I discovered no large cities; and could not obtain any communication with the inhabitants, who all fled at our approach, I continued on west, thinking I should not fail in the end to meet with great towns and cities . . ." He was at the time skirting the coast of Cuba but assuming, of course, that he was in Asiatic waters.

On another occasion he wrote: "The people of this island [Haiti] and of all the others which I have become acquainted with, go naked as they were born, although some of the women wear at the loins a leaf or a bit of cotton cloth, which they prepare for that purpose. They do not possess iron, steel, or weapons, and seem to have no inclination for the latter, being timorous to the last degree. . . .

After they have shaken off their fear of us, they display a liberality in their behavior which no one would believe without witnessing it. No request of anything from them is ever refused, but they rather invite acceptance of what they possess, and manifest such a generosity that they would give away their own hearts. Let the article be of great or small value, they offer it readily, and receive anything which is tendered in return with perfect content. I forbade my men to purchase their goods with such worthless things as bits of platters and broken glass . . . The sailors would buy of them for a scrap of leather pieces of gold weighing two castellanos and a half . . . I thought such traffic unjust."

In all of this, and more, he was charmed. "They are not idolators," he explained, "nor have they any sort of religion except believing that power and goodness are in heaven, from which place they entertained a firm persuasion that I had come with my ships and men. On this account wherever we met them they showed us the greatest reverence after they had overcome their fear. Such conduct cannot be ascribed to their want of understanding, for they are a people of much ingenuity, and navigate all those seas . . ."

Such engaging simplicity did not get in the way of practical necessities. Columbus showed his appreciation of this in a letter to Santangel, who provided the cash for the first voyage: "On my arrival at the Indies I took by force from the first island I came to a few of the inhabitants, in order that they might learn our language."

Other practical necessities cast their shadows over the New World. It had proved difficult to enlist colonists who would risk sailing over the edge of the horizon, even though it be in the company of the "Admiral of the Ocean Seas." A Royal Proclamation was therefore issued ordering "that all and every person . . . who may have committed, or up to the day of publication of this our letter, may commit any murders and offenses, and other forms of crimes of whatever nature and quality they may be . . . shall go and serve in person in Española."

Of the colonists who were persuaded voluntarily to seek their fortunes in the islands, Columbus complained: "All is in favor of the settlers who have taken up their abode there because the best lands are given up to them . . . I should not say so much if these people were married men; but there are not six among them all whose purpose is not to amass all they can, and then decamp with it."

Then this further disillusioning note: "For one [native] woman they give a hundred castellanos, as for a farm; and this sort of trading is very common, and there are already a great number of merchants who go in search of girls. There are at this moment some nine or ten on sale; they fetch a good price, let their age be what it will."

Misunderstandings occurred on both sides. Perhaps that is the easiest way to explain it. The Indians thought that these were gods descending from the sky, and they were properly humble. Everywhere throughout the New World that was the initial reaction. The Indians met the white men full of wonder. They held out their hands to touch their garments, their pale skin. They brought offerings of food and of whatever else they had and prized.

The Europeans knew that they were not gods, and being practical men who had risked their lives and capital investments they were eager to obtain returns. Absconding with natives and carrying them back to Europe served two purposes—it reassured the creditors of the expedition that a new and strange world had been discovered and that perhaps an additional outlay of capital was warranted; while the sale of the natives as slaves, if no other articles of value had been obtained, permitted at least an interest payment on the original investment.[2]

What the Europeans could not appreciate was that they had come face to face with customs, beliefs, habits—cultures—which had been some thousands of years in the forming. Whether these were inferior or superior was inconsequential; they had grown out of an antiquity of their own, and if left to develop were capable of growing into civilizations quite unlike anything that Europe would produce. Already in that New World cities had grown old and fallen into decay and new cities were building.

The practical, enterprising men who sailed the seas and made the discoveries had no insight into any of this, but theirs was not the only failure. The tales which they brought back and published started a chain of speculation, which, while it did not explain the Americans or the American experience, did illuminate some of the recesses in the thinking of the Europeans.

In brief, Columbus and the countless men who followed him into the New World found what they thought was a people living in an age of innocence. They thought this because their own mythology taught them that all mankind once lived in such an age and had fallen from grace. Columbus wrote: "They do not know any religion, and I believe they could easily be converted to Christianity, for they are very intelligent . . . They are a loving people, without covetousness, and fit for anything . . . They love their neighbors as themselves, and their speech is the sweetest and gentlest in the world . . ."

European literature has a long tradition of glorifying the virtuous past. Ovid, writing in the surfeited times of Augustus, resurrected the golden age of antiquity and captured the jaded imaginations of his readers. Tacitus, a generation later, writing his *Germania*, held up to a cynical audience the mirror of a simple and barbaric people.

Montaigne was possibly the first European to find in the accounts of the New World the very virtues which blazed in antiquity and then died out to leave his generation tired and sick. Reading what the mariners had to say of the lands they visited, or perhaps even listening to word-of-mouth accounts, and looking out from his tower upon a world of desperate intrigue and ingenious cruelty (the Massacre of St. Bartholomew was one culmination of the age), he found himself regretting that Plato had not lived to share the new knowledge. Clearly, Montaigne thought, here was a world which surpassed the imagined perfection of the Republic.

Look you, he would say to Plato, here is a nation which "Hath no kind of traffic, no knowledge of letters, no intelligence of numbers, no name of magistrate, nor of politics, no use of service, of riches or of poverty; no contracts, no successions, no partitions, no occupation but idle; no apparel but natural, no manuring of lands, no use of wine . . . the very words that import a lie, falsehood, treason, covetousness, envy, detraction were never heard among them . . . furthermore, they live in a country of so exceeding pleasant and temperate situation, that as my testimonies have told me, it is very rare to see a sick body amongst them . . . They spend the whole day in dancing. The young men go ahunting after wild beasts with bows and arrows. Their women busy themselves therewhilst . . ."

Even the report that these gentle creatures sometimes practiced cannibalism did not disturb the enraptured essayist. "I am not sorry we note the barbarous horror of such an action, but grieved that prying so narrowly into their faults, we are so blinded in ours. I think there is more barbarism in eating men alive than to feed upon them being dead; to mangle by tortures and torments a body full of lively sense, to roast him in pieces, to make dogs and swine to gnaw and tear him as (we have not only read but seen very lately, not amongst ancient enemies, but our neighbors and fellow citizens; and which is worse, under pretense of piety and religion)." Then a final sentence: "We may then well call them barbarous, in regard of reason's rules, but not respect of us that exceed them in all kinds of barbarism."

Not only was virtue seen in simplicity, but the European tradition also supported a suspicion of learning. The notion is best voiced by Erasmus, in one of those passages in *In Praise of Folly* which seem to come from both sides of the mouth at once: "The simple people of the golden age were furnished with no school knowledge. Nature alone sufficed to guide them; instinct to prompt them how to live . . . What would have been the advantage of jurisprudence to men amongst whom bad morals—the sole apology for good laws—had no existence? It is clear to you, I presume, now that those who make wisdom their study, by so doing, make themselves the most miserable of mankind . . . By the immortal gods, then, I solemnly swear to you that no class of men is happier than that of those whom the world calls simpletons, fools, and blockheads!"

Such was the European dream: a land where men were physically handsome and morally virtuous; where one could live without fighting and murdering; where food could be gathered without laboring for it, and where one spent one's days in a perpetual dance. With respect to such desires, perhaps they were not a great deal different from those nurtured by the men who first crossed over from Asia in search of an easier existence.

It was not Rousseau who invented the idea of the Noble Savage. The impulse to believe that such a man of nature existed had long been present in European minds, in the desire to escape the ills and the complexities which their civilization had brought upon them, and in the idealism which ran through Western thought, driving men to believe in the perfectibility of life on earth. It became the very breath of the poetry of Goldsmith, Wordsworth, Coleridge, Southey, Shelley. And it permeated the literature of the continent as well.

Hardheaded men like Dr. Johnson were not beguiled by

oncept of the Noble Savage. "Pity is not natural to Johnson insisted. "Children are always cruel. Savages are always cruel."

This wholly opposite view was a natural enough reaction, but it is to be doubted whether it contributed anything to an understanding of the New World and the men who inhabited it. With a minimum of factual knowledge, Dr. Johnson and others who shared his sentiments reached sweeping conclusions. As when he challenged Boswell with: "The savages have no bodily advantages beyond those of civilized man. They have not better health; and as to care or mental uneasiness, they are not above it but below it, like bears." And on another occasion: "There are men who have preferred living among savages. Now what a wretch must he be, who is content with such conversation as can be had among savages!"

When a traveler is reported to Dr. Johnson as having said, "Here am I, free and unrestrained, amid the rude magnificence of nature, with this Indian woman by my side, and this gun with which I can procure food when I want it. What more can be desired for human happiness?" Johnson was derisive. "It is sad stuff; it is brutish. If a bull could speak, he might as well exclaim: Here am I with this cow and this grass; what being could enjoy greater felicity?"

What Dr. Johnson's blunt skepticism helped to accomplish on the philosophical side, the published accounts of white captives among Indians accomplished for the unreflecting reader. The story of Mary Rollandson's captivity appeared in 1682, six years after her experience with the Indians in King Philip's War. This account, published originally in Cambridge, Massachusetts, had a London edition immediately afterward and altogether thirty editions and reprints were brought out. Probably one of the most widely read early accounts of Indian-white relations, it did nothing to advance understanding.

Although Mrs. Rollandson and two of her children (a third died as a result of exposure) were released after a captivity of about three months, and she appears not to have been subject to any hardships that the Indians themselves were not forced to undergo from cold weather and lack of food, the experience lived in her mind as an indescribable horror. The Indians she thought to be "atheistical, proud, wild, cruel, barbarous, brutish." The flavor of

New England preaching animates some of her passages: "Oh, the roaring, and singing, and dancing, and yelling of those black creatures in the night, which made the place a lively resemblance of hell."

There were many such tales. Cotton Mather was an accomplished purveyor of overwrought picturizations of Indian cruelty and bloodlust. He chilled the blood of his listeners with stories of white captive children having their heads knocked against a tree or an eye gouged out when they cried too much.

Neither extreme was likely to promote understanding. The "sweetest and gentlest" people of Columbus's description could hardly be the brutish creatures discussed by Dr. Johnson and Mrs. Rollandson. They were the same people, racially, yet there seemed to be no middle ground where neutral judgments could be formed.

The most nearly rounded impression of what the Indian people looked like to European observers is to be found in the mountainous anecdote contained in the seventy-three volumes of *Jesuit Relations and Allied Documents* compiled by Reuben Gold Thwaites.[8] The Indian material, fortunately, has been extracted by Edna Kenton and published in two volumes. The observations of native life are especially valuable because of the time span covered by the documents, from 1610 to 1791, and because of the variety of conditions under which the observations were made. The information is often inconclusive or inaccurate or self-contradictory, and judgments which might have seemed unassailable three hundred years ago may seem inadequate today. Yet it would be difficult to find any comparable body of comment on the problems which must arise when men of different cultural heritages meet and try to understand each other.

Frequently the circumstances were far from the best for the promotion of understanding. Thus a French Jesuit wrote in 1639 from his Montreal station: "If you go to visit them in their cabins . . . you will find there a miniature picture of hell—seeing nothing, ordinarily, but fire and smoke, and on every side naked bodies, black, half-roasted, mingled pell-mell with the dogs, which are held as dear as the children of the house, and share the beds, plates, and food of their masters. Everything is in that cloud of dust and if you go within, you will not reach the end of the cabin before you are completely befouled with soot, silt, and dirt."

And he writes of manners: "I found myself very much embarrassed in the beginning; for not daring to cut the meat they gave me in my bark dish, for fear of spoiling the dish, I did not know how to manage it, not having any plate. Finally I had to become all to all, and a savage with these savages. I cast my eyes upon my companion, then I tried to be as brave a man as he was. He took his meat in his open hand, and cut from it morsel after morsel, as you would do with a piece of bread. But if the meat is a little tough, or if it slips away from the knife from being too soft, they hold one end of it with their teeth, and the other with the left hand, then the right plays upon it in violin fashion, the knife serving as a bow . . . If you were to lose your knife . . . you are compelled to take your share in your two hands, and to bite into the flesh and into the fat, as bravely but not so politely as you would bite into a quarter of an apple. God knows how the hands, the mouth, and a part of the face shine after this operation. The trouble was, I did not know upon what to wipe them. To carry linen with you would require a mule. I saw a woman who taught me a secret; she wiped her hands upon her shoes, and I did the same . . ."

Social practices were as baffling as physical circumstances, according to a 1634 report. "We have kept here [at Montreal] and fed for a long time a sick savage, who came and threw himself into our arms in order to die a Christian . . . All his fellow savages were astonished at the good treatment we gave him; on his account his children brought a little elk meat, and they were asked what they wished in exchange, for the presents of the savages are always bargains. They asked some wine and gunpowder, and were told that we could not give them these things; but that, if they wished something else that we had, we would give it to them very gladly. A good meal was then given them, and finally they carried back their meat, since we did not give them what they asked for, threatening that they would come after their father, which they did; but the good man did not wish to leave us . . .

"Do not think that they act thus among themselves; on the contrary they are very grateful, very liberal, and not in the least importunate toward those of their own nation. If they conduct themselves thus toward our French, and toward other foreigners, it is because, it seems to me, that we do not wish to ally ourselves with them as brothers,

which they would very much desire. But this woul
us in three days; for they would want us to go with   ,
and eat their foods as long as they had any, and then they
would come and eat ours as long as it lasted; and when
there was none left, we would all set to work to find more
. . . If you carry on your affairs apart from them, despising
their laws or their customs, they will drain from you, if
they can, even your blood. There is not an insect, nor
wasp, nor gadfly, so annoying as a savage."

The difficulties were more subtle even than that. One
priest wrote in 1710: "These people [evidently the Hurons]
seek a reputation for liberality and generosity; they give
away their property freely and very seldom ask any return;
nor do they punish thieves otherwise than with ridicule and
derision. If they suspect that anyone seeks to accomplish an
evil deed by means of false pretenses, they do not restrain
him with threats, but with gifts. From the same desire for
harmony comes their ready assent to whatever one teaches
them; nevertheless, they hold tenaciously to their native
belief or superstition, and on that account are the more
difficult to instruct. For what can one do with those who in
word give agreement and assent to everything, but in reality
give none?"

Occasionally an individual Indian could be diabolically
exasperating, as in the case of a certain Sorcerer—to use
the term which the priest insisted on using. For years,
before the Jesuits came, according to Le Jeune, the Sorcerer
had been living a life of ease by tricking his people into
believing that he possessed supernatural powers, which
enabled him to help his friends and destroy his enemies.
Le Jeune naturally took upon himself the task of proving
that the Indian was an impostor, and it was equally natural that the Indian shaman should perceive the Jesuit's
design and take measures to countervail him. Le Jeune does
not spare himself in reciting the embarrassments which he
suffered at the hands of his rival. Thus the Indian would
brag about his prowess with women and the priest, bristling
in indignation, would preach on the evils of promiscuous
love.

"I told him," says Le Jeune, "that it was not honorable
for a woman to love any one else except her husband; and
that, this evil being among them, he himself was not sure
that his son, who was there present, was his son. He replied,
'Thou hast no sense. You French people love only your own

children; but we all love the children of our tribe.' I began to laugh, seeing that he philosophized in horse and mule fashion . . ."

It was some time before Le Jeune caught on to one trick which the shaman was practicing on him. He would have Le Jeune pronounce words, drilling him patiently in correct pronunciation. Later when the priest used them he would produce an uproar in his audience. Only much later would someone reveal that he had been speaking obscenities. One gets the impression that the shaman was never outfaced.

There is no gainsaying that these Jesuits achieved insight. Father Ragueneau must have been a particularly acute observer. He wrote in 1648: "In addition to the desires that we generally have that are free—or, at least, voluntary in us—which arise from a previous knowledge of some goodness that we imagine to exist in the thing desired, the Hurons believe that our souls have other desires which are, as it were, inborn and concealed. These, they say, come from the depths of the soul, not through any knowledge, but by means of a certain blind transporting of the soul to certain objects . . .

"Now they believe that our souls make these natural desires known by means of dreams, which are its language . . .

"Now the Hurons do not seek to ascertain whence this power, both for good and for evil, comes to the soul; for as they are neither physicists nor philosophers they do not inquire very deeply into those matters . . .

"In consequence of these erroneous ideas, most of the Hurons are very careful to note their dreams, and to provide the soul with what it has pictured to them during their sleep . . ."

The ideas may have seemed erroneous to Father Ragueneau, but the modern psychiatrist would probably find good sense in this, as well as in a further passage from the same writer: "The Hurons recognize three kinds of diseases. Some are natural, and they cure these with natural remedies. Others, they believe, are caused by the soul of the sick person, which desires something; for these they cure by obtaining for the soul what it desires. Finally the others are diseases caused by a spell that some sorcerer has cast upon the sick person; these diseases are cured by withdrawing from the patient's body the spell that causes his sickness."

This same Father Ragueneau wrote what ought to be the classic admonishment to all missionaries, anthropogists, administrators, indeed to all students and workers who deal with the customs and beliefs of a people other than their own. He closed his narrative with saying: "Had I to give counsel to those who commence to labor for the conversion of the savages, I would willingly say a word of advice to them . . . One must be very careful before condemning a thousand things among their customs, which greatly offend minds brought up and nourished in another world. It is easy to call irreligious what is merely stupidity, and to take for diabolical working something that is nothing more than human; and then, one thinks that he is obliged to forbid as impious certain things that are done in all innocence, or at most are silly, but not criminal customs . . . It is difficult to see everything in one day, and time is the most faithful instructor that one can consult . . ."

And Father Le Jeune wrote: "They do not comprehend our theology well, but they comprehend perfectly our humility and our friendliness, and allow themselves to be won."

At other times and in other places on the continent there were similar first encounters between white men and Indians. What the white men saw and reported is always interesting, sometimes amusing, occasionally so vivid as to make us feel that we ourselves are present, observing with our own eyes and forming our own judgments. Over and over we are impressed with how difficult it is to see a people as they are, not as we conceive they ought to be.

One observer was John Lawson, who traveled among the Indians of the Carolinas at the beginning of the eighteenth century. His *History of Carolina* was published in London in 1709.[4]

Of the Congaree Indians, one of the Siouan tribes which disappeared under the impact of white settlement, Lawson wrote: "These are a very comely sort of Indians, there being a strange difference in the proportions and beauty of these heathens. Although their tribes or nations border upon one another, yet you may discern as great an alteration in their features and dispositions as you can in their speech, which generally proves quite different from each other, though their nations be not ten or twenty miles in distance."

Lawson had an eye for a fine featured woman and never

failed to comment when he encountered one. Of the same Congaree he wrote: "The women here are as handsome as most I have met withal, being several fine fingered [sic] bruettos among them. These lasses stick not upon hand long, for they marry when very young, as at twelve or fourteen years of age."

He comments on a flourishing custom of the time: "The English traders are seldom without an Indian female for his bedfellow, alleging these reasons as sufficient to allow of such familiarity. First, they being remote from any white people, that it preserves their friendship with the heathens, they esteeming a white man's child much above one of their own getting, the Indian miss's ever securing her white friend provisions whilst he stays with them. And lastly, this correspondence makes them learn the Indian tongue much the sooner, they being of the Frenchman's opinion, how that an English wife teaches her French husband more English in one night than a schoolmaster can in a week."

Lawson did not by any means have a good opinion of all the Indians he met, some of whom he found to be lazy and others to be accomplished thieves (of white men's goods). Of the Waxhaw, however, he wrote: "These Indians are of an extraordinary stature . . . I never saw an Indian of mature age that was anyways crooked, except by accident, and that way seldom; for they cure and prevent deformities in the limbs and body very exactly.

"At our Waxhaw landlord's cabin, was a woman employed in no other business than cookery, it being a house of great resort. The fire was surrounded with roast meat, or barbecues, and the pots continually boiling, full of meat from morning till night. This she-cook was the cleanliest I ever saw amongst the heathens of America, washing her hands before she undertook to do any cookery; and repeated this unusual decency very often in a day. She made us as white bread as any English could have done."

He reports what must have been an almost universal custom among Indian tribes: "Whensoever an aged man is speaking, none ever interrupts him, the company yielding a great deal of attention to his tale with a continued silence and an exact demeanor during the oration. Indeed, the Indians are a people that never interrupt one another in their discourse; no man so much as offering to open his mouth until the speaker has uttered his intent."

Not the least of the wonders he reported was that

"amongst women, it seems impossible to find a scold; if they are provoked or offended by their husbands, or some other, they resent the indignity offered them in silent tears, or by refusing their meat." And he adds, "Would some of our European daughters set these Indians for a pattern . . ."

Always in these first encounters, the pattern of friendliness. "They are a loving people," wrote Columbus. When Antonio Espejo journeyed among the Rio Grande Pueblos in 1583, he found a pleasant people, brightly dressed in embroidered cotton costumes, filling their plazas to greet him, offering "a great quantity of turkeys, maize, beans, tortillas, and other kinds of bread," which, the Spaniards thought, was made "with more nicety than the Mexican." When Juan Rodriguez Cabrillo sailed through the Santa Barbara Channel off the California coast in 1542, the people, warm, friendly, came out in many canoes, swarmed over the ships' decks, gave him the names of the many villages that fronted the shore, shared their fish, "fresh and very good."

Always that first friendliness.

As late as the nineteenth century initial contacts were still being made, or earlier contacts were maturing into stable relationships. The quality of the contact was not greatly changed, but depended as always on the intelligence and insight of the principals involved.

Daniel W. Harmon, who managed fur trading posts for the Northwest Company, afterward merged with the Hudson's Bay Company, kept a meticulous journal of his experiences. He was a sober and reflective man, always with a firm grip on what went on around him. He was stationed at a post just west of Lake Winnipeg in March 1802. It was still the dead of winter in the north country, when food begins to give out and cold spells seem to run overlong. It is the very height of the prime fur season, when the trader must view with the strongest disfavor any Indian who comes straggling into the post expecting to be fed and warmed when he should be out gathering in the harvest, which will make the year profitable.

So we can visualize Mr. Harmon frowning in exasperation as he makes his entry for March 20: "The greater number of our Indians have returned from the prairies; as they have brought little with them to trade, I, of course, give them as little; for we are at too great a distance from the civilized world to make many gratuities. Yet the Indians were of a different opinion; and at first made use of some unpleasant language. But we did not come to blows, and are now preparing to retire to rest, nearly as good friends as the Indians and traders generally are. With a few exceptions, that friendship is little more than their fondness for our property, and our eagerness to obtain their furs."[5]

Two months later matters were better. The profits would be earned, after all. He wrote: "All the Indians belonging to this place have now come in with the produce of their hunts, which is abundant; and to reward them for their industry, I clothed two of their chiefs, and gave a certain quantity of spirits to them, and to the others. With this they became intoxicated, and continued so during the night, which prevented our closing our eyes to sleep . . . While in that condition they, like other people, often do things which they will regret in their sober moments."

The quality of the contact had not deepened or become enriched over a span of three hundred years. Something to this effect was in a comment made by another traveler in the north woods, General Sir William Francis Butler, who, in the winter of 1872–73, traveled by dog team from the forks of the Saskatchewan River through Peace River Pass and down the valley of the Fraser River. Writing in the dead of winter at his Saskatchewan River camp, while his thermometer registered seventy degrees of frost, he wrote in his journal:

"In nearly all the dealings of the white man with the red . . . the mistake of judging and treating Indians by European standards has been made. Indian character is worth the study, if we will only take the trouble to divest ourselves of the notion that all men should be like ourselves. There is so much of simplicity and cunning, so much of close reasoning and childlike suspicion; so much natural quickness, sense of humor, credulousness, power of observation, faith and fun and selfishness mixed up together in the red man's mental composition, that the person who will find nothing in Indian character worth studying will be likely to start from a base of nullity in his own brain system."[6]

And he recalls that Goldsmith, when he attempted to teach English in France, concluded that "it was necessary I should previously learn French before I could teach them English."

13

THE WORLD IN FLUX

The Indians, meeting white men for the first time, interpreted what they saw in the light of their own experience and custom, and so made errors of judgment of their own. The difference was that, except for a relatively brief period at the beginning, they lacked superiority in numbers and therefore were never in a position to require the white men to comply with their wishes.

Different Indians expressed their perplexity in different ways, yet a basic similarity ran through their observations. They were at a loss to understand the European's preoccupation with profit-making. Indians were accomplished traders, but trade with them meant an exchange of goods by which each party obtained something useful to himself and gave up something useful to his opposite. No one returned with a surplus.

The Arikara Indian who spoke to the French trader Pierre Antoine Tabeau on the banks of the Missouri River in the winter of 1804 was expressing the confusion of his race when he chided the trader for his apparent lack of generosity. "You are foolish," the Arikara said. "Why do you wish to make all this powder and these balls since you do not hunt? Of what use are all these knives to you? Is not one enough with which to cut the meat? It is only your wicked heart that prevents you from giving them to us. Do you not see that the village has none? I will give you a robe myself when you want it, but you already have more robes than are necessary to cover you."

The Frenchman muttered to himself, and to his journal: "All the logic and all the rhetoric in the world are thrown away against these arguments, and how hope for success in a nation imbued with these principles and always destitute of everything."[1]

Contrary to the impression often created by early commentators—and left unchallenged by most historians—native America was not frozen in a mold of custom and tradition. Change was resisted, as all societies resist innovations that challenge the accepted order of things, but again as in all societies Indians adopted what was useful and posed no threat to their existence.

The history of New World occupation, as we come to know it, is a history of movement, of growth and adaptation. The intrusion of Europeans, with their more varied culture, and the pressure for change exerted by trade goods, proselytizing, and space conquest, can be viewed as but another occurrence in a long process whose beginnings were lost in remote time. The disappearance of big game had been such an occurrence. The diffusion through the Mississippi valley of the religious movement characterized by the construction of massive temple platforms was another major episode. These had stimulated trends and shifts in an evolving life-style.

Tribal societies upon first contact with Europeans were conscious of differences, but they were selective in what they appropriated for themselves. They chose mostly tools, weapons, and equipment, material objects which would enlarge the scope of their own competency. The intangibles of the European, his concern for wealth accumulation and for individual advancement, his aggressiveness toward the environment, and his class-structured society were contrary to the way Indians preferred to live, and did not appeal to them.

The inner dynamic of Indian life, the inertia imparted by generations living in the land, was not to be reduced to inconsequence by strangers seeking to impose a new order. What had been in existence before the stranger arrived would persist, even if impaired and in part destroyed.

The acquisition of the gun and the horse by tribes bordering on or living within the Plains increased the range and the killing power of people who hunted, and they turned some farming people into hunters. But these came late in a long course of New World development.

The commonest explanation for the sudden appearance of horses in North America is that they escaped from De Soto or Coronado or similar expeditions, or were stolen by the Indians from such expeditions. Such an explanation does not stand up under examination.

De Soto kept his horses pretty well together until the party reached the Mississippi, and horses that might have been lost on the eastern side of the river would not likely have reached the Great Plains. After De Soto's death his party wandered on to Texas, badly demoralized, and finally fashioned rude boats on which the members returned to Mexico. Before embarking they slaughtered their horses for food, having failed to get them shipped. The few that were actually turned loose were promptly killed by watching Indians, according to the account of the expedition.

Coronado seems not to have lost any horses on his trip into the Great Plains. He had only thirty horses for forty-two men, and if any had been lost, and particularly if they had been lost by theft, the chronicler of the trip could hardly have failed to mention it. Some of Coronado's horses were taken in retaliation by Pueblo Indians against a Spanish soldier who attempted to rape one of their women. The horses, however, did not survive. When one of Coronado's lieutenants went to the village to try to patch things up, he found that the gates to the village had been closed tight and the horses were being chased around the plaza and shot at with arrows. It turned out to be an interesting new game.

As late as 1630, ninety years after Coronado, a Spaniard observed that the Apache Indians coming to trade at the Spanish settlements carried all their belongings on their backs or on dog travois.

Francis Haines worked out a plausible reconstruction of the process by which Indians obtained their horses.[2] In the beginning, he reasons, the Indian was entirely ignorant about the horse, about its possibilities, its feeding habits. The Indian might even have butchered the animal for food instead of putting it to work. It would take time, and opportunity, to get to know the animal and its qualities.

In 1598 Juan de Oñate formally took possession of New Mexico, bringing with him a colony of four hundred men, of whom 130 had families; a baggage train consisting of eighty-three wagons and carts; and a herd of more than seven thousand head of livestock of all kinds. This settlement, once made, was never abandoned, except for the years following the Pueblo revolt in 1680.

The Spaniards had no intention of making horse users out of the Indians; in fact, they adopted ordinances forbidding Indians to ride horses. As Haines points out, however,

"The Indians were the servants who did all the work, including the care of various kinds of livestock. Inevitably the herdsman learned how to train and use horses, with the mission farm offering him the greater opportunity of learning to ride."

The Pueblo Indians gradually learned the secrets of the mysterious beast, which on many occasions had inspired great fear in Indians first encountering it. This knowledge they imparted to others, or others somehow came by the knowledge. By 1659, at any rate, the Apaches had begun to raid the rancherias and run off the horses. Within the next five years horse raiding had become a well-established practice—in time it would become one of the outstanding institutions of Plains Indian life.

The Pueblo revolt of 1680 produced a sudden increase in the number of livestock in the possession of southwestern Indians, some of which passed on to other tribes. The Pueblo Indians never developed into great horsemen, although they had always been great traders. Trade routes from every direction centered on the Rio Grande country. To Taos, one of the great marketing centers of pre-Spanish days, came buffalo robes and dried buffalo meat, and the hunters from the Plains took home maize and beans and turquoise. Now they would come for horses, and doubtless no price was too high to pay.

By 1690 horses were seen by Spaniards on the Texas gulf coast. At about the same time La Salle's great exploring lieutenant, Le Sieur de la Tonty, reached the Caddo Indians on the Red River of the South and found horses among them. The Pawnee Indians farther north, descendants of earlier farming villagers, began to use horses early in the eighteenth century.

While horses were finding their way eastward, a second line of distribution led northward from Santa Fe to the headwaters of the Snake River. Most of the tribes in the Northern Plains obtained their first horses from the Snake (Shoshone) Indians, beginning about 1700.

What happened to the Indian tribes living in or bordering on the Great Plains with the coming of the horse was a revolution in living habits.[3]

Late in the seventeenth century or at the very beginning of the eighteenth, the Comanches and the Kiowas moved out of the west and northwest into the region between the upper Canadian and Niobrara River drainages. They were hunters before entering the area and now, with the horse, they could range more widely. In their ranging they came into contact with other tribes, from whom they acquired new ceremonies, new types of gear, new ways of organizing for social and political occasions. The daily lives of the people in these two tribes were probably enriched by these contacts.

In contrast were the Cheyenne and Arapaho tribes, agricultural people who occupied permanent villages in the Minnesota area. They, too, moved out into the plains about 1700, going southwestward across the Missouri. Their village life was abandoned, as were the pottery and other material objects which did not lend themselves to light and fast traveling. They probably contributed to the ceremonial life and social forms which developed on the plains, and in turn acquired the gear and weapons which the hunting tribes already had.

Close behind the Cheyenne and Arapaho came the Dakota, or Sioux, who also had been village-dwelling farmers somewhere in the Great Lakes region. Farther north, the Assiniboine, close relatives of the Sioux, who were woodland dwellers as late as 1737, moved southward and westward to the Missouri River. The Cree Indians, forest people, became divided, part of the tribe moving into the open country where they were known as Plains Cree, while the others remained as Woods Cree and continued to hunt with the canoe rather than the horse.

The Mandan, Hidatsa, and Arikara persisted in their old way of life, but behind heavy stockades. They traded corn and beans and other garden produce for meat brought in by the Cheyenne and other erstwhile farmers, who probably retained a taste for such produce.

Other compromises were made by such tribes as the Pawnee, Ponca, Omaha, and Oto. The Pawnee, for example, continued to make pottery, but the style and quality steadily declined. Finally, after they began to use European pots and kettles, the art was forgotten entirely. Soon, too, they gave up their permanent earth-covered houses and moved into buffalo-hide tepees. Much of their old ceremonial life remained, but new ceremonies were added.[4]

The introduction of European trade goods modified the living habits of Indians who never took to the horse. At every port of entry touched by the first Europeans, trade routes reached far back into the hinterland. The French coming up the St. Lawrence Valley, as well as the Dutch and English in the Hudson and Mohawk valleys, while they may not have been aware of it, stimulated trade nerves, the impulses of which reached a thousand miles beyond the headwaters. Long before a white man ever saw a Sioux or Cheyenne or Blackfeet Indian, the lives of these tribes had been affected, competition had been quickened, tastes had been developed which none but European goods would satisfy in full. The landings in what the Spaniards called "Florida," the region stretching from the Mississippi Delta around the peninsula of Florida, touched at river mouths from which lines of travel stretched inland, crossed each other, and intercepted lines from the north and from the west. Mention has been made of the great Pacific road reaching from southern Mexico far into the plateaus of southwestern United States. On the California coast, the rivers which drained into San Francisco Bay, and farther north the Columbia and the Fraser rivers, were the routes by which people and trade goods, parties on missions of war and peace, moved back and forth.

The Europeans who braved the wilderness and took pride in their ability to arrive at a given destination were seldom aware of this Indian traffic. Yet Lake Superior copper was traded to Florida, to Virginia, and westward; Virginia tobacco found its way to Quebec; Minnesota pipestone went up the Ohio River Valley to New York and north into Canada, and Rocky Mountain obsidian came east to Ohio. The great explorations of a De Soto, a Coronado, a La Salle, a Daniel Boone were over well-traveled roads; not wagon roads, to be sure, with wheel ruts to follow, but plainly enough marked once the eye became practiced.

The consequences of these trade routes were felt in the intense competition which immediately developed between tribes. The tribes who were primarily producers of raw materials in the form of furs came into conflict with other tribes, not so favorably situated, who insisted on serving the role of middleman. It was just such a conflict of interest which led the powerful Iroquois Confederacy to wage a war of extermination against tribes who attempted to circumvent the Confederacy and deal directly with the Europeans.

It is not possible to describe with exactness in what respect or to what extent the material life of the Iroquois people was changed by the introduction of European goods. Methods of warfare were doubtless modified, since the weapons of the Europeans would dictate changed tactics. Articles of clothing, possibly foods and methods of cookery would change. In matters of custom and belief and religious practices, change would have come more slowly, since the Iroquois had a highly organized institutional life.

The changes which came to such a tribe as the Blackfeet, lacking the close-knit structure of Iroquois society, were more drastic. The tribe lived at the heart of one of the richest game areas in the northern continent—the country lying between the forks of the Saskatchewan River, from the foothills of the Rocky Mountains to the meeting of the streams east of the Eagle Hills. The grasslands continued right up to the northern fork, where the great forest belt began. This world of grass supported an inexhaustible supply of food, by Indian standards. A people on foot, however, had to be content with a borderline existence.

The horse and the gun came to the Blackfeet country at practically the same time, in 1730. The arrival of these gifts, the iron axe, and the iron knife among people who were pedestrians in a country of boundless horizons, whose only tools and weapons were things of wood and bone and flint, must have been almost beyond wonder. Not the new land, with its lonely distances and harsh winds, but these glittering instruments, would make life easy.[5]

That indeed began to happen. Blackfeet tepees grew larger. Since a dog, the old beast of burden, could not drag the skin covering for a large structure, the average lodge in early days was a small one accommodating six to eight persons. This was reported by a traveler in the Blackfeet country as late as 1754, Oscar Lewis notes. By 1830, the average lodge was somewhat larger, while some tepees had coverings made of as many as forty buffalo skins and could accommodate almost a hundred people.

To meet the increasing demand for skins, more efficient hunting methods had to be devised and the traditional corral type of trap in which buffalo were impounded was expanded in size. The rate of slaughter increased in proportion.

However, what the Blackfeet consumed was but a small part of the kill. For a number of years they delivered twenty thousand hides annually to the traders at Fort Benton on the Missouri River.

Since the tanning of hides was woman's work, these new demands resulted in increasing the economic value of women and a parallel increase in the practice of polygamy. In 1787, not quite sixty years after the arrival of the horse, David Thompson, trading among the Blackfeet, observed that three or four wives was not an uncommon number, although most men apparently had but one or two. A later visitor, in 1810, found households containing six or seven wives and twenty years later some wealthy men had as many as eight. Evidently the number went on increasing, and reliable authorities of later years knew of instances in which as many as twenty and even thirty women were owned by one man.

The Blackfeet were frank about it. When a missionary reproved them for this practice, a chief said: "Tell the priest . . . that if he wishes to do anything with my people, he must no longer order them to put away their wives. I have eight, all of whom I love, and all have children by me —which am I to keep and which to put away?"

The chief then added the information that these eight wives could prepare a hundred and fifty skins in a year, while a single woman could get only ten skins in shape for the trader.

Wives were paid for in horses, and it naturally followed that wealth in horses preceded wealth in women. Ownership of large individual herds did not become noticeable until 1808, roughly eighty years after the tribe obtained its first horses. By then, individuals owning forty to fifty horses were noted, and one man was said to have had as many as three hundred. Twenty-five years later, the nobleman traveler Prince Maximilian met a Piegan chief who was reported to have from four to five thousand head of horses.

Still another change in custom took place. With the increasing economic value of women, the age at which girls were married dropped from sixteen or eighteen, as reported by Thompson in 1787, to twelve, as reported a hundred years later.

Blackfeet society was weakened by some of this change. Competition in the fur trade became so acute that experienced traders were soon disregarding the formality of dealing only through chiefs and headmen and were bargaining with anybody who had furs to trade. Authority within the tribe began to disintegrate until one of the traders early in the nineteenth century commented that "the natives have now been taught to despise the council of their elders."

Deterioration of another kind took place. A trader

observed: "The Indians long deceived have become deceivers in turn, and not infrequently after having incurred a heavy debt at one post, move to another, to play the same game again."

The Blackfeet are reported to have allowed even their relations with other tribes to degenerate, probably the most serious thing that could have happened to group morale. Thus, Prince Maximilian reported: "The Crows in their visits and negotiations presented the Blackfeet with valuable articles, costly feathered caps, shields, horses, etc., but received nothing at all when they came to the latter, by which all the Indians are incensed against the Blackfeet."

Other tribes may have been as complacent about change as the Blackfeet, but generally change was resisted. Efforts of the Spaniards to suppress the religious observances of the Pueblo Indians, efforts which included the hanging of some medicine men as a warning, resulted in the uprising of 1680, in which the entire Spanish population of New Mexico, numbering 2,800, was driven out of the province, except for some 380 who were slaughtered.

At a grand council in 1744 between British commissioners and delegates from several Virginia tribes, the Indians were urged to send their children to the College of William and Mary, which had been established for the particular purpose of educating Indians.

An Indian spokesman responded to this urging by saying: "We know that you highly esteem the kind of learning taught in these colleges, and that the maintenance of our young, while with you, would be very expensive to you. We are convinced that you mean to do us good by your proposal, and we thank you heartily; but you, who are wise, must know that different nations have different conceptions of things; and you will therefore not take it amiss if our ideas of this kind of education happen not to be the same as yours. We have had some experience of it. Several of our young men were formerly brought up at the colleges in your northern provinces. They were instructed in all your sciences; but when they came back to us, they were bad runners; ignorant of every means of living in the woods; unable to bear either cold or hunger; knew neither how to build a cabin, take a deer, nor kill an enemy; spoke our language imperfectly; were neither fit for hunters, warriors, nor councilors; they were totally good for nothing."

The spokesman added, his eye brightening with amusement: "We are nonetheless obliged by your kind offer, though we decline accepting it; and to show you our grateful sense of it, if the gentlemen of Virginia will send us a dozen of their sons, we will take great care of their education, instruct them in all we know, and make men of them."

The English traveler John Halkett quotes the passage with obvious relish in his *Historical Notes Respecting the Indians of North America* (1825), giving Benjamin Franklin as his source.

Halkett was also impressed by the incident reported by Elias Boudinot (not the Cherokee Indian of that name, but the New Jersey philanthropist whose name the Cherokee adopted), a corresponding member of the Scottish Society for the Propagation of Christian Knowledge. According to Dr. Boudinot's account, two missionaries had been educated by the Society for the specific purpose of going among the Delaware Indians and winning them to Christianity. They carried a letter from the Scottish Society when they appeared before the Delawares, in which the missionaries are quoted by Boudinot as saying:

"We had, by the goodness of the Great Spirit, been favored with a knowledge of his will, as to the worship he required of his creatures, and the means he would bless to promote the happiness of man, both in this life and that which was to come. That, thus enjoying so much happiness ourselves, we could not but think of our red brethren in the wilderness, and wished to communicate the glad tidings to them, that they might be partakers with us."

The Delaware chiefs received the missionaries, but indicated that they would not immediately give them an answer until the letter had been carefully studied and considered in a council of all the leading men. Meantime, the missionaries might, if they chose, instruct the women, but they were to stay away from the men. For fourteen days they considered the contents of the letter. At the end of that time they called the missionaries into the council house. In Boudinot's words again: "They felt very grateful that we had condescended to remember our red brethren in the wilderness; but they could not help recollecting that we had a people among us who, because they differed from us in color, we had made slaves of, causing them to suffer great hardships and lead miserable lives. Now they could not see any reason, if a people being black, entitled us thus to deal with them, why a red color would not equally justify the same treatment. They, therefore, had determined to wait and see whether all the black people amongst us were made thus happy and joyful, before they could put confidence in our promises; for they thought a people who had suffered so much and so long by our means, should be entitled to our first attention."

The missionaries were asked to return to the Scottish Society and say, for the Delawares, that "when they saw the black people among us restored to freedom and happiness, they would gladly receive our missionaries."

This reluctance on the part of the Delaware chiefs was echoed many years later by Red Jacket, the Seneca orator, who in the course of a long complaint to Governor Dewitt Clinton in January 1821 made this allegation: "Another thing recommended to us has created great confusion among us, and is making us a quarrelsome and divided people; and that is the introduction of preachers into our nation. These blackrobes contrive to get consent of some of the Indians to preach among us; and whenever this is the case, confusion and disorder are sure to follow, and the encroachment of the whites upon our land is the invariable consequence. The governor must not think hard of me for speaking thus of the preachers. I have observed their progress, and when I look back to see what has taken place of old, I perceive that whenever they came among the Indians, they were forerunners of their dispersion; and they introduce the white people on their lands, by whom they are robbed and plundered of their property; and that the Indians are sure to dwindle and decrease, and be driven back, in proportion to the number of preachers that came among them."

It has always been a source of surprise and chagrin to white men, turning later into scorn, that Indians showed an unwillingness to abandon their peculiar ways. Finding the Indians friendly and hospitable on first acquaintance, most white men were encouraged to believe that the Indians were eager to shed their traditional habiliments of mind and body. The years of contact expanded into decades and generations, and little progress had been made. A reluctance amounting to stubbornness seemed to possess these red men. Some tribes were obliterated, others were sent packing into deeper wilderness, but remarkably few Indians cast their lot with the white men.

The Marquis de Denonville, Governor General of Canada, writing to his minister, commented: "It has been long imagined that the Indians might be brought near to us in order to Frenchify them, but there is every reason to believe that this is a mistake. Those of the savages who have been brought among us have not become French, and the French who have resided among the Indians have become savages."

14

SYSTEMATIZING THE CONQUEST

The gold taken out of the island of Haiti never amounted to a great deal, but it was enough to set imaginations on fire and to spur the Spaniards on to greater discoveries. Portugal had been pushing out everywhere into unknown waters and unknown lands, far outdistancing any other European power all through the fifteenth century. In this enterprise she had been encouraged by exclusive permission granted by Pope Nicholas V in 1454 to explore the road to the Indies, a detail that Ferdinand and Isabella seem to have forgotten when they sponsored Columbus's voyage.

Columbus returned from his first journey across the western sea—and, as it happened, was blown by a storm into a Portuguese port. Thus the Spanish monarchs, to their annoyance, got their first word of the successful venture from Portuguese sources rather than from the lips of Columbus. The Portuguese king, on the other hand, was wrathful, since he held the papal franchise. He threatened to send his fleet across the Atlantic to take over the new lands which Spain was claiming.

Pope Alexander VI stepped lightly into this situation and in May 1493 drew a north-and-south line one hundred leagues west of the Azores and Cape Verde Islands. (By later negotiation the line was moved to a point 370 leagues west of the Cape Verde Islands, and hence Portugal's title was secured to the coast of Brazil, which her mariners had discovered.)

The pope had his price for this act of arbitration. Spain and Portugal both were to assume as their first duty the conversion of all native peoples to Christianity. They became in effect agents of the Holy See, and in their concern for secular development of the New World they could never overlook this spiritual commission.

Spain thus entered upon her colonial adventure with a lion and a lamb in leash. Economically, she was up to the eyes in debt. The desperateness of her situation is illustrated in a small detail.

The Spanish monarchs had put up six million maravedis to finance Columbus's third voyage. This was at the moment when they were defending Perpignan. Columbus's brother Bartolomé, waiting in Española, had sent over a shipload of Indian slaves. The captain in charge of this cargo sent word to Columbus from Cádiz that he was bringing gold, by which he meant the money he anticipated as revenue from the sale of the slaves. Ferdinand and Isabella were shocked to learn that it was slaves and not gold that had come from the New World. They had already spent the six million maravedis and had counted on reimbursement in good coin.

Mindful of their obligation to Christianize, the monarchs had previously expressed disapproval of such transactions. Only the year before, Columbus had shipped a boatload of natives to Spain after a nine months' campaign against a rebellion in Española. The slaves were consigned to Juan de Fonseca, Bishop of Burgos, the royal minister in charge of Indian affairs. When word of this transaction had reached the royal couple, they suspected that it might not be in keeping with the pope's wishes, and they ordered the bishop to hold the natives in custody until they could get a legal opinion. The bishop, having the captives on his hands and being required to feed them, was relieved of some expense by an additional order: "In order to man certain galleys which the captain of our fleet, Juan de Lezcano, has in our service, we have agreed to send him fifty Indians; wherefore we command you to deliver to this said Juan de Lezcano fifty of the Indians, who are to be from twenty to forty years of age. You will take his receipt for them . . . naming in it all the Indians he receives, with their ages, so that if the said Indians are to be free, the said Lezcano may return those of them whom he has alive, and if they are to be kept as slaves, they may be charged against his salary . . ."[1]

The queen did not like slavery to be too frank or too brutal. There was revenue to be returned to the crown from the slave trade, and that was desirable; only it ought to be slavery by consent, if that were possible. Thus, in 1503, one Cristobal Guerra was permitted by the queen "to take Indian men and women for slaves, without harming them, and he is to take them as nearly as possible with their consent; and in the same manner he may take monsters and animals of any kind, and all serpents and fishes he may desire; and all of this is to belong to him, as has been said, the fourth part being reserved for me . . ."

A little later that year the queen issued general instructions that Indians who resisted the Christian religion might be captured and taken to Spain as slaves, the crown to receive its proper share of the proceeds.

Slavery, however, did not sit well with a Christian conscience, and in 1542 it was prohibited by law. Long before that time, a more subtle institution of forced labor had been devised and put into general operation. This was the system of the encomienda. Since it lay at the heart of Spanish colonial policy, a few details in explanation of its origin will be helpful.

Spain's first years in the New World were troubled. The first settlers, as already remarked, were ex-soldiers, adventurers, bankrupt noblemen, and paroled convicts. Scarcely a working man among them, and even if there had been any who had ever worked the soil, it was unthinkable that a Spaniard should labor if others could be required to work for him. Moreover, supply ships from Spain came infrequently and often did not reach the islands at all. So in those first years, there was the constant threat of starvation. Columbus, seeing how matters were likely to go in the first days of settlement, petitioned the crown to allow the colonists to "use" Indian labor for a year or two. Actually, that was what the colonists started to do as soon as they set foot in the islands, and Columbus was trying to secure legal basis for the practice.

The natives, having failed in their effort at rebellion in 1494–95, resorted to a campaign of passive resistance. As the colonists continued to arrive (2,500 of them in the single year of 1501), Indians simply vanished into the forest, while those who were unfortunate enough to be under close observation refused to plant crops.

On top of that was the equally pressing problem of working the mines. Hunger was a private matter, but the recovery of gold was an affair which interested the crown itself. This posed a dilemma. On the one side was the holy injunction laid down by the pope. On the other was the necessity of financing Spain's effort to defeat the enemies of the Church.

The situation is explored by Lesley B. Simpson in his

study, *The Encomienda in New Spain.* As he found: "The crown's position was not an enviable one. If the colonists were allowed to use native labor, and there was no other labor to use, it was brought sharply to task by the missionaries. If the missionaries were allowed to have their way and make the native population entirely free from domination by the Spanish civilian element, the latter faced bankruptcy and the crown a loss of indispensable revenue. . . . As long as the issue was thus sharply drawn, it will be found that in no case did the crown sacrifice its own interests, which were identical with those of the colonists."

All the questions which would arise in later years in the course of white-Indian contact arose for the first time with the Spaniards. The answers found, the policies pursued, and the failures have a bearing on the answers and the policies of every other European nation which ventured into the New World. What Spain undertook to accomplish, and with what final effect, is of primary interest in any study of Indian and white man.

In an effort to find a way out of the chaos produced by hunger, fear, greed, and gross mismanagement—and to bring home some profits—Isabella created the office of royal governor of the Indies. To that office she named Nicolás de Ovando, one of the strongest men in Spain. The queen's orders to him in 1501 provided the rationale of the encomienda system.

First the note of Christian kindliness: "The Governor is to take great pains in the teaching of the natives in the holy Catholic faith, but no violence is to be done them in the process. They are to be lovingly taught by the religious.

"He is to see to it that they are allowed to go in entire freedom about the island. No one is to rob them, do violence to them, or any harm whatever.

"Wives and daughters of the Indians taken from them against their will are to be returned. If any Spaniards wish to marry native women, it is to be with the consent of both parties and not by force . . ."

Then the note of practical necessity: "Since it will be necessary, in order to mine gold and carry out the other works we have ordered done, to make use of the services of the Indians, you are to compel them to work in our service, paying them the wages you think it just they should have."

In spite of these instructions and of the demand of reform which members of the religious order were already laying before the crown, Ovando hesitated. Taking the queen literally at her word could easily mean the end of the colony, and he was certain that was not what the queen desired. Only a brave man, however, could insinuate to a queen that she did not know where her own best interests lay. Ovando tried to accomplish just that. It was obvious that Indians who were allowed to go about "in entire freedom" could not at the same time be compelled to work, and probably could not even be caught up with and taught by the religious.

Strangely enough, the queen yielded to his argument. Her new order, dated December 20, 1503, tightened the policy.

"As now we are informed that because of the excessive liberty enjoyed by the said Indians they avoid contact and community with the Spaniards to such an extent that they will not even work for wages, but wander about idle, and cannot be had by the Christians to convert to the Holy Catholic Faith . . . and because this can be better done by having the Indians living in community with the Christians of the island . . . I have commanded . . . that beginning from the day you receive my letter, you will compel and force the said Indians to associate with the Christians . . . to gather and mine the gold . . . to till the fields . . . and you are to have each one paid [the wage] you think he should have . . ."

The order ended in a peculiar afterthought: "This the Indians shall perform as free people, which they are, and not as slaves."

The notion was that the Indians would be brought in from their scattered villages—many had retreated into the most inaccessible mountain areas after their first rough brushes with the Spaniards—and congregated in towns in which each Indian family would have a house and a plot of ground for cultivating. Moreover, they were to be persuaded to dress like "reasonable men," to abandon their "ancient evil ways." This last was further elucidated: "They are not to bathe as frequently as hitherto, as we are informed that it does them much harm."

The Indians died rapidly in spite of, or perhaps because of, this solicitude. The population of Haiti has been variously estimated at from 100,000 to 250,000 at the time of discovery. By 1514, according to an official report, the island contained 1,000 Spaniards and 29,000 Indians. Some had been slaughtered, others died of incidental cruelty, a great number were victims of measles, smallpox, and other diseases introduced by the Europeans, and still others, by refusing to plant crops either for themselves or for the Spaniards, starved themselves to death.

So drastic a reduction of population was bad for business. The mines could not be worked adequately, food shortages threatened the entire enterprise, and radical reformers like Las Casas, who would become one of the great figures in colonial reform, were beginning to shout from the rooftops.

In an effort to provide a stopgap, Governor Ovando was authorized to bring Indians into Haiti from neighboring "useless" islands—these being the islands where no gold had been found. The justification for the kidnappings which followed was that the Indians brought into Haiti would have an opportunity of living in contact with Christians and becoming converted. It would appear that many of the exploring expeditions resulting in discoveries from the Carolina coast to the coast of South America were for the purpose of seizing and transporting Indians to Española.

The reformers had their way, however. Investigators sent to the island were so shocked by what they saw that they had no trouble in persuading Ferdinand (Isabella had died in 1504) to issue the laws of Burgos in 1512. This was the first attempt by any European power to enact a code of law in which the respective rights and obligations of a native people and Europeans would be set down. Actually, a reading of the laws must leave one with the feeling that, if this was reform, the natives had better not have too much of it. In the last of thirty-two articles there was a vague promise that "if at any time the Indians should give proof of being able to live under their own government, they were to be allowed to do so, by paying feudal dues." Moreover, women four months pregnant were not to be sent into the mines to work.

Members of the Order of St. Jerome were chosen to administer the new laws by way of insuring fair enforcement. It proved to be practically impossible to abolish or seriously modify any of the practices which had grown up on the island. Colonial proprietors insisted that any reforms, however trivial, would simply ruin them and they might as well pack up and go home.

The monks, baffled, circulated a questionnaire among the planters and mine operators to obtain their views as to what was wrong and what ought to be done. The answers were probably of no help to the Jeronymites, but they throw a strong light on the attitudes of the Indians—attitudes which white men would complain of centuries later. The colonists offered such information as: "The Indians are abandoned to drink and gluttony, vice and laziness. They prefer to live in the woods, eating spiders and roots and other filthy things to living with the Spaniards . . . They do not wish to be subject to anyone, but to be free to enjoy themselves in idleness. They smoke tobacco. They refuse to recite the Pater Noster or the Ave Maria unless they are driven to it . . . Natives can do nothing without direction. They are indeed capable of living as they were accustomed, but not one would dig gold without being driven to it. They have no business sense, as they exchange things of great value for things of no value . . . The Indians love to go about naked, and they hold money and property as of no value . . . They have no sense of shame. When they are punished by the Spanish authorities—by beating or losing their ears, etc.—they have no feeling of guilt. They will not work for wages . . ."

In addition to adopting administrative codes, the Spanish government set up procedures for the management of colonial affairs. In the beginning the Spanish monarchs had handled these matters personally, with the assistance of advisers, such as the Bishop of Burgos. A separate board of managers was created in 1517, with Peter Martyr, the historian, and the Bishop of Burgos among the first members. This board was reorganized as the Council of the Indies in 1524 and this became the supreme legislative and judicial authority in Spanish America. Local authority was vested in a governor general, and Columbus's son, Diego, was the first to hold the title. He was complained against so loudly that a superior court was set up in the colony of Española, to which appeals might be carried from rulings of the governor general. This appeals machinery or *Audiencia* was formally incorporated into the administrative system by a decree of 1524.

The Spaniards possessed an excellent theory of colonial administration, if they could have had effective administrators. They wished to Christianize the Indians and bring them to the European way of life; they sought to achieve a unity of religious belief, of thought, of morals, dress, government, even town planning. The concept was excellent; it had elements of Roman greatness. In formulating it, however, the king's councillors failed absolutely to take the Indians into account. They were working with unknown human material. Basic to the plan of unity was the notion of collecting the natives in convenient settlements. This policy was pushed relentlessly down through the years.

A contemporary historian, Father Torquemada, watched the local administrators as they attempted to put the policy into operation. This was in 1599, when he wrote: "The intention of his Majesty was . . . that the Indians who were scattered in many places without order or government should be congregated and should live in orderly established villages." Perhaps the officials could not distinguish between villages that were orderly and those that were not. In any case, they rounded up everybody and moved them into centralized locations. They insisted on niceties of detail as well: "If a house was a little off the line of the street they wrecked it and ordered it rebuilt in line with the others . . ."

Torquemada also observed that the king had not intended that the Indians should lose their land when they moved in from their scattered ancient holdings; but, he wrote, "There is hardly a palm of land that the Spaniards do not possess . . ." In many instances Indians who were ordered to remove to a central location disappeared entirely into remote mountain areas and were heard from no more. Thus they escaped entirely the unity of religion, thought, morals, etc., which made for administrative perfection. As for those who obeyed and moved as ordered, "All, or nearly all," says Torquemada, ". . . have died."

Two great figures stand out in Spanish colonial history—two men who attempted to place colonial administration on a basis that was sound at once in law and in principles of humane action.

The first of these, Bartolomé de Las Casas, apostle of the Indies, has told his own story, and many writers in addition, notably Sir Arthur Helps, have celebrated his name.[2]

Not so much has been written of the other figure, Francisco de Vitoria, for twenty years, 1526–46, professor of theology at the University of Salamanca. He was one of the leading intellectuals of his age, as his friendship with Erasmus might suggest.

Emperor Charles V, made unhappy by the reports he had been receiving of the conduct of affairs in the New World, directed Vitoria to study the problem and give him the

benefit of his views. Vitoria in 1532 delivered two lectures
which for the first time attempted to define the respective
rights of the aboriginal inhabitants and the Europeans in
the New World. His conclusions are summarized by Professor Simpson:

1. Since unbelief does not preclude ownership of property, the Indians are not precluded from owning
   property, and they are, therefore, the true owners of
   the New World, as they were before the advent of the
   Spaniards.
2. The emperor is not the lord of the whole world, and,
   even if he were, he would not therefore be entitled
   to seize the provinces of the Indians, put down their
   lords, erect new ones, and levy taxes.
3. Neither is the pope civil or temporal lord of the
   whole world. He has no secular power except insofar
   as it subserves things spiritual. He can have no power
   over the dominions of unbelievers.
4. On the other hand, the Spaniards have the right to
   go to the lands of the Indians, dwell there, and carry
   on trade, so long as they do no harm, and they cannot be prevented by the Indians from doing so . . .
   In the event of war the Indians may be despoiled of
   goods and reduced to slavery, as "in the law of nations
   whatever we take from the enemy becomes ours at
   once, and so true is this that even men may be
   brought into slavery to us."
5. The Christians have the right to preach the gospel
   among the barbarians . . . If the Indians do not
   hinder the preaching of the gospel, they cannot be
   warred into subjection, whether they accept it or not.

Vitoria was not thrown into a dungeon for expressing
these frank views upon the rights of the Crown and the
Church. He was not even deprived of his chair at the
university. Indeed his legal views were seized upon by Las
Casas and made the basis of the New Laws, which the
emperor promulgated in 1542. Out of fifty-four items in
this code, twenty-three dealt with Indians, containing these
provisions:

> X. . . . The Indians are free persons and vassals
> of the crown . . .
>
> XXV. Lawsuits among the Indians are to be decided
> . . . according to their usage and custom.

XXVI. We order and command that henceforth for
no reason of war or for any other . . . is any
Indian to be made a slave . . .

XXXIX. In expeditions of discovery no Indians are to
be taken, save perhaps three or four to be used
as interpreters . . . Nothing is to be taken
from the Indians except in fair trade.

Here for the first time a European power recognized
Indian "usage and custom." It was not a new thought with
Charles V. He had been annoyed with Cortés because the
conqueror, after capturing Mexico, had made large grants
of land, together with the population attached to the land,
as compensation to his soldiers. The Emperor issued a sharp
interdict against this, and further ordered that the Indians
"were to be encouraged in their high civilization and urged
to lead an orderly life."

The other notable item in the 1542 Laws is the strict
injunction that "nothing is to be taken from the Indians
except in fair trade." The time would come when the
Supreme Court of the United States would adopt that
principle as a basic tenet of Indian law.

These are beginnings only, things that happened in the
far away and long ago. So it might seem, until looking
closer and listening with a sharper ear, it seems not so far
away and not so long ago. Here is a Dominican saying in
1544: "As everyone knows, the Indians are weak by nature
and not acquisitive, and are satisfied with having enough
to get along on from day to day. And if there is any way to
bring them out of their laziness and carelessness, it is to
make them help the Spaniards in their commerce . . . and
thus they will become fond of commerce and profit. . . ."

The argument will be expressed with tireless repetition
by the French, the British, and by the Congress of the
United States in the next several centuries.

There is something hauntingly familiar also in the part-
ing advice written by Mendoza, the first viceroy in Mexico,
to his successor, on the occasion of assuming a similar office
in Peru in 1550. He wrote: "As far as the Indians are concerned, there have been so many changes that several times
I have said that we are going crazy with so many experiments. After sixteen years in this government . . . I could
swear that I am more confused about them than at the
beginning."

15

THE POLITICS OF TRADE

The French kings had no Vitoria to clarify the problem of land title. Grants were made to individuals and to associations and companies, and invariably these grants were resoundingly broad and all-inclusive. The Marquis de la Roche, for example, in the commission given him in 1598, was in effect made absolute ruler of Canada, Hochelaga, Newfoundland, Labrador, the River of the Great Bay, Norembega, etc., although his title read "Lieutenant General Governor."

He was empowered to make war and peace, to maintain an army, to legislate, to punish and pardon, to found cities and erect fortifications, to grant lands, among other things. But all this power was of little practical effect. The marquis was required to recruit and transport colonists at his own expense, and as it happened he could find no candidates who were willing to go to the New World and become his subjects. Finally he emptied the jails at Rouen and with a band of sixty convicts he crossed the Atlantic and tried to establish himself on probably the one spot where a colony could not succeed, barren Sable Island off the Nova Scotia coast. Fortunately for him if not for his colonists, while he was looking about for another spot, he reported, a storm caught him up and blew him back to France. When a rescue expedition came out five years later, only a dozen survivors were found.

Champlain likewise was broadly authorized to serve as legislator, administrator, and judge, and to grant lands to settlers on terms to be fixed by him. He was succeeded in 1627 by the Company of One Hundred Associates, organized in accordance with Cardinal Richelieu's plan. The plan was to establish "a powerful colony" as a "dependency of the crown," instead of licensing a private enterprise, as was done by the Spanish monarch. The Company was authorized "to improve and settle [land] . . . and to distribute the same to those who will inhabit the said country and to others in such quantities and in such manner as they may deem proper; to give and to grant such titles and honors, rights and powers, as they may deem essential . . ."[1]

The Company never seriously concerned itself with bringing permanent settlers into the country and devoted its attention to the fur trade. In this it was thwarted, however, by the Iroquois Confederacy. When the Confederacy destroyed the Huron Nation, the middlemen upon whom the French depended for their supply of fur, the Company was soon bankrupt and turned in its charter.

Louis XIV, in accepting the surrendered charter in 1663, expressed the French theory of tenure in the New World. The royal deed read: "We have learned with regret not only that the number of inhabitants is very limited, but that even these are every day in danger of annihilation by the Iroquoi . . . We have declared and ordered, that all rights of justice, property, and seigniory, rights to appoint to offices of governor and lieutenant general in the said country, to name officers to administer justice, and all and every other rights granted by our most honored predecessor and father by the edict of April 29, 1627, be and the same are hereby reunited to our Crown, to be hereafter exercised in our name by officers whom we shall appoint in this behalf."

Without examining what title he had to the land or how it had been acquired, the king nevertheless assumed the right to grant title to others.

In chartering a successor, the Company of the West Indies, to take possession of "Canada, Acadia, Newfoundland, and the other islands and continents from the north of Canada to Virginia and Florida," the king made it clear that all legal powers remained in him. When this latter charter was abolished in 1674, for the same failure to promote settlement, a royal order was issued directing that in future no land grants could be made without the approval of the king.

Whether the French, if they had remained in the New World, would have contributed toward a better working relationship between Indians and Europeans cannot now be answered. They were ejected from the scene just at the epoch when principles of law and of administrative practice were beginning to take form in colonial affairs. It seems not at all unlikely that, had the French participated in these New World formulations, the Indians would have been the gainers. No other European people understood so well how to live with the Indians, how to do business with them, and how to hold their respect.[2]

Unlike the Spanish, the French did not start with a theory of administration to which they tried to make circumstances conform. Such plans as they put into operation from time to time grew out of experience accumulated in the New World. This experience told them that Indian tribes and individual Indians differed among themselves. The Indians around the larger settlements of Canada, who were largely Christianized and who fought side-by-side with the French against other Indian tribes, were not to be dealt with according to the formula which proved useful in dealing with the western tribes, who made no alliances with white men and sold their furs to the highest bidder. After Cartier's time the French were never too proud or too fearful to live with the Indians. They had sense enough not to insult an Indian host by ridiculing his manners or his way of life. Neither did they assume that the property of a savage, whether it be furs or women, belonged to the white man. Frenchmen, traveling the length and breadth of the land, completely cut off from any support but that which their own wits could provide, not only prospered but came to be held in affection by the Indians with whom they traded.

From earliest times the French governors-general accorded to Indian leaders that respect which was due the leader of any people, whether encountered at Versailles or in the wilderness. The top officials in New France considered themselves in the role of the diplomatic staff. They had no strong garrison behind them, and they knew that French power in the New World would rise or fall in accordance with their ability to win and hold Indian alliances.

One device used effectively by the French was the annual council with the governor-general or his deputy, to which delegates were invited from the most distant tribes. In Canada this annual council was held at Montreal, while in Louisiana, that vague territory of the Mississippi valley, the meeting place was Mobile. In these council meetings the governor did his best to win the Indians to the French interest, always in the best diplomatic language. At the close of such conferences, the delegates were feasted and given presents. Usually also the Indians came laden with furs and a lively business was done with the merchants. It has been estimated that the governor-general of Canada devoted as much as three months out of every year to Indian affairs.

The fact that the Dutch and the English, their successors on the Hudson River after 1664, made formal purchases of land and treaties of agreement with the Indians was not, initially, the result of any conviction that Indian title in the land could only be acquired by purchase.[3] The Dutch doubtless would have taken what they wanted, if that course had been politic. However, they were operating in an area in which they had European rivals, the French and the British. Henrik Hudson, sailing for the Dutch East India Company, had explored the coast from New England south to Virginia, probed Chesapeake and Delaware bays, and entered New York Harbor, all in 1609. Dutch merchants engaged in the fur trade at Manhattan, starting in 1612, and two years later Fort Nassau, later named Fort Orange, was built near the present site of Albany. Presently, competition drew closer with the settlement at Plymouth and with the coming of the Swedes to Delaware in 1638.

The French, meantime, had started off on the wrong foot with the Iroquois. In the summer of 1609, Champlain accompanied Algonquin and Huron warriors who, with the help of a few French muskets, routed a band of Mohawk Indians near Lake Champlain. This relatively minor incident has traditionally been cited to explain the century and a half of conflict between the French and the Iroquois tribes. Quite likely the motives were more complex, as would be suggested by the reconstruction of events pieced together by George T. Hunt.

Whatever the reason for the difficulties which the French had with the Iroquois, they were real enough, and they supplied a strong incentive to the Dutch and English traders and settlers in the Hudson and Mohawk valleys to place themselves in a favored light. If that meant observance of strict formality in acquiring Indian lands and respecting the political rights of the tribes in all forms of intercourse, they were shrewd enough to act accordingly.

The first Dutch treaty was entered into with the Mohawk nation in 1643. The text of this treaty appears to have been lost, but it is significant that the treaty was made during the fateful decade 1640–50, when the Iroquois were beginning to shape the strategy which would save them from annihilation. A moment's digression will explain this.

The French in Canada on several occasions either were on terms of friendship with various Iroquois tribes or such friendship was being sought by the Iroquois themselves—a fact which lessens the likelihood of any revenge motive enduring from Champlain's time. Evidently a treaty was actually consummated on June 2, 1622, with friendship between the French and the Onondaga as the object. In 1633 and again in 1635 offers of peace were being made by one or another of the five Iroquois tribes.* Efforts were also made by the Iroquois to achieve peace and friendship with the Huron Nation, first in 1641 and again in 1645.

These were urgent matters to the Iroquois, because beaver, the universal medium of exchange, were fast disappearing from the Iroquois country. After 1640 scarcely an animal was to be found in all the territory ranged over by the five nations of the Confederacy. The Dutch at Albany at about the same time clamped down hard on traders who had been selling firearms to the Iroquois, another reason why the latter turned to the French and their allies, the Hurons. The Iroquois knew that their own survival could be achieved only by a plentiful and unfailing supply of European goods, expecially firearms.

Iroquois overtures of friendship to the Hurons were a change in strategy. Previously, in their desperate need for furs to exchange for European goods, the Iroquois had taken to raiding Huron commerce. The Hurons were master traders. They took corn, tobacco, and other products on trade routes that extended from Green Bay in the west to the Saguenay River in the east. The furs which they obtained in exchange the Hurons delivered to the French in Montreal. Their canoes in a single season covered several thousand miles. It was this vast trade economy which the Iroquois were trying to cut into, first by force and then by bargaining.

The bargaining resulted in 1645 in a treaty of friendship,

* Originally the Iroquois Confederacy was composed of five tribes: Mohawk, Oneida, Onondaga, Cayuga, and Seneca. After 1726, the Tuscarora, a North Carolina Iroquoian tribe, joined the Confederacy, which thereafter was frequently referred to as the Six Nations.

in which the Hurons agreed to bring their furs to the Iroquois, and the latter agreed to refrain from further raiding. As a bargain, it was something like a highwayman agreeing to let an innocent victim live, in exchange for his purse. The Hurons made the mistake of believing that they could appear to agree, intending all the while to hand over an empty purse. They were a clever people—the Jesuits considered them intellectually superior to any other tribe—and perhaps they trusted their innate sagacity to extricate them from their trouble.

At any rate, the agreement was made in the summer of 1645. That fall, having collected more furs from the northern tribes than they had obtained in several years, the Hurons sent the heavily laden fleet of canoes—direct to Montreal.

The explosion that followed was devastating. The Iroquois concluded from the Huron action that they had no choice but to exterminate their rivals. They acted so swiftly that in five years' time the Huron Nation, which had numbered thirty thousand, had ceased to exist. Its members were slaughtered, starved, or forced to flee to other tribes. It was never reconstituted.

What part the Dutch treaty of 1643 with the Iroquois played in the strategy than being mapped, does not appear in the record. Wisely, though (and perhaps by agreement), the Dutch remained neutral. They may even have aided the Iroquois in spite of the ban on the sale of firearms.

The total role played by the Iroquois Indians in the rivalry of European powers for the control of North America and in the final shaping of government policy with respect to the Indian tribes has not yet been fully stated. It is best understood with respect to the struggles between England and France, and indeed the contemporary participants in those events spoke their views plainly. Governor Dongan of New York frankly stated that the Iroquois were "the bulwark between us and the French and all other Indians," while in Canada the Governor-General, Denonville, was exclaiming. "Whilst we have the Iroquois on our hands, can we be certain of anything?" The people of Albany in 1720 described the Iroquois as "the balance of the continent of America."

The particulars of the matter are explained by Charles H. McIlwain in his introductions to Wraxall's *Abridgement of the Indian Affairs . . . in the Colony of New York*. The

French all through colonial times until their final defeat attempted to cut a line from the St. Lawrence River to Manhattan Island. The Richelieu River leading from the St. Lawrence to Lake Champlain and the comparatively short portage to the headwaters of the Hudson formed a natural line of advance, which, at a stroke, would sever New England from the other British settlements. Failing repeatedly to take that line, either by purchase or by force of arms, New France was vulnerable at all times.

The same line, which, in possession of the French, would have severed the English settlements, in English hands was a spear point aimed directly at the heart of the French. It left the French in Canada with no choice other than to construct and attempt to garrison two thousand miles of fortifications. They were never able to supply such defensive works or the garrisons either. For that matter, the French were never able to overpower New York colony, though it is doubtful, in McIlwain's analysis, whether the colony could have withstood a concerted attack.[4]

The answer is that the Iroquois stood in the way, furnishing a barrier which neither the resources of the colony nor the natural geography supplied. Sir William Johnson, as agent to the northern Indians down to the opening round of the Revolutionary War, served the English interests better than adequately.

The Iroquois, on their part, had chosen the side they would serve with good reason. An alliance with the French would have meant fighting out with them the same issue which had already been fought, and settled, between the Iroquois and the Huron Nation. It was wiser to stick with the English, who had no forts west of Oswego and who were persuaded by the Iroquois not to trade west of that point. That left the western field open to the Iroquois, to collect all the fur and bring it in to the English. The French were better out of the way, and the Iroquois helped to accomplish just that.

16

THE ROYAL WILL AND PLEASURE

English policy with respect to Indian affairs reached its culmination in the Royal Proclamation of October 7, 1763. It represented ten years of effort and discussion, and yet it was promulgated in such haste, under the pressure of an Indian uprising, that a major political blunder was perpetrated.

The incidents of those ten years have an interest not only because they involve some of the major issues coming to focus between the mother country and the colonies, but also because of the impact they would have on the development of United States Indian policy.

Prior to the final defeat of France in the New World and the transfer of Canada to the British by the Treaty of Paris in 1763, the British home government had not been consistently interested in Indian matters. Each of the several colonies was left to treat with the Indian tribes and to regulate trade as it saw fit. In the beginning the colonies discharged this responsibility with a show of concern for the welfare of the native population.

The laws of Connecticut, New Jersey, and others of the colonies in very early days contained proscriptions against unlawful purchase of Indian lands. The act of the Virginia Assembly of March 10, 1655, for example, provided: "What lands the Indians shall be possessed of by order of this or other ensueing Assemblyes, such lands shall not be alienable by them, the Indians, to any man *de Futuro* . . . without the assent of the Assembly."[1]

A further act, in 1658, directed that "all the Indians of this Collonie shall and may hold and keep those seates of land which they now have, and that no person or persons whatever be suffered to entrench or plant upon such places as the said Indians claim or desire . . ."

Governor Winslow of Massachusetts Bay, writing in 1676,

may have been trying to make a good case for the colony in the war with King Philip which had just closed. In any case, he testified: "I think I can clearly say that before these present troubles broke out the English did not possess one foot of land in this colony but what was fairly obtained by honest purchase of the Indian proprietors. Nay, because . . . the Indians are . . . easily prevailed with to part with their lands, we first made a law that none should purchase or receive of gift any land of the Indians without the knowledge and allowance of our court."

When the English took over from the Dutch in New York in 1664, one of the first legislative acts provided that no purchase of lands from the Indians would be valid unless the tribal leaders were brought by the purchaser before the governor. After purchase was completed to the satisfaction of the Indians, the lands were to be recorded in the colonial office.[2]

William Penn was notably conscientious in this matter. No private person could purchase Indian lands; no purchase was valid unless it were made by Penn himself or one of his commissioners.

In the matter of trading with Indians, practices varied widely. Massachusetts colony was one of the first, by legislative enactment in 1684, to enter the trading field as a public venture and as a means of controlling trade relations. The term "trading house" was actually in use in that colony after 1625, but the term applied to private individuals or associations to whom the Indian trade was farmed. South Carolina adopted the public monopoly plan in 1716. Elsewhere, practices varied, but the tendency was to open the trading privilege to anyone who cared to avail himself of it.

As the issues between France and England pointed toward an inevitable and final clash for control of North America, the British government became aware of the weakness of its Indian policy. The ministers might not have realized this of their own knowledge, but men like Benjamin Franklin and the colonial governors, knowing that the French were every day consolidating their alliances with the Indian tribes, made the most of every opportunity to bring the problem to the attention of the ministers.

The Treaty of Aix-la-Chapelle terminating hostilities between the French and the English in 1748 had not settled the question of control in North America. The French

began immediately to prepare for the next stage in the
contest and maneuvered to gain and hold the loyalty of
Indian tribes wherever they could reach them.

The French were not moved by equity alone in dealing
with the Indian people; none of the European powers had
faced the question of how a civilized nation ought to govern a native area. Spain had a body of administrative law,
but law had not solved the problem. The general practice
of the European nations had been to turn discovered lands
over to private enterprise under a charter or license, without considering what the effect of private exploitation
would be on native property rights or native welfare. The
French sooner than the English had centralized the control
over such enterprise. After Louis XIV revoked the charter
of the Company of the West Indies in 1674, no company
was ever again given exclusive monopoly in the Indian
trade. Individuals and associations were forbidden to enter
the field except under license. This gave the French an
advantage in the competition for Indian support, since it
eliminated the cutthroat private competition, which, among
the English, too often resulted in feeding rum to the Indians and robbing them blind.

England was beginning to have some glimmering that
laissez-faire in colonial matters would end disastrously. The
great franchised companies like the East Indies Company
and the scattered colonies, proprietary and crown alike,
must be brought under centralized control.

In 1753, with the French moving boldly into the Ohio
River valley to win over the Miami, Peoria, Shawnee, and
other tribes of the region, the Board of Trade instructed
the governors of New York, Virginia, Maryland, Pennsylvania, New Jersey, New Hampshire, and Massachusetts to
hold a joint meeting with the Iroquois Nations and
attempt to make a treaty of alliance in the name of the
king. All the colonies with the exception of Virginia came
together at Albany, New York, on June 24, 1754, in a meeting which historians in after years recognized as one of the
first faltering steps toward the formation of a federal
union.[3]

The net result of the Albany Congress was disappointing,
though it provided an important occasion for the colonies
to discuss mutual problems. Even better than did the Board
of Trade, the leaders in the colonies realized the nature of
the problems they faced. They knew the Indians to be dis-

satisfied, ready to go over to the French. This dissatisfaction was many-sided: it resulted from the intrusion of English settlers on Indian lands; from the failure of the British to give presents of guns and clothing to Indian leaders, a practice of the French; and, most acutely, from the unscrupulous methods pursued by English traders. Governor Dinwiddie of Virginia called the traders "the most abandoned wretches in the world." The leaders in the colonies knew of these complaints, but no one colony by itself was capable of remedying the matter. Joint action was required.

The same inability to move mutually applied in the field of military action. Governor William Franklin of New Jersey, Benjamin's son, wrote to the Board of Trade: "The want of union among the colonies must ever occasion delay in their military operations. The first that happens to be called upon postpones coming to any determination till 'tis known what the other Colonies will do; and each of these others think that they have an equal right to act in the same manner."

In an endeavor to meet these pressing needs, the Albany Congress unanimously adopted a plan, drafted by Benjamin Franklin, providing for an executive and a legislative branch. The executive was to be appointed by and to represent the crown, while the grand council would be elected by the colonies. To this grand council was to be given jurisdiction over all Indian affairs, both political and commercial.

The plan came to nothing, for the colonial legislatures failed or refused to ratify it. Since Parliament was not called upon to act until the plan had been ratified by the separate colonies, it could do nothing about promulgating the work of the Congress.

This failure of the colonies tossed the problem back to the home government. The Board of Trade next recommended that a commander-in-chief over all colonial and British forces in America be appointed, to achieve unity of defense; and a superintendent of Indian affairs, to achieve, if possible, uniformity in trade relations. The ministry accepted these recommendations, in consequence of which General Braddock became the first military commander. Two Indian departments were set up, a northern and a southern, over which Sir William Johnson and Edmund Atkin were placed.[4]

Since the activities of these agents were limited to political
matters, trade relations having been left in the colonies in
a last-minute compromise, the situation was not improved.
Further, the appointment of a commander-in-chief over all
military forces, instead of achieving unity, actually
worsened the situation. The final result of the Board of
Trade's efforts to meet the approaching crisis was uncom-
fortably close to zero.

Soon after Sir William Johnson took office as superintendent of Indian affairs for the northern department, he
had his secretary, Peter Wraxall, submit a plan for the
organization of the department. The plan, prepared for the
Board of Trade, proposed "that the Indians be remedied
and satisfied with regard to their complaints about their
lands . . . and that no patents for lands be hereafter
granted but for such as shall be bought in the presence of
the superintendent at public meetings and the sale recorded
by His Majesty's secretary for Indian affairs."

Nothing came of the suggestion, though again it emphasized the need of a policy. Settlers were everywhere moving
in upon Indian country.

A more concrete achievement was the treaty concluded at
Easton in October 1758, in which the colony of Pennsylvania promised to prevent any further settlement west of
the Allegheny Mountains. This treaty was approved and
confirmed by the British ministry, and moved the government one step nearer to recognizing that Indians had a
property interest in their lands which must be protected.

Three years later, in November 1761, a further step was
taken when the Board of Trade, in considering a question
involving settlement in the Mohawk River valley, commented that "the granting of lands hitherto unsettled and
establishing colonies upon the frontiers before the claims of
the Indians are ascertained appears to be a measure of the
most dangerous tendency." The Privy Council, agreeing
with this finding, directed that instructions be sent to governors and other officers forbidding them "to pass any
grants to any person whatever of any lands within or adjacent to the territories possessed or occupied by the said
Indians or the property possession of which has at any time
been reserved to or claimed by [the Indians]."

This order of the Privy Council applied only to the
royal colonies, where legal title resided in the crown.

Nevertheless, it formulated an important policy with respect to lands claimed by the Indians.

These instructions remained in full force until after the Peace of Paris. Then, with the transfer of the extensive French holdings to British jurisdiction, the whole question of expansion and settlement beyond the established colonies came under review.

Lord Shelburne, upon assuming the presidency of the Board of Trade in April 1763, set himself the task of making this review. Concluding that the control over Indian affairs must be centralized in His Majesty's government, Shelburne faced the strategical problem of conveying to the Indian tribes the knowledge that this responsibility had been assumed in London. He proposed to accomplish this purpose "first, by the unity of management; secondly, by a definite boundary, which should be established between the westernmost settled parts of the colonies and the hunting grounds of the Indians . . . thirdly, by imperial regulations for the Indian trade, since the colonies had failed, on account of their rivalries, in . . . restraining the unscrupulous traders."

Shelburne did not intend, by establishing a western boundary and decreeing that settlement should not take place beyond the line, to prohibit westward expansion. He was convinced that some colonies were in need of additional land, not so much because of overpopulation, but because large tracts had been taken up and were being held for speculative purposes. In any case, westward expansion seemed inevitable. His concern was that expansion should be an orderly process and that the interests of the Indians should be protected. Any course which did not allow for consultation with the Indians could only involve the colonies and the mother country in the expense and hardship of fighting the Indians. He saw no necessity for that.

He had three proposals in mind: (1) To permit the Indians to sell their lands within settled areas (the Iroquois, for example, in New York, and the Cherokees, Creeks, and other tribes in the south) directly to the crown, thus eliminating fraudulent deals; (2) to survey a boundary line between the settlements and the areas used by the Indians, excluding from the Indian lands the upper Ohio Valley and allowing settlement in this region; and (3) to relieve the pressure on the Appalachian frontier by encouraging settlement in Nova Scotia and the provinces of East and West Florida.

While the Board of Trade pondered these and other considerations, the Ottawa warrior Pontiac completed his fighting plans among the tribes of the Northwest, and in May 1763 he struck his blow.[5]

The attack had been a long time in the making. The Indians had given repeated warning that they would not keep the peace forever if they continued to be abused by the traders whom the English allowed to go among them and if their lands were to be entered and settled upon without prior agreement.

When in 1760 Major Robert Rogers (Rogers the Ranger) appeared on the Cuyahoga River at the site of today's Cleveland to take over that territory in the name of England after the defeat of the French, Pontiac almost took up arms. If he had not been satisfied that the English had not really defeated the French king, he might have chosen war. As it was, he made Rogers wait a day while, no doubt, he scouted the English party and turned the matter over in his mind.

Rogers shrewdly waited and made his own calculations of his possible opponent. He reported later in his *Concise Account* that Pontiac had "an air of majesty and princely grandeur . . . I had several conferences with him, in which he discovered great strength of judgment, and a thirst after knowledge."

Pontiac let the Rogers party pass, even provided an escort.

But the Ottawa leader was not happy about either that incident or any of the chain of events that had taken place within his lifetime. On a later occasion, as he exhorted his followers to prepare to attack the English, he described a vision in which the Master of Life spoke through him: "The land on which you live I have made for you and not for others. Why do you suffer the white man to dwell among you? My children, you have forgotten the customs and traditions of your forefathers. Why do you not clothe yourselves in skins, as they did, and use the bows and arrows and the stone pointed lances, which they used? You have bought guns, knives, kettles, and blankets from the white man until you can no longer do without them; and what is worse, you have drunk the poison firewater which turns you into fools."

It was more than a fight for land about which Pontiac brooded. But he was practical enough to realize that the land must be taken and held if the Indians were ever to return to the virtues of their fathers.

When General Amherst, Braddock's successor as commander in the colonies, was advised that Pontiac had finally taken to the warpath, he was contemptuous. He had a poor opinion of the fighting qualities of Indians. His forts, strung out from Fort Pitt westward along the Ohio and northward to Michilimackinac at the head of Lake Huron, would turn back the best that the Indians had to send against him.

Pontiac had planned well. He struck suddenly, and simultaneously, all along the line, and the forts fell like so many ripe apples—Michilimackinac, St. Joseph, Miami, Ouiatenon, Sandusky, and Presque Isle. Only Detroit and Fort Pitt resisted successfully, and Detroit was under siege for six months. This is the only instance in the history of Indian fighting in which a siege was maintained for any length of time. It was the more remarkable in that the force making the attack was drawn from several tribes, some of whom had fought against each other not too many years before. Pontiac held them to their purpose of fighting the English by force of personality alone.

By the time Amherst heard the news, early in June, the country west of Detroit had been lost. It was the end of June before the news reached England, and yet it was August before the proposed royal proclamation was discussed.

Two subjects were to be covered by this proclamation: The Indians were to be advised that a definite boundary line would be set up between the settlements and their own lands; and Nova Scotia and the Floridas were to be held out as inducements to settlement by persons who otherwise might seek to enter the region beyond the Appalachians. Having quickly agreed on this strategy, the Ministry proceeded to fall apart, and nothing further happened.

It was September 28 before the cabinet reorganization was completed and the long-postponed proclamation was taken up by the new president of the Board of Trade, Lord Hillsborough. He came cold to the subject, and moreover he is reported to have been a man whose "mind was indeed highly cultured, but it seemed to be rather the information of a gentleman than the knowledge of a statesman" with which he was equipped. This was the opinion of Peter Wraxall, who, in behalf of Sir William Johnson, had been trying for years to get decisions out of the government. Hillsborough, as a result of his unfamiliarity with the subject, allowed the proclamation to be loaded down with other details than those previously agreed upon.

News of Pontiac's successes was becoming known in the London streets, and the Ministry moved fast. By October 1 a draft had been referred to the attorney general for opinion and by the fifth it had the approval of the Privy Council. Two days later the King signed the proclamation, and the New York packet, which had been held from sailing until the document was executed, finally departed with copies for the American colonies.

The blunder, which the ministers committed in their haste, and a consequence of burdening the proclamation with extraneous matters, came to light soon after its publication. It was a blunder which required ten years to repair.

Briefly, the Treaty of Paris, concluding the Seven Years' War, had provided that French Canadian law with respect to property should not be disturbed by the transfer of sovereignty. French property law differed from English law of the same period, since it embodied feudal dues and privileges derived from the Middle Ages with only minor changes. The English might not think them good laws; nevertheless they were the laws and customs which the French Canadians knew, and the treaty had promised that they would not be disturbed. The Proclamation of 1763, unintentionally it is true, appeared to invalidate French law by including the Province of Quebec, along with Nova Scotia and the Floridas, as regions in which settlement was to be encouraged, and by providing that "all persons inhabiting in or resorting to our said colonies may confide in our royal protection for the enjoyment of the benefit of the laws of our realm of England . . . [Courts would be established] for hearing and determining all causes, as well criminal as civil, according to law and equity, and as near as may be agreeable to the laws of England."

This provision, which was to have been an inducement to newcomers to settle in the wilderness, was a staggering blow to the French Canadians when they understood that it meant the abolition of their familiar laws and customs and the substitution of English law. Until the passage of the Quebec Act, June 22, 1774, successive ministries wrangled over this piece of maladroitness, with Lord Hillsborough exclaiming: "It never entered into our idea to overturn the laws and customs of Canada, with regard to property, but that justice should be administered agreeably to them."

Returning to the Indian provisions of the Proclamation of 1763, some of the language is worth having in mind as later events are recounted.[6]

It first declared that "it is just and reasonable, and essential to our interest, and the security of our colonies, that the several nations or tribes of Indians with whom we are connected, and who live under our protection, should not be molested or disturbed in the possession of such parts of our dominions and territories as, not having been ceded to or purchased by us, are reserved to them, or any of them. . . ."

It then commanded that no civil or military official presume, "upon any pretext whatever, to grant warrants of survey, or pass any patents for lands beyond the bounds of their respective governments . . . or any lands beyond the heads or sources of any of the rivers which fall into the Atlantic Ocean from the West and Northwest . . ."

"And we do further declare it to be our royal will and pleasure . . . to reserve under our sovereignty, protection, and dominion, for the use of the said Indians, all the lands and territories lying to the westward of the sources of the rivers which fall into the sea from the west and northwest as aforesaid;

"And we do hereby strictly forbid, on pain of our displeasure, all our loving subjects from making any purchases or settlements whatever, or taking possession of any of the lands above reserved . . ."

It provided also that "if at any time, any of the said Indians should be inclined to dispose of the said lands, the same shall be purchased only for us, in our name, at some public meeting or assembly of the said Indians . . ."

The final sections prohibited private persons from trading with the Indians except by license, and provided that criminal offenders who escaped into Indian country could be arrested by military officers and Indian agents and returned to the settlements for trial. In the haste of drafting and securing approval of the document, the king's ministers failed to authorize either the military or civilian peace officers to take action in the case of crimes committed in the Indian country.

17

COLONIALISM ENDS

The same public indignation which kept the colonies in a turmoil and finally brought about the repeal of the Stamp Act was responsible for the failure of the British government to achieve an overall Indian policy.

The ministry of Lord Halifax, which had assumed charge of the government just prior to the publication of the Proclamation of 1763, immediately formulated a plan for establishing a centralized department of Indian affairs, which would be independent of both the military commander and of the colonial governors. Except for details, it was the scheme which had been under discussion since the Albany Congress. The plan is interesting because, while it was never put into operation, the men who would afterward sit in the Continental Congress were obviously familiar with its provisions and must have approved of many of them, even though they opposed the Halifax ministry. When it came their turn to write the laws, as members of the Congress, they adopted much of the program.

The Halifax plan proposed a northern and southern district, with the Ohio River forming approximately the boundary. Complete control of all political relations with Indian tribes was to be retained in the Indian department, and no military officer or colonial governor could participate in a meeting with Indians without first obtaining the concurrence of the district superintendent; the colonial governors at the same time were to be kept informed on Indian affairs in the colony. Detailed regulations were to be issued governing trade, replacing all prior enactments of the several colonies. Provision was made for the trial of criminal matters. To finance this program, the cost of which, including the payment of salaries, was estimated at twenty thousand pounds per year, it was proposed to levy a tax on the fur trade. Authority to levy such a tax required an act of Parliament, and that was enough to put the plan on the shelf. Taxation had become too thorny an issue.[1]

Failure to put this or any similar comprehensive plan into effect meant that some compromise program had to be worked out. The government was still committed by its official proclamation to protect Indian lands and to regulate Indian trade.

Like so many compromises, the reorganization plan for the Indian department issued by the Board of Trade on March 7, 1768, was so conceived as to achieve the least of any of the possibilities open to it. In the absence of adequate funds (a failing that often overtakes the best of government plans), it is questionable whether any constructive labors could have been carried on. Not only were the superintendents of the two districts inadequately provided with staff help but the garrisons, which might have been effective in enforcing the land policy, were withdrawn. The government still proposed to protect the Indian boundary, while control over trade was returned to the colonies. This pleased no one.

In October 1765 the governors of Virginia and Pennsylvania were instructed to remove the settlers who had been crossing the mountains into the Indian territory. General Gage, then commander of colonial troops, was instructed to give assistance. It was found, however, that settlement had proceeded at such a pace that a major military operation would have been required to carry out the instructions. As for the control of trade, that had become such a mare's nest that several governors would gladly have seen the responsibility assumed elsewhere.

The last specific achievement of British administration was the establishment of the much-discussed boundary between the colonies and the Indians. The Proclamation of 1763 had indicated only that the Appalachian watershed should separate the settled country from Indian country, without taking into account that Indian lands in the north and in the south lay east of the watershed and that some white settlements had previously, with the consent of the Indians, moved west of such a dividing line. In the rush to get the proclamation issued these finer points were left for later negotiation.

Some negotiations had actually been undertaken before the issuance of the proclamation. It will be recalled that following the failure of the colonies in the Albany Congress to effect a centralization of control over Indian affairs, the Board of Trade had created a northern and a southern department or superintendency, and that Edmund Atkin had been appointed to the southern department. He was succeeded in this office by John Stuart in 1761.

The Indians of the area, Cherokee, Creek, Choctaw, Chickasaw, and lesser groups, complained constantly of the encroachments on their land. Stuart called a general conference of the governors of the southern provinces, and this meeting convened at Augusta, Georgia, in the autumn of 1763. Here the Indians brought their complaints against trespassing white men. A spokesman for the Creek Nation remarked, with more than ironical intent, that "the red men were formerly ignorant, but God Almighty and the King of England had made them otherwise."

A treaty was entered into at Augusta, the most important provision of which was the establishment of a line between the province of Georgia and the Indians living westward, with a further understanding that this boundary line would be continued northward until a western boundary for all the Atlantic colonies had been established.

By the autumn of 1765 this line had been run to the northern boundary of South Carolina. Agreement had also been reached with respect to the boundary of North Carolina, although this line was not surveyed until 1767.[2]

When it came to Virginia, that colony objected, since she felt that her claims to western lands were valid and should not be reduced by any action of her own. The Board of Trade insisted, and Virginia agreed to a conference with the Indians and other interested governors. This meeting took place at Fort Stanwyx in October 1768 and was attended, according to an eyewitness, "by about 3,400 Indians, and much fewer women and children than I ever saw at any treaty before, occasioned by their staying at their villages to secure their corn."

At Fort Stanwyx a line was agreed upon, starting in northern New York near the east end of Lake Ontario, running in a southerly direction to the Delaware River, then westerly to the Allegheny, down that river to the Ohio, and along the Ohio to the mouth of the Tennessee, where it joined the line which had been run as the western boundary of North Carolina.

In the earlier discussions, when Lord Shelburne was

president of the Board of Trade, and the matter of establishing a boundary was first brought up, it was not intended that this should be a permanent line dividing the country into a region of white settlements and Indian. Rather it was proposed that expansion should be under appropriate controls, that from time to time negotiations for land sales should be undertaken with the tribes involved, that satisfactory compensation would be paid to the Indians, and that white settlement would not take place until agreement had been reached and the Indians had withdrawn. Later ministers, however, were fearful of western expansion. They reasoned that the movement for independence would be fostered by encouraging growth in population and resources. The failure to establish an adequate administrative agency removed any possibility of managing a controlled westward movement.

When, therefore, the maintenance of the boundary line between the colonies and the Indians was made a function of the imperial government by the Indian Reorganization Plan of 1768, it meant that the government had decided to maintain a permanent boundary if possible. There would be no negotiations looking toward further expansion.

By adopting such a policy, the government fostered the building up of pressures against Indian territorial holdings. And, of course, it never succeeded in checking movement into the West.

What might have been the subsequent development if Britain had remained in control is speculation of an unfruitful kind. During and immediately following the Revolutionary War, British colonial officials, first in the American colonies and later in Canada, made use of every opportunity to warn the Indians that they would be robbed of their lands by the new nation and to promise the tribes full protection of their holdings if they would give their allegiance to the king. By that time, however, England had lost her opportunity to legislate and administer effectively in the field of Indian affairs.[3]

One of the last echoes we have of the functioning of British-Indian policy is a complaint in July 1774 from a spokesman for the Iroquois Indians. The complaint reflected conditions among the Iroquois, but it reflected equally well conditions all along the frontier. Indian villages everywhere were swarming with lawless vagabonds, according to Superintendent Stuart of the southern department, and they were carrying on every species of trade, with every sharp practice ever devised.

Said the Iroquois spokesman: "The provinces have done nothing and the trade has been thrown into utter confusion by the traders being left to their own will and pleasure and pursuit of game, following our people to their hunting grounds with goods and liquor, where they not only impose on us at pleasure, but by means of carrying these articles to our scattered people, obstruct our endeavors to collect them, which we might easily have effected if the traders had been obliged to bring their goods to Niagara or other markets, as before."

The final effect of British policy was such as to make it impossible to protect the Indians in their land rights. The king's ministers had in effect created a great Indian reservation where, in Professor Alvord's words, "the land was to remain untouched by the plow and where no settlement of white men should disturb the peace of the primeval forest."

Having created what was finally intended as an impermeable barrier, the ministers did nothing to stem the fast-running current already pouring westward. Instead, the duty of enforcing the imperial decree was transferred to the colonial governments, who were to keep their citizens in check.

The Indians had not a chance in such a combination.

PART 3

Supplanting a People

"The first subject to which we would call attention of the governor, is the depredation daily committed by the white people upon the most valuable timber on our reservations. This has been the subject of complaint for many years. . . .

"Our next subject of complaint is the frequent theft of our horses and cattle by the whites, and their habit of taking and eating them when they please, and without our leave.

"Another evil arising from the pressure of the whites upon us, and our unavoidable communication with them, is the frequency with which our Indians are thrown into jail, and that too for the most trifling causes.

"In our hunting and fishing, too, we are greatly interrupted. Our venison is stolen from the trees where we have hung it to be reclaimed after the chase. . . . The fish which, in the Buffalo and Tonnewanto creeks, used to supply us with food, are now, by the dams and other obstructions of the white people, prevented from multiplying, and we are almost entirely deprived of that accustomed sustenance.

"The greatest source of all our grievances is, that the white men are among us. . . ."

—Red Jacket, Seneca, in a letter to Governor DeWitt
Clinton, January, 1821

". . . We have no prisons; we have no pompous parade of courts; we have no written laws; and yet judges are as highly revered among us as they are among you, and their decisions are as much regarded.

"Property, to say the least, is as well guarded, and crimes are as impartially punished. We have among us no splendid villains above the control of our laws. Daring wickedness is here never suffered to triumph over helpless innocence. The estates of widows and orphans are never devoured by enterprising sharpers. In a word, we have no robbery under the color of law."

—Joseph Brant, Mohawk

18

NATIONALISM BEGINS

The failure of the colonies to cooperate in time of mutual danger, which had characterized their behavior under British rule, became a luxury they could not afford once they undertook to maintain their separate sovereignty.

The centralized controls, which the colonies had resented in the mother country, became one of the necessities of life in their new status.

These were but two of the first lessons the rebelling provinces had to learn, and in both cases the reality which taught the lesson was the problem of dealing with the Indian tribes.

Time could not be wasted either in learning the lessons. Britain made strenuous efforts to hold the Indians loyal and was not above offering guarantees of property protection, which, in the light of her past failures to make good on similar promises, were no better than bribes. Gifts of money and clothing, which she had spurned to offer in competition with the French, were now quickly forthcoming. Counteraction was urgent.

The rebellious colonies proved themselves capable of acting in the emergency.

On Friday, June 16, 1775, in the chambers of the Continental Congress then sitting in Philadelphia, George Washington was offered the commission as commander-in-chief of the American forces, which he accepted at once. In the very next order of business the Congress, by unanimous resolution, appointed a committee of five to report what steps ought to be taken "for securing and preserving the friendship of the Indian nations."[1]

A month later the committee, which included Philip Schuyler of New York and Patrick Henry of Virginia, recommended measures "to strengthen and confirm the friendly disposition toward these colonies which has long prevailed among the northern Indians, and which has been lately manifested by some of those to the southward . . ." The Congress responded by establishing Indian departments for the northern, middle, and southern regions and appropriating $23,333.34 out of a slim treasury to meet the costs of the three departments. The commissioners were authorized "to take to their assistance gentlemen of influence among the Indians, . . ."

There was no condescension in the urgent note directed by the Congress in those same days to be sent to the Six Nations. "Brothers, in our consultation we have judged it proper and necessary to send you this talk, as we are upon the same island, and that you may be informed of the reasons of this great council . . ." The letter concluded: "This is a family quarrel between us and Old England . . . We desire you to remain at home, and not join on either side, but keep the hatchet buried deep."

In August of that summer a neutrality pact was negotiated with the Six Nations, which, among other items, agreed to provide gunpowder for the Indians for hunting purposes. This was at a time when Congress was urging tobacco growers to dig up the earthen floors of their tobacco warehouses in order to reclaim saltpeter. Money was also provided to engage two blacksmiths and an interpreter, who were to reside among the Indians and be of assistance to them.

When in 1777 two white men, George Walton and George Taylor, presuming to act in the name of the United States, tried to persuade the Six Nations to enter into a treaty by which the Indians would have ceded certain lands, Congress immediately repudiated the men and directed the commissioners for the northern department to look into the matter and reassure the Indians.

Two years later, when the officer in command at Pittsburgh, Colonel Brodhead, reported that settlers had crossed the Ohio River and had entered Indian lands on the north bank of the river, Congress called upon the governor of Virginia "to endeavor to prevent a repetition of the trespasses." The colonel had seized the trespassers and destroyed their buildings, and he was supported in these actions.

These were all urgent matters in which a wrong decision could have serious consequences.

The diplomatic policy of the Congress was not wholly successful with the Six Nations of Iroquois, at least two of the tribes siding with the British, their ancient ally. While this was resented in Congress, it was also recognized that any attempted coercive action might only spur the Indians on to greater effort in behalf of the British. The more choleric members insisted that the Indian tribes which had been guilty of depredations against Americans should be required to pay in land cessions, the land to be added to "such state as may have a prior right [November 1779]."

This proposal opened up a question of public policy which completely obscured the original motion to take punitive action against the Indians. The question had to do with determining who should have the right to extinguish Indian title. It was settled tentatively at the time by the adoption of a resolution reading, as to that part: "No land [shall] be sold or ceded by any of the said Indians, either as individuals or as a nation, unless to the United States of America, or by the consent of Congress." Certain of the states were prepared to challenge the policy, since it imposed a limitation on local freedom of action, which looked suspiciously like the very issue over which they were at war with England.

This seems to have been one of the first clashes between the advocates of centralized control and those who favored states' rights. One party at the outset insisted that relations with the Indian tribes were the primary concern of the national government, in which no state and no private individual should intervene. On September 14, 1786, for example, the Congress transmitted a formal request that Virginia abstain from making war upon Indians who had been raiding her borders. If Virginia had a just complaint, it should be referred to the national government for appropriate action. A minority in Congress opposed this view.

This prior right of Congress was embodied in the Articles of Confederation, the ninth of which provided that "the United States in Congress assembled shall also have the sole and exclusive right and power of . . . regulating the trade and managing all affairs with the Indians, not members of any of the states. . . ." Here followed a proviso insisted upon by those states which were fearful of giving too much control into the hands of a central government: "Provided, that the legislative right of any state within its own limits be not infringed or violated."

The Continental Congress did not act specifically to make its broad powers effective until the close of the war. On September 22, 1783, three weeks after the signing of the Treaty of Versailles, it issued a proclamation which prohibited "all persons from making settlements on lands inhabited or claimed by Indians . . . and from purchasing or receiving any gift or cession of such lands or claims without the express authority . . . of Congress"; concluding, "it is moreover declared that every such purchase or settlement, gift or cession, not having the authority aforesaid, is null and void, and that no right or title will accrue in consequence of any such purchase, gift, cession or settlement."

A comparison of this text with the Royal Proclamation of 1763 reveals that the transfer of sovereignty resulted in no change of policy. In two other actions of the Congress certain principles laid down under British rule were adopted or extended to meet the changed situation.

The first of these was the Ordinance of August 7, 1786, providing for the regulation of Indian affairs. The Ordinance consisted of four sections: (1) it created an Indian department divided into two districts, northern and southern, over which the secretary of war was given jurisdiction (not until the middle of the following century would Indian affairs be taken out of the War Department); (2) traders were required to give bond, be of good character, and operate under license; (3) no official associated with the administration of Indian affairs could engage in Indian trade; and (4) where any transaction of the Indian department might interfere with the legislative rights of the states, the superintendent was directed to "act in conjunction" with the states.

The second was the Ordinance to regulate the Northwest Territory, adopted July 13, 1787, of which the third section, dealing with the subject of education, contained this declaration: "The utmost good faith shall always be observed towards the Indians, their lands and property shall never be taken from them without their consent; and in their property, rights, and liberty, they never shall be invaded or disturbed, unless in just and lawful wars authorized by Congress; but laws founded in justice and humanity shall from time to time be made, for preventing wrongs being done to them, and for preserving peace and friendship with them."

These actions in Congress were designed to answer the

complaints registered by the Indians and to give assurance of the friendly intentions of the new government. The Indians had reason to complain, for they had been witnessing a steadily growing volume of traffic across the mountains since the years preceding the outbreak of the Revolution. The British had not been able to check the traffic, for the reasons already suggested, and there was an unhappy possibility that the anger of the Indian tribes would be turned against the Americans in a fresh outbreak similar to the Pontiac uprising.[2]

The Indians who had participated in the war on the side of the British did so out of a conviction that the king could and would protect their interests. British propaganda helped to further this notion, as the delegates in Congress were well aware. Apart from the propaganda, however, the Indians felt that they, as much as the American revolutionaries, were fighting for freedom and security. By the end of 1773, at least 60,000 white men had settled in the area between Pittsburgh and the mouth of the Ohio, where they had no business going under British rule. Flatboats, built and floated on the Ohio at Pittsburgh, carried family after family with household goods, machinery, and livestock to the fertile lands below. Lord Dunmore's war, fought on the eve of the Revolution, started as a dispute between the rival claims of Virginia and Pennsylvania over ownership of the land at the Monongahela-Allegheny junction. In its effect, it turned out to be a war of annihilation directed at the Shawnee tribe.

It is not surprising, in view of these developments, that Joseph Brant, the shrewd Mohawk leader whose sister had married Sir William Johnson, should have taken himself off to England at the beginning of the conflict. During the winter of 1775–76 he obtained the promise of Lord Germain, secretary of state for the colonies, to see that all the land grievances of the Six Nations were promptly settled. The Six Nations, it is true, had entered into a neutrality pact at Albany in the summer of 1775, but the Continental Congress up to that point had given no guarantees to respect Indian interests—and who knew how long there would be a Continental Congress?

Hostilities between the United States and Great Britain ceased on February 14, 1783, after a preliminary discussion of peace terms. The Indians received their first information of this development from the British. The Congress made no effort to inform the Indians until the month of May, when the secretary of war was instructed to transmit the notice. When the emissary reached Brant, at Niagara, the Mohawk sent word back that the Indians wanted their lands guaranteed before they participated in treaty negotiations.

The Indians were not consulted at any stage of the discussions. This was criticized in England, where it was pointed out that in the Treaty of Fort Stanwyx in 1768, when the boundary running north and south between Indian country and the several colonies was finally completed, the government had placed itself under obligation to protect the Indian lands. England should have insisted, according to these critics, that she was without power to relinquish lands still held in Indian ownership.

The Indians did not protest further the failure to consult them, and adopted a watchful attitude as representatives of the United States went among the tribes talking treaties, boundaries, peace, and friendship. In November and December 1786 two meetings were held near the mouth of the Detroit River with representatives from the Iroquois Nations and from the Hurons and Wyandottes (both fragments of the once powerful tribe destroyed by the Iroquois 140 years before), Delawares, Shawnees, Ottawas, Chippewas, Cherokees, and the tribes along the Wabash River. At the second of these meetings the Indians joined in a letter addressed to their "Brethren of the United States of America."[3]

The letter expressed frustration: "It is now more than three years since peace was made between the King of Great Britain and you, but we, the Indians, were disappointed, finding ourselves not included in that peace, according to our expectations . . . We thought we were entering upon a reconciliation and friendship with a set of people born on the same continent with ourselves, certain that the quarrel between us was not of our own making. In the course of our councils, we imagined we hit upon an expedient that would promote a lasting peace between us.

"Brothers," the letter suggested, "all treaties carried on with the United States, on our part, should be with the general voice of the whole confederacy, and carried on in the most open manner, without any restraint on either side; and especially as land matters are often the subject of our councils with you, a matter of the greatest importance and of great concern to us, in this case we hold it indispensably necessary that any cession of our lands should be made in the most public manner, and by the united voice of the confederacy."

In this, doubtless, the great council had followed the advice of the Iroquois spokesmen, who knew the value of confederation. Perhaps also the hard voice of an Iroquois supplied the text of the next passage: "Brothers . . . you have managed everything respecting us your own way. You kindled your council fires where you thought proper, without consulting us, at which you held separate treaties, and have entirely neglected our plan of having a general conference with the different nations of the confederacy . . .

"Brothers . . . let us have a treaty with you early in the spring. Let us pursue reasonable steps; let us meet half-way, for our mutual convenience. . . . We beg that you will prevent your surveyors and other people from coming upon our side of the Ohio River."

The letter was alluding to treaties made in 1784 and 1785 with representatives of the Six Nations, and the Wyandotte, Delaware, Chippewa, and Ottawa tribes, respectively. The treaties would have conveyed lands to the United States, but without compensation to the Indians. The tribes complained of this, as well they might. Reports of their dissatisfaction reached Congress from many sources, with rumors of outbreaks or threatened outbreaks in the Northwest.

Finally in October 1787, Congress issued instructions to the governor of Northwest Territories, Arthur St. Clair, directing him "to examine into the real temper of the Indian tribes inhabiting the northern Indian department . . . The treaties which have been made, may be examined, but must not be departed from, unless a change of boundary, beneficial to the United States, can be obtained."

The letter written from the mouth of the Detroit River the preceding winter was in the hands of Congress on the occasion of writing these instructions. Hence the significance of the concluding sentence: "Every exertion must be made to defeat all confederations and combinations among the tribes, and to conciliate the white people inhabiting the frontiers, towards them."

St. Clair followed his instruction zealously. He succeeded in negotiating new treaties in 1788, which in effect confirmed the concessions made by the Indians in the 1784 and

1785 agreements. He had succeeded in arousing latent hostilities among the tribes, which led them to act disadvantageously to their own interests. As he reported, "The reason why the treaties were made separately with the Six Nations and the Wyandottes, and more westerly tribes, was a jealousy that subsisted between them, which I was not willing to lessen, by appearing to consider them as one people—they do not so consider themselves; and I am persuaded their general confederacy is entirely broken. Indeed, it would not be very difficult, if circumstances required it, to set them at deadly variance."

General St. Clair had won that round, but there was no "deadly variance" among some of these same tribes when they met him on the Wabash on November 4, 1791. Neither was their confederacy quite as thoroughly broken as he had reported. True, the force which the Miami warrior, Little Turtle, had at his disposal was inferior in numbers to the American force led by St. Clair as major general, but several tribes were represented, and they were all eager to drive home the point.

This they did in an efficient manner. In a surprise attack they overwhelmingly defeated the general, just a day's march out of Fort Wayne.[4]

19

BASIC TENETS

Henry Knox, first secretary of war and the first federal official in charge of Indian affairs, was as dissatisfied with the treaties of 1784 and 1785 as were the Indians.

He also disagreed with the opinion then prevalent in Congress, that the United States, by winning the war with Great Britain, had thereby become absolute owner of the soil.[1]

In reporting to President Washington on May 23, 1789, Knox found that serious trouble was rapidly building up on the western frontier. Ever since the conclusion of the war, acts of hostility had been committed. White settlers were murdered along the Wabash River. Indians had even crossed the Ohio, beyond their recognized boundary, to kill and burn. There were demands that the Indians be exterminated and the western lands be cleared of them once and for all. Knox was not impressed by appeals of that nature. He had a fair idea of what was happening.

His report ran: "The injuries have been so reciprocal, that it would be a point of critical investigation to know on which side they have been the greatest."

He counseled against punitive action: "When the impartial mind of the great public sits in judgment, it is necessary that the cause of the ignorant Indians should be heard as well as those who are more fortunately circumstanced. It well becomes the public to inquire before it punishes; to be influenced by reason, and the nature of things, and not by its resentments."

He proceeded to analyze the situation for the president. One of the principal sources of trouble at the moment was the territory centering around the Wabash River, where such tribes as the Delawares, Wyandottes, Chippewas, Ottawas, Miamis, Piankeshaws, Weas, Shawnees, and remnants of others were all bunched together. For some of these, the country north of the Ohio and westward from the Pennsylvania border was the native habitat; but for others—Wyandotte, Ottawa, Delaware, Shawnee—it was country into which, more or less recently, they had been driven by the encroachments of white men upon their original homes in the north or the east.[2]

Considering their diversity of language and background and the traditional rivalry of many of them in the days before white settlement, they had accommodated themselves to each other and to the crowded environment as best they could. General St. Clair might comment that their confederacy was falling apart. In this, he completely misunderstood what was happening before his eyes. Pontiac had formed the first alliance only some twenty years before. Now some of the same tribes were coming together in a last effort to preserve their lands. Land was vital, and they pleaded with the United States not to separate them into hostile camps in which each would be kept ignorant of what the others had bargained away, possibly without any right of ownership to convey. "Brothers," they wrote in their letter of December 18, 1786, "we wish to pursue just steps, and we are determined they shall appear just and reasonable in the eyes of the world."

Knox could not have knowledge of all this background, but he knew and reported that the tribes in the Northwest had from 1,500 to 2,000 able-bodied warriors. An expedition to exterminate the Indians and their towns could not be undertaken with an armed force of less than 2,500 men. Knox had just come through the Revolutionary War, in which he had participated in every action of any consequence, from the siege of Boston to the surrender of Yorktown, and he knew something about organizing and supplying an army. The $200,000 which he estimated would be required to raise, equip, and maintain a force necessary to defeat the Indians in a six months' period was simply not available. It was "a sum far exceeding the ability of the United States to advance," in view of previous obligations. Moreover, resort to arms seemed to him as unnecessary as it was economically infeasible.

A policy of conciliation, or peaceful settlement and orderly expansion, would mean savings to the treasury. He estimated that the entire Indian population east of the Mississippi numbered 76,000 (which probably was too low), and that this number could be absorbed or peacefully moved out of the area over a fifty-year period at an annual expenditure of $15,000. He reasoned: "As the settlements of the whites shall approach near to the Indian boundaries established by treaties, the game will be diminished, and the lands being valuable to the Indians only as hunting grounds, they will be willing to sell further tracts for small consideration. By the expiration, therefore, of the above period, it is most probable that the Indians will . . . be reduced to a very small number." A system of coercion, on the other hand, would cost infinitely more and would accomplish no greater objective in the end.

Quite apart from this dollar-and-cents reasoning, principles of public policy were involved, which he was unwilling to see ignored.

Henry Knox seems to be one of the unknown great men of the national history. His record of accomplishments is enough to have made any two or three men gratefully remembered. Biographical material is far from abundant.

He was the citizen-soldier par excellence. With no military training, other than that obtained as a militiaman for a few years prior to the Revolution, he became Washington's chief artillery officer. In time, so well did he master the science of gunnery, he would have the satisfaction of having his effectiveness praised by the enemy. His skill in placing guns to get the most out of a limited armament at the siege of Yorktown moved Washington to comment that "the resources of his genius supplied the deficit of means."

By the end of the war, Knox had risen to the rank of major general. Possibly Washington prized his unquenchable optimism above all other gifts in his fellow officers—it was a quality that had carried through the darkest hours. To Knox, evidently, the country is indebted for the establishment of the military academy which later became West Point, and he was responsible for the first arsenal at Springfield. He was the moving spirit in the founding of the Society of the Cincinnati, of which he was the first secretary and Washington the first president.

He was made secretary of war in March 1785, while Congress still operated under the Articles of Confederation. With the adoption of the Constitution and the organization of the first cabinet, he was continued in that office and so remained until December 1794.

Knox was no lawyer—he had been a bookseller in Boston until the approaching revolution ruined his business—yet his reasoning was remarkably similar to that which the United States Supreme Court would follow in Indian cases years later. Facing the question whether the United States ought not to proceed by force against the Indians, assuming the means to be available, he could not escape the conclusion that any nation desiring to establish its characters "on the broad basis of justice, would not only hesitate in it, but reject every proposition to benefit itself, by the injury of any neighboring community, however contemptible and weak it might be, either with respect to its manners or power."

He saw no alternative, practical or just, to the negotiation of treaties, in which rights and limits would be explicitly defined and in which the United States would bind itself to the strictest observance of the terms. He pointed out, in his report to the president, "the Indians being the prior occupants, possess the right of the soil. It cannot be taken from them unless by their free consent, or by the rights of conquest in case of a just war. To dispossess them on any other principle, would be a great violation of the fundamental laws of nature . . ."

As to the notion that the treaty of peace with Great Britain had invested the United States with the absolute title to all Indian lands, he found that the Indians had quite a different view of the matter: ". . . The Indians are greatly tenacious of their lands, and generally do not relinquish their right, excepting on the principle of a specific consideration . . ." In this, he thought, they were asking only what was justly due them.

In short, the United States having "come into the possession of sovereignty, and an extensive territory, must unavoidably be subject to the expenses of such a condition."

He concluded his recommendation to the president: "The time has arrived, when it is highly expedient that a liberal system of justice should be adopted for the various Indian tribes within the limits of the United States."

His reasoning persuaded Washington, who directed his secretary of war to renegotiate the treaties of 1784 and 1785 on a basis of paying money compensation for land. As it turned out, the matter of the northwestern boundary was not settled without bloodshed and defeats for both Generals Harmar and St. Clair. William Henry Harrison then took hold, and at the battle of Fallen Timbers [in 1794] broke the Indian resistance.

No magic in words could compel men to act with a decent regard for the rights of others; Knox had no illusion there. He realized that a solemn treaty would not be kept unless the United States took active measures to secure its enforcement. "All treaties with the Indian nations," he commented, hearing that a treaty with the Cherokee Indians had been violated, "however equal and just they may be in their principles, will not only be nugatory but humiliating to the sovereign, unless they shall be guaranteed by a body of troops . . . There can be neither justice nor observance of treaties, where every man claims to be the sole judge in his own cause and the avenger of his own supposed wrongs . . . In such a case, the sword of the Republic only, is adequate to guard a due administration of justice, and the preservation of the peace."

In this, Knox discovered what would prove to be the fatal flaw in the nation's policy with respect to the Indians. He had a clear view of the future indeed when he wrote referring to the violation of the Cherokee treaty by white settlers going on Cherokee lands: "If so direct and manifest contempt of the authority of the United States be suffered with impunity, it will be in vain to attempt to extend the arm of government to the frontiers. The Indian tribes can have no faith in such imbecile promises, and the lawless whites will ridicule a government which shall, on paper only, make Indian treaties, and regulate Indian boundaries."

He thought it unfortunate that so many Indian tribes inhabiting the eastern seaboard at the time of the first settlements had become extinct. Would it not have been better, he wondered, if perseverance had been used to impart knowledge and skills possessed by the white men in order that this "part of the human race" might have been saved from destruction?

In his report to the president dated July 7, 1789, Knox made two suggestions which, in fact, were adopted by the president and by the first Congress and became part of the basic national policy. Pointing out that the great source of Indian wars arose in disputes about boundaries, he urged that no state should be free to deal with Indian tribes over land matters since any dispute between the state and the tribes involved could plunge the nation into a war not of

its own making. Accordingly the authority and consent of
the national government should be deemed indispensable
in any action whose consequences would be a national
responsibility. Further, the Indian tribes ought to be dealt
with as foreign nations, not as the subjects of any particular state, and therefore "the general sovereignty must possess the right of making all treaties, on the execution or
violation of which depends peace or war."

His second suggestion was that the national government
should issue a statement of policy, in the form of an act of
Congress, which would at once make clear how the United
States intended to deal with the Indian tribes. "It would
reflect on the honor of the new government," he wrote,
"were a declarative law to be passed, that the Indian tribes
possess the right of the soil of all lands within their limits,
respectively, and that they are not to be divested thereof,
but in consequence of fair and bona fide purchases, made
under the authority, or with the express approbation, of the
United States."

Such a declarative law had been anticipated by Section 3
of the Northwest Ordinance of 1787. In fact, since Knox
was secretary of war and in charge of Indian affairs at that
time, it is to be assumed that he was responsible for the
idea, if not the actual language, of that section. Now, following his recommendation to President Washington, the
same principle was incorporated in the Act of August 7,
1789. (Incidentally, of thirteen laws passed in the first session of Congress, four dealt with Indian matters.)

In the following year, the first Indian Trade and Intercourse Act of July 22, 1790, established in the national
government that prior authority which Knox had made as
his first suggestion. Section 4 of the Act provided, "no sale
of land made by any Indians, or any nation or tribe of
Indians within the United States, shall be valid to any person or persons, or to any state . . . unless the same shall be
made and duly executed at some public treaty, held under
the authority of the United States."

Washington's own views were closely akin to those of
Henry Knox—indeed they were the views of most men, in
or out of Congress, who were not intent on profiting out of
Indian lands. Writing to James Duane in Congress, September 7, 1783, Washington anticipated the problem, which,
year after year, would come before Congress for solution
and would never be solved, so long as any lands remained

in Indian ownership. His letter ran: "To suffer a wide extended country to be overrun with land jobbers, speculators, and monopolizers, or even with scattered settlers, is in my opinion inconsistent with that wisdom and policy which our true interest dictates, or that an enlightened people ought to adopt; and, besides, is pregnant of disputes both with the savages and among ourselves, the evils of which are easier to be conceived than described. And for what, but to aggrandize a few avaricious men, to the prejudice of many and the embarrassment of government? For the people engaged in these pursuits, without contributing in the smallest degree to the support of government, or considering themselves as amenable to its laws, will involve it, by their unrestrained conduct, in inextricable perplexities, and more than probably in a great deal of bloodshed."[3]

He, too, was in agreement with the British policy of establishing and maintaining a definite boundary between Indian and white land. In the same letter to Duane he proposed the issuance of a proclamation which would make it a felony for any person to survey or settle beyond the line. "Measures of this sort," he wrote, "would not only obtain peace from the Indians, but would, in my opinion, be the means of preserving it. It would dispose of the land to the best advantage, people the country progressively, and check land jobbing and monopolizing, which are now going forward with great avidity, while the door would be open and terms known for everyone to obtain what is reasonable and proper for himself, upon legal and constitutional grounds."

Patrick Henry, as governor of Virginia through this period, tried to prevent the citizens of his state from going on Indian lands. In a proclamation dated January 6, 1785, he expressed the desire of his office to remove all causes of jealousy and suspicion from the minds of the neighboring tribes of Indians, "and to evince a disposition to act with friendship and justice towards them . . ." He then commanded "all the commissioners, surveyors, and other persons to suspend the taking possession, or surveying, of any lands on the northwest side of the Ohio River, or below the mouth of the River Tennessee, until they shall legally be authorized so to do." Persons who had already taken possession of such lands were ordered to withdraw.[4]

When citizens of the state of North Carolina crossed the mountains into the Cherokee country and attempted to erect the state of Franklin, Governor Henry was alarmed. The encroachment, he felt, "must certainly produce hostility, if not quickly retracted." Virginia had its own agent, Colonel Joseph Martin, representing it among the Indians, and the North Carolinians tried to persuade the colonel to join forces with them, presumably to get Virginia to support their enterprise. Martin was cautious, and so was Governor Henry. He advised his agent that if the Cherokees should become openly hostile, "you are to communicate to the Indians in some fit and proper manner, a solemn and pointed assurance, that the state of Virginia is not party, aiding, or assisting in the encroachment."

The North Carolinians were using a familiar argument in justification of the invasion of the Indian land: The Indians were nomadic hunters, therefore they could not make the best use of the land and ought to give way to white tillers of the soil. It was notable, however, as Governor Henry pointed out in a letter to the Virginia delegates in Congress, that the first lands preempted by the whites were the towns and the cleared fields which the Indians had been planting for generations before any white man was in sight. Henry's letter concluded: "I have little hope that either justice or policy will have much influence on their proceedings."

Thomas Jefferson, as secretary of state, wrote a formal opinion on the question of Indian land title, which is substantially in agreement with what Chief Justice Marshall would write some years later. Jefferson had been requested to comment on the validity of a grant of land made by the state of Georgia to a private land company (the Yazoo Company). The land in question had not previously been acquired from the Indians, but the charter granted by the state contained a proviso purporting to authorize the individual members of the land company to take measures for extinguishing the Indian title, that is, by purchase. The question was, by what authority could the state issue such a charter?[5]

Jefferson's opinion, dated May 3, 1790, ran: "A society, taking possession of a vacant country, and declaring they mean to occupy it, does thereby appropriate to themselves as prime occupants what was before common . . . If the country, instead of being vacant, is thinly occupied by another nation, the right of the native forms an exception to that of the newcomers; that is to say, these (the newcomers) will have a right against all other nations, except the natives. Consequently, they have the exclusive privilege of acquiring the native right by purchase or other just means. This is called the right of pre-emption, and is become a principle of the law of nations, fundamental with respect to America. There are but two means of acquiring the native title. First, war; for even war may, sometimes, give a just title. Second, contracts or treaty.

"The states of America, before their present union, possessed completely, each within its own limits, the exclusive right to use these two means of acquiring the native title, and, by their act of union, they have as completely ceded both to the general government."

This thesis would be central to the violent controversy in which Georgia would be involved a generation later.

Henry Knox had concluded that armed force would be needed to obtain respect for Indian treaties. Jefferson seemed to be hopeful that extreme measures might not be needed, as in the case of a state which refused to abide by a decision of the national government. At least he wrote: "Respect and friendship should, I think, mark the conduct of the general towards the particular government, and explanations should be asked and time and color given them to tread back their steps before coercion is held up to their view."

White men could see clearly what ought to be done to defend the rights of the Indians, if that was any comfort to the Indian. Forty years later, when force alone could have protected the Indians, it was withheld, and the Indians east of the mountains lost everything they owned.

Preserving the land in Indian ownership was not the end of the problem. Without land the Indians could only perish. But, even though they be possessed of land, conditions in their country had changed so that unless other things were done for them, and by them, they might still perish. Jefferson urged: "Encourage them to abandon hunting, to apply themselves to the raising of stock, to agriculture and domestic manufacture, and thereby prove to themselves that less land and labor will maintain them; and bring within their reach more and more of the things which would help them to make the transition. . . . Develop in them the wisdom of exchanging what they can spare and we want [land], for what we can spare and they want [the arts of civilization]."

That was a sufficient statement of the problem. Would there ever be a sufficient interest in the fate of the original settlers in America to achieve a solution of the problem?

"The ultimate point of rest and happiness for them," Jefferson wrote, "is to let our settlements and theirs meet and blend together, to intermix, and become one people."

Such a goal called for the free play of self-determinism; it could not be achieved unilaterally, by one party defining the terms and compelling acceptance.

20

THE LAWGIVER

The pope of Rome had determined that the dwellers in the New World were real men—*utpote versos homines*—and not beasts. The emperor's adviser had concluded that they were "the true owners of the New World." The king of England had proclaimed it as his will that they not be disturbed in the peaceful possession of their lands.

All of these opinions, findings, and conclusions are reflected in Chief Justice John Marshall's writings on Indian questions. His are the decisions to which the courts of later days have repeatedly turned, occasionally to elaborate upon them, but never to overturn them. The legislative and the executive arms might withhold what John Marshall said should be delivered, but rarely the courts.

It was unfortunate for the Indians that much of what Marshall said, in the era in which he said it, should have caused political hackles to come up stiff and hostile. His judicial reasoning might be ever so deep and true; those who were his political opponents—and at the time he wrote his Indian opinions there were few men in Congress whom he could call friend—were prepared to defeat if they could everything he uttered. In his last years he was a kind of Don Quixote left over from the Federalist days of old John Adams. He had an imperious belief in the sovereignty of the federal state, which on every offered occasion he reinforced.[1]

The age which produced Andrew Jackson was moving as fast as it could away from the doctrine of centralized control. It would move into nullification, then into secession and civil war, before a balance was reestablished. John Marshall, looking at Andrew Jackson's record in 1828 in the heat of the presidential campaign, saw what was happening and was moved with wrath.

"Should Jackson be elected," he wrote to a friend, "I shall look upon the government as virtually dissolved."[2]

The words would come back to do John Marshall a disservice. That might make no difference to Marshall, an old man coming to the end of his days, but the disservice reached out to the Indians and tipped the balance against them.

Marshall summarized the historical situation in *Johnson* v. *MacIntosh*, 8 Wheaton 543. He wrote: "On the discovery of this immense continent the great nations of Europe were eager to appropriate to themselves so much of it as they could respectively acquire. Its vast extent offered an ample field to the ambition and enterprise of all, and the character and religion of its inhabitants afforded an apology for considering them as a people over whom the superior genius of Europe might claim an ascendancy. The potentates of the old world found no difficulty in convincing themselves that they made ample compensation to the inhabitants of the new by bestowing on them civilization and Christianity in exchange for unlimited independence. But as they were all in pursuit of nearly the same object, it was necessary, in order to avoid conflicting settlements and consequent war with each other, to establish a principle which all should acknowledge . . .

"The exclusion of all other Europeans necessarily gave to the nation making the discovery the sole right of acquiring the soil from the natives and establishing settlements upon it. It was a right with which no Europeans could interfere. It was a right which all asserted for themselves, and to the assertion of which all others assented.

"The relations which were to exist between the discoverer and the natives were to be regulated by themselves . . .

"In the establishment of these relations the rights of the original inhabitants were in no instance entirely disregarded, but were necessarily, to a considerable extent, impaired. They were admitted to be rightful occupants of the soil, with a legal as well as a just claim to retain possession of it and to use it according to their own discretion . . .

"While the different nations of Europe respected the rights of the natives, as occupants, they asserted the ultimate dominion to be in themselves; and claimed and exercised, as a consequence of this ultimate dominion, a power to grant the soil, while yet in the possession of the Indians. These grants have been understood by all to convey title to the grantee, subject only to the Indian rights of occupancy."

Marshall was called upon to decide two fateful questions for the Indian people. These questions were bound up with political issues of the day, and Marshall answered them in full awareness of their effect on national affairs. But that did not make his decisions any less valid. The men who followed him on the bench, even members of the legislative branch in later times, would find reason and justice in his words.[3]

The first of these questions in its immediate scope had to do with the political nature of an Indian tribe; but, as analyzed and discussed by Marshall, it had also to do with the nature of contract. This aspect of the issue was one which in Marshall's thinking, went to the fundamental nature of society. Governments which could ignore or modify contracts at will were not governments in any good social sense. Property which could not be protected by contract was not property. Marshall might have had imperfect information on the living habits of the Indian people, as he displayed in certain passages of the *Johnson* v. *MacIntosh* opinion, but he saw clearly enough that once Indians were admitted to be human they could not be denied the rights enjoyed by human beings without endangering all human rights.

The fact that Indian tribes had placed themselves under the protection of England or the United States or any other power, as was frequently done in early treaties, was in the nature of an agreement between the tribe and the contracting nation that they would deal exclusively with each other. The Indians would not go to trade with any other power, nor would they look to any other power for political support. The contracting nation offered to restrain its own citizens or the citizens of other nations from encroaching on the Indian land and to protect the Indians from acts of violence. As Marshall viewed this relationship, "the Indians perceived in this protection only what was beneficial to themselves—an engagement to punish aggression against them. It involved, practically, no claim to their lands, no dominion over their persons . . . Protection does not imply the destruction of the protected."

It was necessary to distinguish, however, between the

sovereign right of self-government and absolute independence. The state of Georgia in 1828 and 1829 adopted
measures incorporating Cherokee territory as part of the
state, annulling all Cherokee laws and substituting the laws
of the state. The Cherokees carried the matter directly to
the Supreme Court in a suit to enjoin the state from enforcing these measures.

In this instance the Court had only one issue to determine, and that was whether the Cherokee Nation quali-
fied under the judiciary article of the Constitution as a
foreign state, competent to bring action in the Supreme
Court against one of the United States. The Court ruled
that the Cherokee Nation was not wholly independent and
sovereign and therefore did not qualify. It reasoned: "It
may well be doubted whether those tribes which reside
within the acknowledged boundaries of the United States
can, with strict accuracy, be denominated foreign nations.
They may, more correctly, perhaps, be denominated domestic dependent nations . . . They and their country are considered by foreign nations, as well as by ourselves, as being
so completely under the sovereignty and dominion of the
United States that any attempt to acquire their lands, or
to form a political connection with them, would be considered by all as an invasion of our territory and an act of
hostility."

The question whether Georgia had the right to incorporate Cherokee territory to itself and to annul Cherokee
laws was not argued in *Cherokee Nation* v. *Georgia*.

The issue was argued, however, in a second case, *Worcester* v. *Georgia,* decided in 1832. In writing the Court's
opinion in this case Marshall made an exhaustive study of
Indian-white relations, examining the charters of all the
English colonies, the treaties made by England and the
United States with the several Indian tribes, and such
international law as then existed governing relations
between nations. The question of the right of an Indian
tribe to maintain its sovereignty in the face of attacks from
a state had an obvious application. The tribe might not be
deemed to occupy the status of an independent foreign
nation, but it partook of sovereignty, and any attack upon
its rights of sovereignty by a state was by indirection or
analogy an attack upon the central government.

Marshall reasoned carefully: "The Indians had always
been considered as distinct, independent, political commu-

nities, retaining their original natural rights, as the undisputed possessors of the soil, from time immemorial, with the single exception of that imposed by irresistible power, which excluded them from intercourse with any other European potentate than the first discoverer of the coast of the particular region claimed; and this was a restriction which those European potentates imposed on themselves, as well as on the Indians . . . The settled doctrine of the law of nations is, that a weaker power does not surrender its independence—its right to self-government—by associating with a stronger, and taking its protection.

"The Cherokee Nation, then, is a distinct community, occupying its own territory, with boundaries accurately described, in which the laws of Georgia can have no force, and which the citizens of Georgia have no right to enter, but with the consent of the Cherokees themselves, or in conformity with treaties, and with the acts of Congress."

The second basic question with which Marshall dealt was the nature of Indian title in the land. This question also involved the larger right of the central government to exercise sovereignty to the exclusion of the individual states and to have the sole right of extinguishing Indian title.

Lands were not given to the Indian tribes—a fact which is as rarely understood in our day as it was when John Marshall wrote his opinion. The language of certain treaties might lend color to the notion that gifts of land had been made to Indians. The first treaty between the United States and the Cherokee Indians, made in 1785, provided that a tract should be "allotted to the Cherokees for their hunting ground." This might sound as if the United States had marked off a portion of the public domain and indicated that the Indians might go there to hunt. As Marshall pointed out, the reverse of this situation was the case.

The Cherokee Indians were agreeing to cede to the United States certain lands lying outside of the stipulated boundary and the word "allotted" simply meant that the boundary was agreed upon. The words "hunting ground" similarly were not intended to place a limitation or a qualification on the type of occupancy right the Indians were to have. Marshall commented, "To the United States, it can be a matter of no concern, whether their whole territory was devoted to hunting grounds, or whether an occasional village, and an occasional cornfield interrupted, and gave some variety to the scene. These terms had been used in their treaties with Great Britain, and had never been misunderstood. They had never been supposed to imply a right in the British Government to take their lands, or to interfere with their internal government."

Moving over to the question of prior authority between the national and the state governments, Marshall argued that "the treaties and laws of the United States contemplate the Indian territory as completely separated from that of the states; and provide that all intercourse with them shall be carried on exclusively by the government of the Union."

He pointed out that, at the outbreak of the Revolutionary War, "the necessities of our situation produced a general conviction, that those measures which concerned all must be transacted by a body in which the representatives of all were assembled, and which could command the confidence of all; Congress, therefore, was considered as invested with all the powers of war and peace . . . They employed diplomatic agents to represent the United States at the several courts of Europe . . . and on the same principles Congress assumed the management of Indian affairs . . .

"Such was the state of things when the Confederation was adopted. That instrument surrendered the powers of peace and war to Congress, and prohibited them to the states . . . This instrument also gave the United States in Congress assembled the sole and exclusive right of 'regulating the trade and managing all the affairs with the Indians, not members of any of the states; provided, that the legislative right of any state within its own limits be not infringed or violated.'" The ambiguity of this last proviso had been removed in writing the Federal Constitution. The new instrument gave a clear grant of power to Congress to regulate commerce with foreign nations, among the several states, and with the Indian tribes.[4]

Marshall covered one other subject, which, before he had been dead many years, would be hotly discussed. This was the question of how seriously an Indian treaty was to be regarded. Cynicism on this subject would soon turn to firm conviction that treaty-making with Indian tribes was a farcical game to which the United States should not lend dignity. The more powerful the United States became and the greater the opinion American statesmen had of themselves, the more popular this attitude became.

John Marshall felt no loss of dignity in discussing Indian treaties. He answered the cynics of his own day: "It is said, that these treaties are nothing more than compacts, which cannot be considered as obligatory on the United States, from a want of power in the Indians to enter into them. What is a treaty? The answer is, it is a compact formed between two nations or communities, having the right of self-government. Is it essential, that each party shall possess the same attributes of sovereignty, to give force to the treaty? This will not be pretended, for, on this ground, very few valid treaties could be formed. The only requisite is, that each of the contracting parties shall possess the right of self-government, and the power to perform the stipulations of the treaty . . ."

There could be no question of the power of Indian tribes to perform the obligations and responsibilities imposed on them in treaties with the United States. "In the management of their internal concerns, they are dependent on no power. They punish offenses, under their own laws, and in doing so they are responsible to no earthly tribunal."

For those who in afteryears felt that the treaties had been a farce and a waste of time, he left these questions to answer: "We have made treaties with them; and are those treaties to be disregarded on our part, because they were entered into with an uncivilized people? Does this lessen the obligation of such treaties? By entering into them, have we not admitted the power of this people to bind themselves, and to impose obligations on us?"

Thus were laid the foundations.

For three hundred years there had been intercourse between Indians and whites. They had traded. They had made presents to each other. They had profited from their contacts. So long as they were not in direct competition for a piece of earth, they were able to live together. But once they were in conflict, the Indians never had more than one choice: either they gave way, or they were destroyed.

Since John Marshall's day the record of what happened is much too complicated and monotonous to be followed in a brief space. The monotony would come, not because nothing happened, but because the same thing happened repeatedly in so many different forms and at so many different places, and always with such similarity of results. The Indians lost; the white men justified their actions.

The complete record can be suggested by pausing to examine three isolated incidents. The incidents are isolated in time, but one flows from the other with an inevitability that could be taken for logic.

The first of these has to do with the agitation to clear the eastern seaboard of its Indian population, which culminated in the removal to the territory west of the Mississippi in the 1830s.

Next in the sequence is the action taken by Congress in 1871 to terminate treaty-making as a method of dealing with the Indian tribes.

Finally, what was designed as the last official act, the act of magic which would turn red men into white: the General Allotment Act of 1887.

21

THE FRONTIER SWALLOWS THE LAW

The white settlers from the older eastern area were not
philosophers or lawyers carrying in their heads the thesis
of aboriginal occupancy rights. Even if some of them had
been warned to stay out of the Indian country, when they
got to the top of the mountains and looked westward, they
saw such an incredible immensity that it must have seemed
absurd to pretend that there was not room enough for
everybody. They need not drive the Indians out, they might
have reasoned in those earliest years; they wanted only a
small piece of infinity for themselves. It is quite unlikely
that the white settlers moving in, household by household,
one on the heels of another, had any clear conception of
the mighty irruption which was taking place west of the
mountains.

Charles and Mary Beard, in *The Rise of American Civilization*, have filled in some of the details of that first expansion. First of all, eleven new states were added to the
original thirteen by 1825, the close of President Monroe's
administration. The population had multiplied nearly
threefold, and at the close of the period "there were more
inhabitants in Kentucky and Tennessee than in Massachusetts, Rhode Island, Connecticut, and Vermont combined."[1]

Quoting again from the Beards: "The rapidity with
which these immigrants from all quarters subdued the
wilderness almost surpasses belief. In 1775 there were not
more than five thousand whites in the Mississippi valley,
outside of New Orleans, and they were mainly French families clinging to their old posts. In 1790 there were about
110,000 white people in that region. Within another decade
the number rose to 377,000. The national census of 1830

gave 937,000 to Ohio, 348,000 to Indiana, 157,000 to Illinois, 687,000 to Kentucky, and 681,000 to Tennessee . . ."

In the single year 1787, more than 900 flatboats cast off from Pittsburgh, transporting 18,000 men, women, and children, 12,000 head of livestock, and 650 wagons, all going down river to join others who had preceded them.

Francis Baily, a young Englishman of twenty-two, who would later establish a reputation as an astronomer, spent the year 1796–97 traveling in America. He went down the Ohio on a flatboat launched at Pittsburgh and left a memorable record of the experience. His cataloging of some of the natural resources is a picture of bounty itself.[2]

"The woods all over this western country produce a variety of spontaneous kinds of grass, some of which grows three or four feet high, and affords nourishment for the cattle, which the settlers let loose to graze thereon. They also abound in a variety of natural flowers and herbs, which at the approach of spring regale both the eye and the sense of smelling with the most agreeable diversity and profusion. There are also to be found a number of wild fruit trees, such as gooseberry, plum, cherry, grape, apple, and many others. But the chief beauty in this way to the settler is the variety and size of the timber, which is plentifully scattered over the country, and consists of oak, maple, beech, buttonwood, dogwood, buckeye, walnut, hickory, and many others, which are only to be found in the first rate uplands and bottomlands. I have seen oak trees, and those not uncommon, which measure near four feet in diameter at the bottom, and which have a straight trunk without a single branch for seventy feet; and from that part to the termination of the upper branch it has measured seventy more; and these immense trees I have seen cut down for the sole purpose of making a few shingles; and even for the sake of killing a poor bear who had taken refuge therein . . ."

His observations on pioneer society suggest that he may have been dismayed at times by what he witnessed. Anyone entering the wilderness, he wrote, "must expect to meet a race of people rough in their manners, impatient of restraint, and of an independent spirit, who are taught to look upon all men as their equals and no farther worthy of respect from them than their conduct deserves . . . They are a race which delight much to live on the frontiers, where they can enjoy undisturbed, and free from the controls of any laws, the blessings which nature has bestowed upon them. As soon therefore as plantations begin to multiply around them, and an increase of population begins to deprive them of these blessings, they sell their little possessions, and with the money arising from it they stock themselves with clothes and other necessaries and move off to cultivate some other part."

A second class follows the first, somewhat more refined in their manners and slightly more willing to yield to authority. They, too, move on, however, and "it is not till the third succeeds that you meet with any kind of society that is at all desirable." For an old-world visitor, even this was probably a concession.

The policy advocated by Henry Knox of paying for what was taken, made a favorable impression on young Baily. "The Indian title to these lands is not wholly extinct," he notes, and continues, "from the policy which the United States are pursuing, there is every reason to expect that the Indians will never have reason to reproach the white people with unjust encroachment on their territory. Congress have found it to be much more beneficial and advantageous to purchase what land they want, than to attempt to force it by the sword ..."

He commented on Indian-white relations: "The great cause of so many quarrels with the Indians has been, that the latter have always looked upon the attack of individuals as expressive of the disposition of the whole nation ... and it is worthy of note, that the most violent prejudices exist on both sides ... so much so, that I have heard them talking with the same unconcern of killing an Indian, as of killing a deer or a turkey; and with a savage exultation they would mimic him in his dying agonies; and I would venture to pronounce that it would be impossible to find a jury in the back parts of America, who would bring anyone in guilty of murder, for causing the death of an Indian."

Perhaps it was Daniel Boone who most truly reflected the American character which was forming out there on the front line of settlement. Baily met the old colonel alone in a canoe with a dog and a gun on the lower Ohio. In the course of a long interrogation, he asked the old trailblazer whether it did not give him a secret satisfaction to watch the progress of the settlements he had carved out of the woods. Boone shook his head in the negative. The folks in the settlements, he thought, had "got too proud." Of all the land that had been given to him as his share in opening up Kentucky, he had divided it among his relatives and had moved on, "unwilling to live among men who were shackled in their habits, and would not enjoy uncontrolled the free blessings which nature had bestowed upon them." He told Baily that he was heading for the farther wilderness to trap beaver and "enjoy the pleasures arising from a secluded and solitary life."

Here was one white man at least who must have come close to appreciating the country for what the Indians saw and felt in it. He left the Englishman disconcerted.

The pressures were not entirely the pressures engendered by landless easterners or European immigrants going west to better their fortunes. Southern agriculture was beginning a boom period which would carry right on down to the Civil War and turn cotton raising into big business. The cause for this lay not in agriculture itself but in improved mechanical devices for handling raw cotton and processing it. The introduction of the cotton gin, in 1794, following soon after the invention of greatly improved spinning machinery, resulted in enormously increased demands for cotton. In the twelve-year period 1791–1803 cotton exports from the United States jumped from 200,000 to 40,000,000 pounds annually.

In writing of this period, Vernon L. Parrington remarked: "Here was an enormous vested interest, the economic life of the South, that could not suffer its present or future profits to be put in jeopardy by any political party on any pretext. Its well-being and its prestige were both at stake."[3]

Parrington was interested particularly in noting what effect increased agriculture demand had on the institution of slavery. The effect it had on Indian land holdings in the South was disastrous, for the Indians. Someone, someday, will need to make a close study of the connection between the booming cotton industry and the demand for Indian removal. Here we can only suggest that the relationship was direct and immediate.

It was in the South and particularly in Georgia that the demand to move the Indians took its most spectacular form. Also it was there that the carefully formulated federal policy and the carefully enunciated doctrines of John Marshall met their first defeat.

Georgia had a consistent record of holding out against central authority. Most of the original thirteen colonies, under the language of their charters, had claims to western land. These charters referred vaguely to territory extending to the southern sea, but no one had a clear notion at the time of what lay beyond the Atlantic seaboard. During or immediately following the Revolution all the colonies, with the exception of Georgia, ceded to the national government their ill-defined claims to western lands. In the case of the colonies which were indebted to the national treasury for their share of national defense costs, the land cession was accepted by Congress in satisfaction of the indebtedness.

Georgia offered to turn over her western lands to the United States, but she insisted on being reimbursed to the extent of $170,000, which she claimed it had cost her to acquire title or to defend herself against Indian attacks.[4] The offer was rejected. Next she attempted to sell some thirty-five million acres, the greater part of the territory now occupied by the states of Alabama and Mississippi, to private speculators for a total sum of about $500,000. This was the notorious Yazoo Company incident, on which Thomas Jefferson had written his opinion, holding that the land was not Georgia's to grant away. He had also expressed an unwillingness to use coercive measures against Georgia, but as it happened the question did not arise. The proposed sale had been put through the legislature with such indications of fraud that a convention of citizens of the state condemned the action and demanded its repeal, which followed.

Meantime, the state was establishing a reputation as the most intransigent champion of states' rights. It had been the Georgia delegates who insisted, when the Articles of Confederation were under discussion in the heat of the Revolutionary War, that the legislative right of the state could not be infringed in any negotiation between Congress and an Indian tribe.

In 1794 the United States Supreme Court reviewed an action brought by a Mr. Chisolm, a citizen of South Carolina, against the state of Georgia, for moneys due him, and upheld the lower court in a decision favoring the plaintiff. The lower house of the Georgia legislature, upon being informed that the decision had gone against the state, resolved "that any federal marshall, attempting to levy on the territory of this state, or on the treasury, by virtue of an execution, by the authority of the Supreme Court of the United States, for the recovery of any claim against the said state of Georgia, shall be guilty of felony, and shall suffer death, without benefit of clergy, by being hanged." The action was not concurred in by the upper house.

When in 1802 Georgia finally consented to a relinquishment of her claims to western lands, it was on condition that the United States reimburse her to the extent of $1,250,000, which she claimed to have expended in connection with the lands, and, more important, she required that the United States extinguish, "at their own expense, for the use of Georgia, as soon as the same can be peaceably obtained on reasonable terms, the Indian title" to any lands still in Indian possession within the borders of the state. These conditions were accepted by the United States and would be a source of trouble in the years ahead.

Georgia had tried on several occasions immediately after the Revolutionary War to win land concessions from the Creek Indians. Her methods were cynical, though no worse than the methods followed elsewhere on the frontier. Having in 1773 inveigled a spokesman representing two out of a confederation of Creek towns to agree to the sale of a fairly large area of their traditional lands, she tried to hold the entire Creek Nation bound by the agreement.

It so happened that the leader of the Creeks at that time was a half-blood, Alexander McGillivray, whose Scottish father had married a daughter of one of the leading Creek families.[5] The elder McGillivray had been a successful Indian trader, who had invested the profits from his trade in Savannah real estate. He remained loyal to Britain during the war and his property was confiscated—an action which did not inspire the son's love for the state of Georgia.

Alexander died in 1793, before he was quite thirty-five years of age, and for almost ten years prior to his death he held off the land-hungry Georgians and had both the United States and Spain seeking his alliance. Physically he was frail, and throughout his entire career he was beset by agues and fevers. Moreover, he made no pretense of being a brave man and joked about his lack of military ability. Sea travel made him unheroically sick. These were failings which ordinarily would have disqualified him for leadership in an Indian tribe. McGillivray was not, however, an ordinary person. His extensive correspondence, most of which has been collected by John W. Caughey, reveals an exceedingly acute mind and a master strategist. His orthography may have been irregular—he had only a few years of schooling—but he was always to the point.

When Georgia sent an agent, Daniel McMurphy, to get McGillivray and the other Creek leaders to agree to the spurious treaty, the agent took no pains to disguise his contempt for the Indians. McGillivray wrote to the Spanish commander at St. Augustine: "I have not been able to learn how the Americans Considers our late Conduct to them respecting our lands, they had Sent up an Agent & for what purpose I know not without it was to play the fool, which he performed with Considerable Insolence & then took a French Leave of the Nation."

McGillivray's answer to the Georgians, when they proceeded to settle on the lands which the two towns had bargained away, was to negotiate a treaty with Spain, in which that country agreed to supply the Creeks with ammunition and to protect Creek lands to the extent that those lands fell within Spanish limits. Spain did not want to risk a war, hence the ambiguity of this last provision; but she was willing to supply arms secretly and let the Creeks fight their own battle. This actually was all the support the Creeks wanted.

The first efforts of the United States to intervene, in 1785–86, met with no success with either the Georgians or the Creeks. There was, however, a growing conviction at the national level that Indian wars were unnecessary, expensive, and could only damage the nation's reputation in the eyes of the world. Urged on by Henry Knox, a continuing effort was made by United States commissioners to negotiate a treaty with the Creek Nation. Finally, in 1790, when it appeared that Spanish backing would never be stronger than a rope of sand, and that Spain was interested in keeping the Indian trade but not in protecting Indian territory, McGillivray agreed to go to New York to discuss the terms of a treaty with President Washington and his cabinet.

Nothing quite like it had happened before. An Indian—not a full-blood, to be sure, but by Creek custom an Indian by virtue of his mother's blood—traveled across country with all the notoriety and public entertainment usually accorded a visiting potentate from abroad. Upon his arrival in New York, his party of twenty-six warriors and headmen was met at the dock by the leaders of Tammany Hall and escorted up Wall Street to Federal Hall, where Congress was in session. Later the party visited the president and Governor Clinton; Secretary Knox was host at a dinner.

Knox took a personal hand in the negotiations which followed. A treaty was concluded on August 7, 1790, the public signing of which took place a week later. This was reported in the *Pennsylvania Packet and Daily Advertiser*: "Yesterday the treaty of peace and friendship between the United States and the Creek nation was solemnly ratified by the contracting parties, in Federal Hall, in the presence of a large assembly of citizen . . . At twelve o'clock the President of the United States and his suite—General Knox, the commissioner; the clerks of the department of the secretary of war; colonel McGillivray, and the kings, chiefs, and warriors of the Creek nation being assembled, the treaty was read by the secretary of the President of the United States.

"The president then addressed colonel McGillivray, the kings, chiefs, and warriors; he said that he thought the treaty just and equal; stated the mutual duties of the contracting parties; which address was communicated, sentence after sentence, by Mr. Cornell, sworn interpreter, to all of which the Creeks gave an audible assent.

"The president then signed the treaty, after which he presented a string of beads as a token of perpetual peace, and a paper of tobacco to smoke in remembrance of it: Mr. McGillivray rose, made a short reply to the president, and received the tokens."

The signatories to the treaty were Washington, Jefferson, and Knox, for the United States; McGillivray and his twenty-three Creek headmen. Richard Morse, chief justice of the state of New York, Richard Varick, mayor of the city of New York, and other officials, signed as witnesses.

By the terms of this treaty Georgia gained the territory she claimed by reason of the disputed treaty. The Creeks on their part were to be paid $1,500 annually for an indefinite period; the United States solemnly guaranteed the Creek lands within the limits of the United States west and south of the boundary agreed on; any citizen of the United States who settled on Creek lands without permission forfeited the protection of the United States; no citizen could enter Creek territory without first obtaining a passport from a governor of one of the United States or from the military.

Georgia was not happy over the treaty, in spite of the confirmation of her title to the disputed lands. In Caughey's

words, the Georgians "fulminated against it as a betrayal
. . . and an admission that Georgia had been in the wrong
in the entire controversy . . . and a questionable exercise of
the powers entrusted to the central government by the new
Constitution." Congressman James Jackson of Georgia
denounced the treaty, which, he said, had ceded away
"3,000,000 acres of land guaranteed to Georgia by the Constitution." As if that were not bad enough, the government
had "invited a savage of the Creek Nation to the seat of
government, caressed him in a most extraordinary manner,
and sent him home loaded with favors."

The resistance offered by the Creek Indians to unlawful
encroachment on their lands was by no means singular
with them; resistance equally determined was offered by the
Choctaws, the Chickasaws, and the Cherokees. On the part
of the Cherokees, notably, there was a realization that what
had happened could not be undone; time could not be
rolled back and the events of the past century obliterated.
Change had come, and either they must adjust to that
change or they would soon cease to exist as separate people.

The Cherokees were an extraordinary people. William
Bartram, the itinerant botanist, who knew the Cherokees
well during the Revolutionary War period, spoke of the
women as "tall, slender, erect, and of a delicate frame,
their features formed of a perfect symmetry, their counte-
nance cheerful and friendly, and they move with a becoming grace and dignity." And of Cherokees generally he
wrote: "Their disposition and manners are grave and
steady; dignified and circumspect in their deportment;
rather slow and reserved in conversation . . . and are ready
always to sacrifice every pleasure and gratification, even
their blood and life itself, to defend their territory and
maintain their rights."[6]

Among those who took the lead in urging change, was
the full-blood Cherokee who was named by his people "The
Buck," but who, when he went north to be educated at the
foreign mission school at Cornwall, Connecticut, assumed
the name of Elias Boudinot, the New Jersey philanthropist.

The boy not only finished the course, but managed to
marry the daughter of one of the benefactors of the school
—an event that almost caused a riot in the quiet Connecticut town.[7]

For years the mission school had preached the necessity
of bringing the Word to the heathen, but when one of

their daughters decided to join the heathen and devote her life to one of them, the agents of the school, which included Lyman Beecher, found that their "duty as honest men" compelled them to condemn Elias Boudinot and the girl, Harriet R. Gold. Such a union was an "insult to the known feelings of the Christian community"; it sported "with the sacred interests of this charitable institution." Seeking to extricate themselves from any blame, the agents declared: "For those who have been guilty of this outrage upon public feeling, we can offer no apology; all we have to request is that the Christian public will not condemn the innocent with the guilty . . . Let the blame fall where it justly belongs."

Harriet Gold went to live among the Cherokees where, confounding her captious critics, she found affection and happiness.

Elias Boudinot completed the course at Andover Theological Seminary and in 1826 traveled through the north, speaking to church groups, hoping to build up support for the Cherokee people in the crisis which was already shaping on the horizon. He wanted the white people to understand what his tribe had accomplished and why they were entitled to remain unmolested while they worked out their adjustment to the new order.

Speaking before the First Presbyterian Church in Philadelphia in 1826, he reported: "It is a matter of surprise to me, and must be to all those who are properly acquainted with the condition of the aborigines of the country, that the Cherokees have advanced so far and so rapidly in civilization. But there are yet powerful obstacles, both within and without, to be surmounted in the march of improvement . . . In defiance, however, of these obstacles, the Cherokees have improved and are rapidly improving. . . . At this time there are 22,000 cattle; 7,600 horses; 46,000 swine; 2,500 sheep; 662 looms; 1,488 spinning wheels; 172 wagons; 2,948 plows; 10 sawmills; 31 grist mills; 62 blacksmith shops; 8 cotton machines; 18 schools; 18 ferries; and a number of public roads. In one district there were, last winter, upward of 1,000 volumes of good books . . . Most of the schools are under the care and tuition of Christian missionaries, of different denominations."

The Cherokee Nation was going forward, beyond any question. Sequoya had invented his alphabet in 1821 and plans were afoot to issue a newspaper. Boudinot was to be the first editor of the paper, the *Cherokee Phoenix*.

In 1827 a written constitution proclaiming a "sovereign and independent nation" was drafted. It provided for a principal officer called the "chief," a bicameral legislature, a supreme court, and a code of laws. The instrument was adopted July 4, 1827, and the first election under it, a year later, was quiet and orderly. A missionary who had been asked to serve as an election official reported: "There was nothing of that intrigue and unfairness which is to be seen at elections in some of the civilized states."

By that time, too, the New Testament had been translated into Cherokee.

These accomplishments were not everywhere the occasion for congratulations. On the contrary, they were disturbing to many Georgians and even to many who were part of the national government at Washington. A letter written to the editor of the *Family Visitor* at Richmond, dated September 2, 1825, indicates even more clearly than Elias Boudinot's report at Philadelphia why southern planters might be disturbed. The Cherokees were growing prosperous, as Boudinot's report might have indicated; but there was more to it than that. The writer of the Richmond letter was David Brown, one of the educated Cherokee young men, of whom it was said that he knew Greek better than he knew his own language.[8]

He wrote: "The natives carry on considerable trade with the adjoining states; and some of them export cotton, in boats, down the Tennessee to the Mississippi, and down that river to New Orleans . . . Cotton and woolen cloths are manufactured here; blankets, of various dimensions . . . Almost every family in the nation grows cotton for its own consumption . . . Nearly all the merchants in the nation are native Cherokees . . . The population is rapidly increasing; in the year 1819 [the population had been estimated at] 10,000 souls. An actual census taken in 1825 showed, native citizens, 13,563; white men married into the nation, 147; white women married into the nation, 73; African slaves, 1,277 . . . If we judge the future by the past, to what number will the Cherokee population swell in 1856?"

This contemplated population growth was in itself a disturbing forecast, yet it probably was not nearly so disquieting as what Brown wrote next:

"White men in the nation enjoy all the immunities and privileges of the Cherokee people, except that they are not eligible to public office. In the above computation of the present year, you perceive that there are some African slaves; they have been, from time to time, brought in and sold by white men; they are, however, generally well treated, and they much prefer living in the nation to a residence in the United States. There is hardly any intermixture of Cherokee and African blood. The presumption is, that the Cherokee will, at no distant day, cooperate with the humane efforts of those who are liberating and sending this proscribed race to the land of their fathers."

More than the growing prosperity of the Cherokees, more than their adaptation to civilized modes of life and their increasing population, this suggestion that the Cherokees might be contemplating the freeing of their slaves must have set many Georgians to thinking that the time had come to take action.

22

BEYOND THE GREAT RIVER

"We view all rights secured to us by solemn treaty, under the constituted authority, rights secured to us by the blood of our fathers, and which we will never yield but with our lives."

It was Andrew Jackson, not an oratorical Indian, expressing himself. The year was 1812, and Jackson was annoyed because the federal agent in the Choctaw Nation was insisting that all persons passing through the nation should carry passports, as provided in the treaty with the Choctaw Indians and stipulated in orders issued by the secretary of war.

The agent, Silas Dinsmore, had a problem on his hands. Slaves had been escaping from the settled areas and traveling into and beyond the Choctaw country, without benefit of passport. Dinsmore wrote to Washington: "I feel very much embarrassed with respect to a proper conduct to be pursued respecting Negroes passing through this country without a passport. By the last mail I received letters stating, with urgent importunity, that four Negroes had absconded . . ."

It was brought to Jackson's attention that this Choctaw agent, in his honest effort to enforce his instructions, had insisted that white persons passing through the country with Negro slaves in their party possess passports for the Negroes. Jackson, as a citizen of west Tennessee, protested vigorously that a treaty existed between his section of the state and the Choctaw Nation promising free use of the highways through tribal territory. "My God," he wrote the secretary of war, "is it come to this? . . . Can the secretary of war, for one moment, retain the idea that we will permit this petty tyrant to sport with our rights secured to us by treaty?"[1]

It was a strange sentiment for Andrew Jackson to express when, less than five years later, he would write to President Monroe, on the occasion of the latter's first inauguration: "I have long viewed treaties with the Indians an absurdity not to be reconciled to the principles of our government."

But then, Jackson's part in ambushing the Indians and forcing their removal west of the Mississippi was remarkably devoid of logic or honorable motives.

The idea of removal did not originate with Andrew Jackson. It may have originated in Jefferson's thinking; at least he appears to have been the first person in public office to suggest such a course. Jefferson's plan, however, would have been noncoercive and would have been carried out in an orderly manner over a period of years.

Jefferson first contemplated the proposal in 1803, while he was considering what ought to be done with the newly acquired Louisiana territory. Some question had been raised as to the constitutionality of the president's action in acquiring the territory. While he was satisfied that he had the authority, he thought it might be expedient not to create new states within the purchased area until a constitutional amendment could be adopted.[2]

His proposed amendment, drafted in July 1803, was devoted almost entirely to protecting Indian interests in the land. It would have authorized the Congress to make exchanges of land owned by the United States in the territory (that is, lands not occupied by Indians or in which the title had been secured by purchase or agreement from Indians) for lands held by Indians east of the Mississippi. He would have included in such an amendment a provision that "the rights of occupancy in the soil, and of self-government, are confirmed to the Indian inhabitants as they now exist."

His advisers persuaded him that this might be an awkward provision to embed in the Constitution. "We could not disturb their rights of occupancy without a formal alteration of the Constitution," wrote the secretary of the navy.

That Jefferson did not intend forceful removal of the Indians is clearly indicated by his attitude toward them and their future in the nation. Writing to Benjamin Hawkins, the agent to the Creeks in February 1803, Jefferson outlined what might have been a successful long-term plan, if it had been adopted: "I consider the business of hunting as already become insufficient to furnish clothing and subsistence to the Indians. The promotion of agriculture, therefore, and household manufacture, are essential in their preservation, and I am disposed to aid and encourage it. This will enable them to live on much smaller portions of land . . . while they are learning to do better on less land, our increasing numbers will be calling for more land, and thus a coincidence of interests between those who have such necessaries to spare, and want lands. . . . Surely it will be better for them to be identified with us, and preserve the occupation of their lands, then be exposed to the many casualties that may endanger them while a separate people."

Benjamin Hawkins at the time was working toward this very end. A man of independent means and good social position in his native North Carolina, Hawkins spent twenty years with the Creek Indians, helping them to get started in commercial agriculture, stock raising, and small home industry. The War of 1812, in which part of the Creeks took up arms with Tecumseh, ruined this enterprise. Hawkins died in 1818, before a fresh start could be made.

Some Indian tribes voluntarily suggested removal to western lands. Several thousand Cherokees had moved to Arkansas in the early years of the century. In 1803 and again in 1807 the Shawnees requested a tract of land to which they might remove, together with the Wyandottes, Delawares, and Miamis. No action was taken on these requests. Such Indians as moved beyond the Mississippi did so on their own initiative and no lands were set aside for them.[3]

Georgia began to use pressure. The lands which had been settled by the whites in Georgia were, on the whole, the poorer lands. Many found themselves in the pine barrens of the coastal plain, which, before the application of commercial fertilizer, were regarded as almost worthless for agriculture. The Indians, long before the arrival of the white man, had given up these coastal lands and had moved farther back, where the soils were deeper and richer. The planters of Georgia were making this discovery for themselves, and with the demand for cotton increasing year by year, they would not long be denied.

They had grounds for grievance besides. The compact of 1802, by which the state relinquished its claims to western lands and which established the present western boundary of the state, required that the national government extinguish the Indian title "as soon as the same can be peaceably obtained on reasonable terms." The lands in this case would become public domain of the state, not of the nation.

Georgia's representatives in Congress, as well as her own officials at home, repeatedly charged that the federal government was not keeping faith with the state. Parcels had been added from time to time, but not at all in the quantity or at the rate of acquisition to satisfy the Georgians. In a memorial to Congress in 1822, the state complained: "It has been the unfortunate lot of our state to be embroiled in the question of territorial rights almost from the commencement of her existence . . . The state of Georgia claims a right to the jurisdiction and soil of the territory within her limits."

At this juncture the Creeks and Cherokees decided that they would not sell or cede another foot of territory. They had been bargaining away parcels of land for many years and had come to the conclusion that they needed what was left for themselves and their children.

Neither President Monroe nor President Adams was willing to force the issue. Monroe pointed out that the compact with Georgia could not be fulfilled without the consent of the Indians, peaceably and on reasonable terms, and he also declared in his message to Congress of March 30, 1824, "that the Indian title was not affected in the slightest circumstance by the compact with Georgia." The representatives of that state, of course, were not to be conciliated. If the Cherokees would not remove peaceably, they insisted, then it became the duty of the United States to employ force.

The hesitancy at the White House vanished when Andrew Jackson took up his residence there.

Whether Jackson was ignorant of the policies which had prevailed and the law which had been built up, or whether he chose to ignore them is immaterial, since the effect of his actions would have been the same in either case. The opinion he had of Indian treaties—"an absurdity not to be reconciled to the principles of our government"—had not altered with the years. He had also a notion that lands had been reserved to the Indians for hunting grounds, and that as quickly as the game was destroyed or driven away, "the right of possession, granted to the Indians for the purpose of hunting, ceases, and justice, sound policy, and the constitutional rights of the citizens would require" that the lands be made available for white settlement. If Indians refused to relinquish their occupancy, the mere fact that a treaty appeared to protect them should not stand in the way.

Departing completely from previous proclamations and policies and from the guarantees contained in many treaties, Jackson declared in a letter to President Monroe (March 1817): "The Indians are the subjects of the United States, inhabiting its territory and acknowledging its sovereignty. Then is it not absurd for the sovereign to negotiate by treaty with the subject? I have always thought, that Congress had as much right to regulate by acts of legislation, all Indian concerns as they had of territories; there is only this difference, that the inhabitants of territories, are citizens of the United States and entitled to all the rights thereof, the Indians are subjects and entitled to their protection and fostering care."

"Now," he wrote to Secretary of War Calhoun in 1820, "it appears to me that it is high time to do away with the farce of treating with Indian tribes."

Curiously, the Indians of the southern tribes regarded Andrew Jackson as their friend. He would tell them that he never talked to them with a forked tongue, and they believed him. He would send secret agents among them, with secret public funds to be used in purchasing gifts for those whose influence was most needed—and the Indians never doubted his motives.

Jackson knew that the Indians would have to go. He knew that he intended to use the full weight of his office in forcing them to go. But he would put a good face on the matter.

In a very brief first inaugural address, he took time to say: "It will be my sincere and constant desire to observe toward the Indian tribes within our limits a just and liberal policy, and to give that humane and considered attention to their rights and their wants which is consistent with the habits of our Government and the feelings of our people."

The first draft of his first annual message has an interesting passage, in which he proposed to say: "The policy of the Government [toward the Indians] has been gradually to open to them the ways of civilization; and from their wandering habits, to entice them to a course of life calculated to present fairer prospects of comfort and happiness . . . It will not answer to encourage them to the idea of exclusive self-government. It is impracticable. No people were ever . . . capable of carrying into execution a social compact for themselves until education and intelligence was first introduced."

He must have decided that the argument was not sound. The record which the Cherokee Indians had been making for themselves belied the argument. The passage was not used, and in place of it he inserted a recommendation that the Congress consider "the propriety of setting apart an ample district west of the Mississippi . . . to be guaranteed to the Indian tribes as long as they shall occupy it." And where, moreover, they would be "secured in the enjoyment of governments of their own choice. . . ."

West of the Mississippi, they would be capable of governing themselves; east of the Mississippi, they would require "education and intelligence."

When the new state of Mississippi joined Georgia in adopting legislation subjecting the Indians within their borders to state laws, the Indians turned their eyes to Washington. It was the eve of Jackson's inauguration. Georgia adopted its measure on December 20, 1828, and Mississippi on February 4, 1829. The states must somehow have been informed of what Jackson's attitude would be.

The measures were clearly in violation of existing treaties between the United States and the tribes. Treaties, along with the Constitution and the statutes, were part of the laws of the United States which the president took an oath to uphold. The Georgia and Mississippi measures were also in violation of the statute adopted in the very first session of Congress, providing that "in their property, rights, and liberty [the Indians] never shall be invaded or disturbed, unless in just and lawful wars authorized by Congress." They violated as well the Trade and Intercourse Act of 1790, which directed that federal law only should apply to crimes committed by non-Indians against Indians within Indian country and to crimes committed by an Indian away from his country, in any state or territory. No provision was made for the application of state law under any circumstances.

Jackson chose to ignore the incompatibility. In his first annual message he indicated that he was powerless to take any action against Georgia and Mississippi, defending his position by citing the constitutional limitation that "no new state shall be formed within the jurisdiction of any other state." His argument ran: "It is too late to inquire whether it was just . . . to include [the Indians] and their territory within the bounds of new states." In this he disregarded what had been legal policy that, until the title had been extinguished, Indian lands were not within the jurisdiction of any state. Even Georgia had acknowledged as much in the compact of 1802, in which she required that the United States purchase the Indian title at a "reasonable" cost.

Soon after his inauguration Jackson sent agents among the Cherokees, the Creeks, Choctaws, and Chickasaws, instructing the agents to "say to them as friends and brothers to listen to the voice of their father, and their friend. Where they now are, they and my white children are too near to each other to live in harmony and peace . . . Beyond the great river Mississippi, where a part of their nation has gone, their father has provided a country, large enough for them all, and he advises them to remove to it. There their white brethren will not trouble them, they will have no claim to the land, and they can live upon it, they and all their children, as long as grass grows or waters run, in peace and plenty . . . Where they now are, say to them, their father cannot prevent them from being subject to the laws of the state of Mississippi."

The Choctaws, who were the recipients of the above message, were not beguiled. One of their leaders wrote to Colonel Ward, agent for the federal government: "We have no expectation that, if we should remove to the west of the Mississippi, any treaties would be made with us, that would secure greater benefits to us and our children than those which are already made. The red people are of the opinion that, in a few years the Americans will also wish to possess the land west of the Mississippi . . . We have no wish to sell our country and remove to one that is not fertile and good, wherever it is situated. . . . During your residence in our nation as United States agent, you have seen what improvements we have made in those things which are for our good and the good of our children. And here it is, in this very land that we wish to reside and make greater improvement until we become a happy people."[4]

Everywhere, the answer was the same. The Indians felt that they had sold as much land as they could afford to let go, if they were to survive.

In July 1829 gold was discovered in the northeastern corner of Georgia, and the last act of the drama was ready for staging.

Within a short time after news first went out, some 3,000 men had rushed to the diggings, in defiance of three different legal codes: (1) federal law, which prohibited anyone from settling or trading on Indian lands without a special license; (2) Georgia mineral entry law; and (3) the laws of the Cherokee Nation, which also required a permit of anyone entering to settle or trade.

When federal officials attempted to enforce the laws of the United States and arrested citizens of Georgia, the local judge before whom the prisoners were brought wrote to the governor: "When I saw the honest citizens of your state paraded through the streets of our town . . . for no other crime than that of going upon the soil of their own state . . . I never so distinctly felt, as strong as my feelings have been on that subject, the deep humiliation of our condition in relation to the exercise of power on the part of the general government within the jurisdiction of Georgia."

President Jackson then withdrew the federal troops in the area and left the state completely in control. The state legislature responded by adopting a measure on December 22, 1830, by which it became illegal for any Cherokee legislative body to meet, except to execute land-sale agreements, or for any Cherokee officials to hold a session of court. Then, striking at the missionaries who had been defending the Cherokees, the legislature made it an offense for any white person to reside in the Cherokee Territory after March 1, 1831, without a license from the governor.[5]

Meantime, at President Jackson's urging, bills providing for the removal of the eastern tribes had been introduced in both houses of Congress. The debate was interesting, though futile, from the Indians' point of view. The country by that time was aroused by the administration's evident determination to carry out its plan of removal regardless of prior commitments by the United States to protect the Indians in their property. While the bills under discussion were permissive only and did not authorize forceful removal, it was generally understood that force would be used if necessary. Petitions began to pour in upon Congress, urging a due regard for the rights of the Indians. Civic groups, religious organizations, and private citizens in Massachusetts, Ohio, New Jersey, Pennsylvania, Virginia, New York, and Maryland expressed their concern.

Senator Frelinghuysen of New Jersey talked for two days against the Senate bill. His argument ran: "By immemorial possession, as the original tenants of the soil, they hold a title beyond and superior to the British crown and her colonies and to all adverse pretensions of our confederation and subsequent union. God, in his providence, planted these tribes on this western continent, so far as we know, before Great Britain herself had a political existence. I believe, sir, it is not now seriously denied that the Indians are men, endowed with kindred faculties and power with ourselves . . . With this conceded, I ask in what code in the laws of nations, or by what process of abstract deduction, their rights have been extinguished . . . Is it one of the prerogatives of the white man, that he may disregard the dictates of moral principles, when an Indian shall be concerned?"[6]

On the House side, Congressman Storrs of New York spoke of the fallacy of pretending to remove the Indians for their own good from a community where they had pleasant homes, churches, and schools, to a wilderness where hostile tribes would be their only neighbors. Then he attacked President Jackson for embarrassing Congress by apparently repealing the trade and intercourse law and other protective devices.

The measure first passed the House. In the Senate, amendments were proposed to protect the tribes from state action until removal was effected and to respect treaty rights, but these proposals were lost. Four days after passing the House, the bill was adopted in the Senate and was before the president for signature. He approved it on May 28, 1830.

It was at this point that the Cherokees, seeing themselves defeated in every effort to adapt themselves to white civilization and to obtain protection from the Executive, turned to the white man's court. For the Cherokees, more than legal principles were involved. It was as if they were giving the white man every opportunity to prove how treacherous he could be. Two details out of the crowding events that followed revealed as much as they would ever again need to know on the subject.

It will be recalled that in 1829 the Georgia legislature extended state law to Cherokee territory and at the same time annulled Cherokee laws. Subsequently a Cherokee, named Corn Tassel, was tried for murder in a state court, and was convicted. The tribe through its attorney, William Wirt, sued in the United States Supreme Court for a writ of error, and the state was called upon by the Court to show cause why such a writ should not be issued.

The governor referred the matter to the legislature, with a statement of his views, that "so far as concerns the executive department, orders received from the Supreme Court in any manner interfering with the decisions of the courts of the state in the constitutional exercise of their jurisdiction will be disregarded, and any attempt to enforce such orders will be resisted with whatever force the laws have placed in my command."

The legislature not only concurred in these views, but moreover directed the governor to send instructions to the county authorities where the Cherokee was detained to carry out the execution of the sentence. Corn Tassel was therefore hanged before the matter ever reached the Supreme Court.

The next test arose out of the Georgia Act of December 22, 1830, which made it unlawful for a white person to reside in Cherokee territory without taking an oath of allegiance to the state and obtaining a permit from the governor, agents of the United States being excepted. The missionaries stationed in the Cherokee country immediately adopted a resolution in which they objected to the requirement and expressed the view that removal of the Cherokees from their ancestral lands would work hardships on them. The missionaries were then invited to leave the country. Upon their refusing to do so, they were arrested.

Seven of the nine missionaries were supported out of private funds, yet technically they might be classed as United States agents, since they disbursed Cherokee tribal funds as appropriated out of the Treasury. The secretary of war, however, disclaimed any of them as agents of the government, with the single exception of Samuel A. Worcester, who was postmaster at New Echota.

In order to remove this last ambiguity, Jackson ordered the dismissal of Worcester. Thus all the missionaries were equally exposed to Georgia law.

The missionaries were given a second chance to leave the

country peaceably. The alternative was four years at labor in the state penitentiary. Two men refused to le..., Worcester and Elizur Butler. They were rearrested, whereupon they appealed to the Supreme Court. The question: Could a state government extend its laws over Indian territory?

The answer was given in the negative, as already pointed out [*Worcester* v. *Georgia*]. The Cherokee Nation, a distinct community, occupied its own territory, in which the laws of Georgia could have no force. Accordingly, "the act of the state of Georgia, under which the plaintiff was prosecuted, is consequently null and void, and the judgment a nullity," Marshall wrote.

At last the white man had vindicated himself. His law would uphold and protect an Indian as well as another white man.

But not so. The final lesson had yet to be learned.

The governor of Georgia, reporting to his legislature on November 6, 1832, declared that the decision of the Court was an attempt to "prostrate the sovereignty of this state" and that he intended to resist it. He refused to release Samuel Worcester. Butler previously had taken the oath of allegiance, and eventually Worcester would do so.

Here it was that John Marshall's opposition to Andrew Jackson turned victory to ashes for the Cherokee people. Horace Greeley reports that Congressman George N. Briggs of Massachusetts was with President Jackson when word of the Court's decision was reported to him. Jackson is supposed to have commented: "Well, John Marshall has made his decision: now let him enforce it!"

So they all moved, the Cherokees, Choctaws, Chickasaws, Creeks, Seminoles, the Kickapoos, Wyandottes, Ottawas, Pottawatomies, Winnebagos, Sac and Fox (after a last-ditch fight led by Black Hawk), Delawares, Shawnees, Weas, Peorias, Miamis, Kaskaskias, Piankeshaws—all went to the land beyond the Mississippi.

Count de Tocqueville was on hand to witness the beginning of this sorrowful journey, what the Indians afterward would refer to as the Trail of Tears. The Count reported: "At the end of the year 1831, whilst I was on the left bank of the Mississippi, at a place named by Europeans Memphis, there arrived a numerous band of Choctaws. These savages had left their country, and were endeavoring to gain the right bank of the Mississippi, where they hoped to find an asylum which had been promised them by the American government. It was then the middle of the winter, and the cold was unusually severe; the snow had frozen hard upon the ground, and the river was drifting huge masses of ice. The Indians had their families with them; and they brought in their train the wounded and the sick, with children newly born, and old men upon the verge of death. They possessed neither tents nor wagons, but only their arms and some provisions. I saw them embark to pass the mighty river, and never will that solemn spectacle fade from my remembrance. No cry, no sob, was heard amongst the assembled crowd; all were silent. Their calamities were of ancient date, and they knew them to be irremediable. The Indians had all stepped into the bark which was to carry them across, but their dogs remained upon the bank. As soon as these animals perceived that their masters were finally leaving the shore, they set up a dismal howl, and, plunging all together into the icy waters of the Mississippi, swam after the boat."[7]

At a later point in his narrative, de Tocqueville summarized with excellent insight what had taken place on the continent up to that point. "The Indians," he wrote, "in the little which they have done, have unquestionably displayed as much natural genius as the peoples of Europe in their greatest undertakings; but nations as well as men require time to learn, whatever may be their intelligence and their zeal. Whilst the savages were endeavoring to civilize themselves, the Europeans continued to surround them on every side, and to confine them within narrower limits . . . With their resources and acquired knowledge, the Europeans soon appropriated to themselves most of the advantages which the natives might have derived from the possession of the soil . . . and the Indians have been ruined by a competition which they had not the means of sustaining. They were isolated in their own country, and their race only constituted a little colony of troublesome strangers in the midst of a numerous and dominant people."

23

WESTWARD THE COURSE

The Removal Act of 1830 was a peculiar law. After all the talk by Jackson and by leaders in Congress in disparagement of Indian treaties, it might have been expected that Congress would eliminate all doubt in the matter by making Indian tenure entirely dependent on the will of the Congress or the executive branch.

Nothing so drastic was attempted. The act merely provided that "it shall and may be lawful for the president" to set aside any land belonging to the United States, to which Indian title had previously been acquired, "for the reception of such tribes or nations of Indians as may choose to exchange the lands where they now reside. . . ."

More important, the law authorized the president "solemnly to assure the tribe or nation with which the exchange is made, that the United States will forever secure and guarantee . . . the country so exchanged with them."

The status quo would be restored, once the Indians had crossed the river. That was the promise of the legislation.

One thing led to another, however. First, the lawmakers discovered that they had forgotten to leave a corridor to the Pacific, and before very long that began to seem exceedingly important.

During the debates on Indian removal and during the decade that followed no one thought much about the region west of the Mississippi. It was believed that the region between the ninety-sixth meridian and the Rocky Mountains was worthless. As late as 1856 the superintendent of Indian affairs located at St. Louis reported that no part of the Kansas and Nebraska territories, with the exception of a narrow belt, was suitable for agriculture.

Information about the Pacific coast was more favorable. Oregon had begun to fill up with settlers from 1842 on;

in that year, in fact, it was deemed advisable to appoint an Indian agent for Oregon while the country was still under a kind of joint occupation by England and the United States. Discovery of gold in California in 1848 was all that was needed to change the national attitude toward the far West overnight.

By that time treaties had been made with all the eastern tribes, and with many trans-Mississippi tribes as well, defining boundaries and solemnly guaranteeing permanent possession—as contemplated by the 1830 law. A map of the United States for the decade 1840–50 would show Indian country stretching from the Red River in the south to the River Platte in the north. Actual occupation by Indians extended all the way to the Canadian border, but the Sioux, Cheyenne, Crow, and other tribes in the northern area were scarcely known, much less their habitat. The Indian removal treaties, together with the Indian Intercourse Act of 1834, prohibited settlement west of a line starting at Fort Smith and running northward through the mouth of the Kansas River, a line roughly corresponding with the present Arkansas-Oklahoma and Missouri-Kansas boundaries. The Removal Act had moved the Royal Proclamation of 1763 westward a thousand miles and set it in operation again.[1]

The proposals in Congress to organize the Kansas and Nebraska territories, whatever other considerations became involved, and apart from the debates over slavery which quickly dominated the issue, originated as a plan to open a corridor to the Pacific coast. The Oregon and Santa Fe trails in operation after 1840, both of which took off in the northern section of the Indian country, required a wide and safe zone for the movement of traffic. Before long, plans for a transcontinental railroad were being debated.

For the time being, however, such settlers as crossed the Mississippi were obliged to turn south into Texas or north into Iowa, avoiding the Indian country.

The proposal to organize an Indian territory had some support in Congress. It had been discussed earlier, in 1834, and indeed Thomas Jefferson had contemplated a similar measure. The territory would be placed under the president, who would name a governor. There were some differences in the various plans, but generally it was proposed that the member tribes would elect delegates to a general council, which would be the legislative body. Some versions also proposed that a delegate from this Indian territory would represent it in Congress and eventually the territory might be admitted as a state of the Union.[2]

The discussion finally reduced itself to the immediate problem of moving the Indians out of the path of westward progress. Requests to organize Nebraska territory had been presented in Congress since 1844, and were renewed almost annually down to 1853. Even the Wyandotte Indians, who had been moved to the Kansas River from the region north of the Ohio, joined in these requests, though they would doubtless be required to move once more.

The Congressional delegations from the southern states uniformly opposed all bills to organize Kansas and Nebraska, since under the terms of the Missouri Compromise the new territories would have the right to exclude slavery. The southern representatives varied their attack from time to time by adverting to Indian occupancy rights. Congressman Howard Hughes of Texas led the opposition to a Nebraska bill in 1853 by arguing that until Indian title to the land in Nebraska had been extinguished with the consent of the Indians, the United States had no business organizing a territory. A champion of the bill retorted that, according to his understanding, judged by "Texas morals and politics" the Indians had no rights whatever.

The upshot was the passage of the Kansas-Nebraska Bill on May 30, 1854, opening to white settlement, territory which, less than a quarter of a century earlier, had been set up under solemn promises as Indian country. "Say to them," Jackson had instructed an agent who was about to visit the Chickasaw Indians, "their father, the President, will lay off a country of equal extent . . . He will establish landmarks for them never to be moved, and give them a fee simple title to the land. You must be prepared to give assurance of permanency of title, and dwell upon the idea that they will never be asked to surrender an acre more . . ."

Discovery of gold in Colorado in 1859 and in Montana in 1861 brought the clash between Indian and white man out into the Great Plains, where it would be fought to a conclusion. When the smoke and dust of that conflict subsided, the free moving days of the native Americans would be ended forever.

The stream of traffic over the Oregon and Santa Fe trails to the Pacific Northwest and to California suddenly began to wheel out in new directions. A commissioner of Indian affairs reported to Congress: "Since the discovery of gold in the vicinity of Pikes Peak, the emigration has immensely increased; the Indians have been driven from their local haunts and hunting grounds, and the game so far killed off or dispersed, that it is now impossible for the Indians to obtain the necessary subsistence from that source."

An agent on the Upper Platte noted: "This great wave of emigration to the prairie west is moving onward with greatly increased velocity. It is beyond human power to retard or control it, nor would it be wise to do so, even were it possible."

A Sioux Indian, Bear Rib, addressed an Army captain: "My brother, to whom does this land belong? I believe it belongs to me. Look at me and at the ground. Which do you think is the oldest? The ground; and on it I was born . . ."[3]

Presently it was a shooting war on the Cannonball River, in the Killdeer Mountains, on the Powder River. The United States was insisting that a road be opened up through the Powder River country to reach the gold fields in southern Montana. The Sioux were as determined to prevent this invasion of their remaining hunting ground.

It must be said for the Sioux that they did not want to start the shooting. When Colonel Sawyer was sent out from Sioux City in the spring of 1865 to open a road from Laramie to Bozeman, the Sioux war chief, Red Cloud, tried psychology.

First he protested orally, and got nowhere with the colonel. Then he gathered his forces and for days on end stalked the survey party. At one point he held it under siege for fifteen days. No one was hurt, only the Indians made a good deal of noise. When the colonel, considering himself under orders to survey a road, refused to turn back, Red Cloud raised the siege and resumed his stalking tactics.

By an unfortunate mischance, a soldier was killed. He had strayed too far from the party, and an Indian dropping arrows around his head, let one drive to the mark. Fighting might have broken out then, but Red Cloud withdrew. His young men were getting restive. Sawyer completed the task assigned without further incident.

Shooting followed that summer of armed neutrality. It seemed as if at any moment a general uprising would sweep the entire length of the frontier. To forestall this, Congress in July 1867 created a Peace Commission consisting of three army officers not below the rank of brigadier general, the commissioner of Indian affairs, and the chairman of the Senate committee on Indian affairs. The commission was directed to call together the chiefs and headmen of all the bands and tribes then engaged in more or less open warfare, to remove "all just causes of complaint," and "establish security for persons or property along . . . the thoroughfares of travel to the western territories."[4]

Further, the commissioners were required to select a district or districts of sufficient area where all the Indian tribes occupying territory east of the Rocky Mountains might be established on permanent reservations.

In issuing instructions the Senate indicated that it had no intention of departing from historic policy. The Peace Commission was advised that any district or districts selected for the Indians would be approved by Congress, and thereafter would "be and remain permanent homes for said Indians to be located thereon, and no persons not members of said tribes shall ever be permitted to enter thereon without the permission of the tribes interested, except officers and employees of the United States."

The commissioners appointed in due course made the long journey up the Missouri by boat and afterward traveled out to various meeting places where councils were held with the different branches of the Sioux Nation, and with the Cheyenne, the Arapaho, the Crow, Assiniboine, and other northern plains groups. In all, eleven treaties were negotiated, were submitted to the Senate, and almost without delay were approved by President Johnson.

The eleven treaties called for an expenditure of almost $4.5 million, about twice the amount provided in the annual operating budget of the Bureau of Indian Affairs for the fiscal year 1868.

After the annual supply bill had passed the House in the first session of the Forty-first Congress, the Senate amended it by adding the items of expenditure called for in the eleven treaties. Generally these expenditures were in the form of annuity payments, though rations, tools, and other items were included. This was intended as compensation for the considerable areas of land which the several tribes agreed to cede to the United States.

The Senate amendments precipitated a debate between the two branches of Congress which lasted for two years, and when the clamor had finally died away, the Indians found that one more breach had been made in the bulwark protecting their historic rights.[5]

The lower house said at the outset that the day of treaty-making with the Indians was done. The members in charge of the appropriation bill declared flatly that they would not agree to any payment of funds called for by the eleven treaties, or by any other treaties that might be submitted in future. The speakers on the Senate side were better versed in history and constitutional law, but it mattered not the least.

President Grant's administration had just come into office, and, as so often happens with a new administration, the leaders in Congress insisted on reviewing the entire course of administration and satisfying themselves that policy and procedure were correct.

Congressman (later Senator) Henry L. Dawes of Massachusetts, who was in charge of the Interior appropriation bill on the floor, stated the situation frankly: "I do not feel competent to discuss any special policy at this time, [but] I am of the opinion that a new administration, just taking upon itself the responsibilities of the Government [ought] to develop its own policy in reference to these Indians as well as other matters."

One member even doubted the existence of the tribes or bands with which the commissioners had negotiated, except "in the minds of some Indian traders and speculators." When he asked the committee chairman (Mr. Dawes) to indicate in what part of the country the tribes lived and to give their populations, the chairman had to admit: "My acquaintance with these citizens of the United States has been of so recent a character that I am unable to answer the gentleman."

Into such hands had the Indians fallen.

The House had a serious charge to bring against the Senate. Indian affairs, then, as now, were complex, specialized, involving great labor, and accomplishing nothing in the way of votes. Consequently, when Indian treaties came up for ratification, the Senate chamber was sometimes empty of all but the presiding officer, the chairman of the Indian committee, and the ranking minority member. The House was able to cite instances in which ratification of an Indian treaty was proposed by a single member, was opposed by the same number, and the deciding vote was cast by the presiding officer. Deliberations such as these, the House could point out, had resulted in a proposal to spend $4.5 million on some Indian tribes that no one had heard of.

It was a gilded age. Fortunes were kicked out of the grass roots. The Civil War was over and every man who could shake off old ties was traveling to what was quickly becoming the fabled West to make a stake. What the Spaniards had missed when they came up the coastal road from old Mexico in search of the Seven Cities of Cibola, had been found at last on Cherry Creek, in Oliver Gulch, in the Coeur d'Alene. Who knew where it might be found next?

It was western men who were most aggressive in disparagement of the Indians and in attempting to destroy the protected position which law and the consciences of men had built around them. Senator Yates of Illinois, for example, condemned the legislative record of Congress because "it treated the Indians as the owners of the land." He enlarged upon that theme: "They never owned a foot of land. They were roving savages. They never owned and could not own land. They could not understand the title to land. They never claimed land. We treat them as the owners of land. That is all wrong. The Indians cannot be civilized; they will not be civilized; they do not want to be civilized . . . We must treat them as savages."

Senator Stewart of Nevada, having similar convictions, argued that since it cost money to deal honorably with Indians, it must be wrong. He thought that Indian treaties were a "sham" and he insisted that wherever the word "treaty" was used in the appropriation bill the expression "so-called" should be inserted in front of it. "Every dollar appropriated for Indians," he declared, "tends to prevent the Indians from becoming civilized, teaches them to live in idleness. . . . I do not believe that the Indians can ever become civilized without labor."

The Spaniards, it will be recalled, were troubled because the Indians avoided contact with Christians and preferred to live in the woods "eating spiders and roots and other filthy things to living with the Spaniards." The best way to overcome all this, they thought, was to make them labor in the mines.

Pomeroy of Kansas replied to Stewart: "When we were weak and the Indians were strong, we were glad to make treaties with them, and live up to those treaties. Now we have grown powerful and they have grown weak, and it does not become this great nation to turn around and trample the rights of the weak." But Stewart was not deflected from his line of reasoning. "I am opposed to taxing white men to feed the Indians," he answered.

It would be unjust to leave the impression that westerners were uniformly hostile to the Indians. Congressman Smith of Oregon, for one, brushed aside the argument that treaty-making with the Indians had been abused. The fact that the Senate did not turn out in full force to discuss an Indian treaty was no reason for insisting that the lower house should be made a party to negotiations with the Indian tribes; adding the House to the proceedings was no guarantee that intelligent action would result. The Constitution had provided that the President and the Senate were to have the responsibility of treating with Indian tribes. The House had no more right to insist on sharing this function than it had to claim a right to participate in the deliberations and decisions of the Supreme Court.

Most eloquent of all in defense of the Indians was Senator Casserly of California. He was one of not more than half a dozen who had taken the trouble to read the history of Indian relations and to study the court decisions, to judge from the character of the debates. He pleaded with those who would abolish treaty-making that mere change in procedure would not solve difficulties; only time would do that. "Time will solve it if we have patience, either by the disappearance of the dwindling races or by their voluntary acceptance of the relations of citizenship."

Most telling was his closing statement: "I know what the misfortune of the tribes is. Their misfortune is not that they are red men; not that they are semi-civilized, not that they are a dwindling race, not that they are a weak race. Their misfortune is that they hold great bodies of rich lands, which have aroused the cupidity of powerful corporations and of powerful individuals . . . I greatly fear that the adoption of this provision to discontinue treaty-making is the beginning of the end in respect to Indian lands. It is the first step in a great scheme of spoliation, in which the Indians will be plundered, corporations and individuals enriched, and the American name dishonored in history."

The House, however, was able to put a good appearance on its motives, whatever they might be; and in appropriation matters, it always had the final say. Representative

Clarke of Kansas rationalized the position of the House: "The remnants of the Indian tribes which exist in the United States, ought to be dealt with as we deal with any other class of people. The laws of the United States ought to be as effective over our Indian reservations as they are effective over any other part of the country."

Senator Harlan of Iowa, chairman of the Senate committee on Indian affairs, was finally instrumental in swinging the Senate to accept the terms insisted upon by the House. He reasoned: "I have been of the impression for years that there was no necessity for negotiating and ratifying treaties with Indians; that all our intercourse with them could be regulated by law, by statutory provisions, just as well as by treaty; that on the whole it was much safer to submit all these propositions to both branches of Congress than to submit them only to the Senate."

Much more was said, but Harlan's view carried in the end. When the Appropriation Act for 1871 passed, it included a rider providing: "Hereafter no Indian nation or tribe within the territory of the United States shall be acknowledged or recognized as an independent tribe or power with whom the United States may contract by treaty."

Ordinarily Congress will not permit the incorporation of substantive law in an appropriation act, but in this case no objection was heard.

The Congress was not by this language denying that Indian tribes were "domestic dependent nations," as John Marshall described them. Congress merely said that, as a matter of policy, it would not in the future treat with Indian tribes as independent powers. A succeeding Congress might at any time declare the policy to be in error and return to the earlier practice, as established by the first president under the Constitution.

24

SOLUTION BY LAW

Having decided that there was nothing wrong with its Indian policy that could not be cured by legislation, the Congress in the years following 1871 resorted to statutory devices. Until that time, laws limited in application to Indians were relatively few, and usually these were enacted for the purpose of carrying out treaty provisions. When the *Handbook of Federal Indian Law* was compiled by Felix S. Cohen in 1940, in the course of which a survey was made of the entire field of Indian law, it was found that approximately four thousand statutes had been adopted, most of them after 1871.[1] The number has continued to increase since then.

While many of these laws dealt with trivia, the unhappy feature was that too many were of general application and attempted to enforce uniform requirements on a people who differed in language, custom, economic activities, religious practices—in everything including racial origin. The treaties were each directed to a particular tribe, and during the treaty-making period little attempt was made to regulate internal affairs. The amount of control that can be vested in a few thousand statutes and the regulations to implement the statutes, can come rather close to the absolute.

White men worried over the lack of enthusiasm they detected in the Indians for European civilization, ideas, religion. A note of injured feelings is present in the complaints of the Spaniards that the Indians did not care to live near them. This concern led to numerous devices or plans by which the interest of the Indians would be captured and, presumably, their conditions bettered. A common notion was that the task of civilizing would be speedily accomplished if, by some means or other, the Indians would adapt themselves to the European property sense—if they would become acquisitive and if they would develop private proprietorship.

The Dominican monks, reporting on conditions in Mexico in 1544, observed that "the Indians are weak by nature and not acquisitive, and are satisfied with having enough to get along on from day to day. If there is any way to bring them out of their laziness and carelessness, it is to make them help the Spaniards in their commerce . . . and thus they will become fond of commerce and profits."

The Jesuit Father Biard writing from Montreal in 1616 had a similar reaction, if not the remedy: "This nation [the Montagnais] takes little care for the future, but, like all the other Americans, enjoys the present . . . As long as they have anything, they are always celebrating feasts, and having songs, dances, and speeches."[2]

Education by example was a favorite method advocated in the English colonies. When Plymouth colony in 1685 settled Indian families on tracts of land the purpose was to teach husbandry, as well as to provide for the inalienability of the land. Similar experiments were carried out with the Mohican Indian settlement at Stockbridge, Massachusetts, and with the Delaware Indians at Brotherton, New Jersey.

An ambitious plan of this nature was proposed by the Countess Huntington and submitted to Patrick Henry soon after the close of the Revolutionary War. She wrote that she had "long reflected with pain on the condition, both in a religious and civil light, of the Indian nations in North America." She suggested that a large tract of land be set aside for joint settlement by Indians and "decent industrious, religious people, of exemplary lives and manners." The Indians, seeing their European neighbors enjoy more comfortable ways of living and observing "their modes of cultivation and their mechanic arts," would be instructed accordingly. The experiment was not attempted, since Virginia had just turned over to the national government its unappropriated western lands in payment of its share of the recently acquired national debt.[3]

Henry Knox reflected on various aspects of the problems facing the Indian people. In one of his reports to the president he included the suggestion: "Were it possible to introduce among the Indian tribes a love for exclusive property, it would be a happy commencement of the business [of civilizing them].

"This might be brought about by making presents, from time to time, to the chiefs or their wives, of sheep and other domestic animals; and if, in the first instance, persons were appointed to take charge, and teach the use of them, a considerable part of the difficulty would be surmounted."[4]

In 1816 Secretary of War William Crawford urged similar views: "The idea of separate property in things personal universally precedes the same idea in relation to lands. This results no less from the intrinsic difference between the two kinds of property, than from the different effects produced by human industry and ingenuity exerted upon them . . . To succeed perfectly in the attempt to civilize the aborigines of this country, the government ought to direct their attention to the improvement of their habitations, and the multiplication of distinctive settlements."[5]

Crawford proposed that in any future treaty for the purchase of lands from the tribes, provision be made to reserve a section of land for each Indian who cared to make a permanent settlement in the ceded area, to which eventually he should be given title in fee simple.

He explained: "These views are substantially founded on the conviction that it is a true policy and earnest desire of the government to draw its savage neighbors within the pale of civilization . . . It will redound more to the national honor to incorporate, by a humane and benevolent policy, the natives of our forests in the great American family of freemen, than to receive with open arms the fugitives of the Old World, whether their flight has been the effect of their crimes or their virtues."

In views and sentiments such as these lay the origins of the General Allotment Law of 1887—which was the culmination of a consistent statement of purpose of those who from earliest times had expressed a desire to preserve and to better the Indian race. As early as 1609 the governor of Virginia had proclaimed that the purpose of the English in their relations with the Indians "was not to supplant and roote them out but to bring them from their base condition to a farre better."[6]

The fact that there were selfish, exploitive interests who looked upon the Indians and their property as fair game was recognized and was a matter of concern to officialdom in colonial times as well as under United States rule. It was charged, during the debates on the proposal to adopt the allotment law, that these selfish interests would profit more than would the Indians from a policy of individualizing ownership and eventually investing the fee title in individual Indians. Spokesmen in Congress and the civic and religious leaders who favored the measure were firm in the conviction that the measure would benefit the Indians alone. The Indians were universally opposed to the legislation, but no one wanted their views.

Reservation of land for exclusive Indian use was a fairly common practice in the colonies. Virginia had worked out a reservation plan by 1656, and in 1658 commissioners for the united colonies agreed to a system of setting aside lands for the purpose. Connecticut had Indian reservations in 1680. The lands in these first reservations were left in community ownership and the first effort to divide a common holding into individual parcels occurred in Massachusetts in 1746. The general court in that year created land committees and placed in charge of these committees the various reserves which from time to time had been set aside for the Indians. Among the duties of these land committees was to make assignments of crop and meadowland to such Indians as showed an interest in improving a farm.

Except for the recommendations made by Knox, Crawford, and others, the allotment idea received no notable support until after the Civil War. In the removal treaties for the eastern tribes, it is true, provision was made for individual Indians to remain behind on selections of land, which might then be patented to them. A number of Choctaw families remained in Mississippi by this arrangement, but the idea was not encouraged by the white community.

The commissioner of Indian affairs in 1870 thought that he detected an increasing demand from the Indians to have their tribal lands divided up into individual holdings. He urged a policy of "giving to every Indian a home that he can call his own."

This was a strange recommendation, indeed, since the commissioner in question was an Indian, Eli S. Parker, the first Indian to hold the office. He was a member of the Seneca tribe, one of the Iroquois Six Nations, who had always protected their tribal interests with vigilance. Parker had been aide to General Grant, to whom he owed his appointment, and perhaps he no longer felt himself identified with the concerns of his tribe. In the previous year he had expressed the opinion that the treaty system ought to be abolished as a method of dealing with the Indian tribes.

He wrote: "As civilization advances and their possessions of land are required for settlement," legislation rather than treaties should be resorted to in terminating the Indian interest. Only a few years previously Parker had been campaigning vigorously to secure compliance with certain treaty rights of his Seneca tribe.

Carl Schurz, as secretary of the interior in 1877, became an advocate of allotments, arguing that "the enjoyment and pride of individual ownership of property [is] one of the most effective civilizing agencies." His identification with liberal causes would help to satisfy many that dividing up Indian land was in the interest of progress.[7]

The first general allotment bill was introduced in Congress in January 1879, and from then until its adoption in 1887, it was under constant discussion in Congress, before missionary groups, in the annual reports of the commissioner and the secretary of the interior, and out on the reservations, where agents were instructed to urge Indians to favor the idea.

Practically everything that was said for and against the idea was said at the very beginning, in the debates which took place in the third session of the Forty-sixth Congress, from December 1880 to March 1881.

The provisions of the bill as introduced and explained by Senator Coke were simple: it authorized the president to subdivide any Indian reservation, with the consent of the Indians, into individual parcels, a specific tract or allotment being assigned to each individual Indian; the lands might not be sold for a period of twenty-five years; and lands remaining after the assignments had been made would be purchased by the government and would become available for settlement by non-Indians. The Coke Bill was endorsed by both the commissioner of Indian affairs and the secretary of the interior.

Senator Pendleton of Ohio was one of the first to speak in support of the bill. "They must either change their mode of life or they must die," he asserted, with an assurance that must have disconcerted any Indian who might have been listening. "We may regret it, we may wish it were otherwise, our sentiments of humanity may be shocked by the alternative, but we cannot shut our eyes to the fact that that is the alternative, and that these Indians must either change their modes of life or they will be exterminated . . . In order that they may change their modes of life, we must change our policy . . . we must stimulate within them to the very largest degree, the idea of home, of family, and of property. These are the very anchorages of civilization; the commencement of the dawning of these ideas in the mind is the commencement of the civilization of any race, and these Indians are no exception."

The General Assembly of the Presbyterian Church of the United States urged these and other worthy sentiments, in a memorial supporting the bill: to elevate the Indian, "give him a home with a perfect title in fee simple; protect him by the laws of the land, and make him amenable to the same; give him the advantage of a good education; and grant him full religious liberty."

Senator Plumb of Kansas offered an amendment which would have enlarged the opportunity for white men to avail themselves of Indian land values. He proposed that land allotted to Indians might be leased to white men, under such conditions as the secretary of the interior might impose. Senator Dawes attacked the proposal sharply: "I had an impression that this was a measure the purpose of which was to induce the Indian to cultivate the soil and get some interest in the soil that would induce him to become a cultivator of it and to derive all the incidental advantages in the progress of civilization which come from industry rewarded. This amendment . . . will furnish employment for the white man and food for the Indian without employment."

Plumb's colleague, Senator Ingalls, then answered in a vein of sarcasm, which suggested that he, at least, was not moved by any humanitarian interest in securing the advancement of the Indians. "It has been said that this [amendment] would result in the establishment of a landed aristocracy. Now, sir, the Indians today are the only unadulterated genuine aristocracy in this country. They are a peculiar and chosen people, like the children of Israel, having hereditary titles and privileges: possessing vast untaxed areas of the public domain, over which they roam at will in savage pastime . . . they burn, murder, and plunder with impunity; they contribute nothing, and never have contributed anything to the welfare of society. Yet they have for generations been maintained in insolent idleness or audacious hostility by the voluntary contributions of millions of money from the public revenue . . . They have for centuries maintained a receding but almost insuperable barrier to the progress and advance of American civilization; so that at the expiration of more than two centuries of efforts to evangelize, to Christianize, to civilize, to exterminate, or to conquer, the American Indian presents the same characteristics and exhibits the same problem today as that which confronted the earliest colonists . . . The stubborn fact remains that, in spite of diseases, wars, exposures, and migrations, there are nearly as many Indians today as there were in 1620."

This was not actually the case—the eighth census had shown an Indian population in the United States of 294,431, as against an estimated population for the same area of approximately 800,000 at the time of discovery. It was a striking fact, however, that the Indians had survived in larger numbers than many persons realized. Ingalls's remarks moved Senator Morgan of Alabama to say that he had never heard the Indians attacked so savagely and mercilessly, but that in effect the Kansas senator had pronounced a great eulogy on the Indian race.

Senator Dawes was not at the beginning a principal advocate of the proposed legislation. He would become so in time and would take over the management of a subsequent bill, introduced under his own name. It was as the Dawes Act that the allotment idea became law.

The evidence which Indians were able to muster in opposition to the Coke Bill in the Forty-sixth Congress must have proved difficult to answer on rational grounds. The presentation of evidence actually was limited to that submitted in the form of a petition by the Five Civilized Tribes. These were the same Cherokees, Choctaws, Chickasaws, Creeks, and Seminoles who had been moved out of the Southeast at the cost of such anguish. That they had retained their vigor is demonstrated by the Cherokee record. Members of that tribe owned 67,000 head of cattle, 108,000 swine, 13,000 horses—all of which had been accumulated since the end of the Civil War, when everything they owned had been stolen or destroyed. Moreover, a recent census showed only sixteen who gave their occupation as hunters and five as fishermen, while 3,549 were listed as farmers in a population of 5,169 males over the age of eighteen. In the year 1881 they had exported 1,200 bales of cotton.[8]

With respect to the Coke Bill, the petition declared: "Our people have not asked for or authorized this, for the reason that they believe it could do no good and would only result in mischief in their present condition. Our own laws regulate a system of land tenure suited to our condition, and much safer than that which is proposed for it.

"Improvements can be and frequently are sold, but the land itself is not a chattel. Its occupancy and possession are indispensable to holding it, and its abandonment for two years makes it revert to the public domain. In this way every one of our citizens is assured of a home.

"The changed individual title would throw the whole of our domain in a few years into the hands of a few persons. In your treaties with us you have agreed that this shall not be done without our consent; we have not asked for it and we call on you not to violate your pledge with us."

Quite apart from these moral grounds, the petition recited a good practical reason against allotments. "A large portion of our country, and at least two-thirds of the Indian country, are only suitable for grazing purposes. No man can afford to live by stock raising and herding who is restricted to 160 or even 320 acres, especially on lands away from water."

White men in the thousands would prove the wisdom of that statement, by their personal failures, in attempting to live on the quarter-sections conveyed to them under the Homestead Act.

For the senators who failed to read the petition of the Five Civilized Tribes, Senator Teller of Colorado labored prodigiously to make the facts apparent. He detected considerable confusion in the minds of his colleagues. Senator Butler, for example, remarked: "Quite a number of these Indians are producing corn, wheat, and cattle. . . . I should like to ask the Senator [Teller] how they produce cereals unless they have some idea of a title to land?"

Elementary as it must seem, Teller had to remind the senator from South Carolina that when John Smith landed within a few miles of the national capital he found the Indians raising corn, tobacco, beans, and other products on fields, which were owned in common. He tried to explain what this meant. "The civilized Indians in the Indian territory hold all their land by a common tenure, and yet they do not work an acre of it in common any more than white men would do under the same circumstances. Each Indian goes upon the reservation and takes for himself such land as is unoccupied and works it, and he works it just as long as he sees fit . . . When he abandons it and goes away from it then any other Indian may step in and take his place. Knowing that fact, and knowing that the Indians protect these possessions with as much scrupulous honesty as we protect the fee simple title, I say that when it is asserted that they will not work because the title is not secure, it is nonsense."

He could find no evidence that the Indians wanted their common-owned lands divided and individualized. This seemed to him to be a matter of some importance. If they were not requesting it and the measure were to be adopted in the absence of their knowledge or support, would it accomplish what was intended? He agreed that they wanted title to the land. "They know what a paper title from the Government means, and they want the title not to themselves, but to their tribe; they want it where it will be understood that they cannot be disturbed; they want it so that an act of Congress cannot move them without their consent."

It occurred to him also that the proponents of the allotment law were attempting to reverse the natural order of things. He argued: "When an Indian becomes civilized, when he becomes Christianized, when he knows the value of property, and when he knows the value of a home . . . then he is prepared to take land in severalty, and . . . to take care of the land after he has got it."

Finally, Senator Teller's predictions of the ultimate result of an allotment law were remarkably accurate, as the passing years would prove. This was something that could not be appreciated in the heat of debate, but it does indicate that his reasoning was basically sound. He had read rather widely in the history of Indian affairs and he was familiar with the report made by Jedediah Morse in 1822, in which the confident prediction was made that within ten or fifteen years of that date the Indians would be civilized and the difficulties then apparent would be resolved. Teller cited the report as a warning against the expectation that any legislation which attempted to do all things for all Indians could succeed.

Addressing the Senate in one of his long harangues, Teller predicted: "You propose to divide all this land and to give each Indian his quarter-section, or whatever he may have, and for twenty-five years he is not to sell it, mortgage it, or dispose of it in any shape, and at the end of that time he may sell it. It is safe to predict that when that shall have been done, in thirty years thereafter there will not be an Indian on the continent, or there will be very few at least, that will have any land . . .

"It is in the interest of speculators; it is in the interest of the men who are clutching up this land, but not in the interest of the Indians at all; and there is the baneful feature of it that when you have allotted the Indians land on which they cannot make a living the secretary of the interior may then proceed to purchase their land, and Congress will, as a matter of course, ratify the purchase, and the Indians will become the owners in a few years in fee and away goes their title."

Then a last shouting challenge: "If I stand alone in the Senate, I want to put upon the record my prophecy in this matter, that when thirty or forty years shall have passed and these Indians shall have parted with their title, they will curse the hand that was raised professedly in their defense to secure this kind of legislation, and if the people who are clamoring for it understood Indian character, and Indian laws, and Indian morals, and Indian religion, they would not be here clamoring for this at all."

Teller went on to become secretary of the interior, 1882–85, and then to return to the Senate and participate in the final round of discussion on a later draft of the bill.

By that time sentiment in and out of Congress in favor of the allotment principle had greatly increased in intensity. It offered a theory of social development which fitted in exactly with ideas then current, of evolution as a growth from the simple to the complex, from the herd to nineteenth-century man. It seemed right to many minds even in the absence of information about Indians and their property systems.

Senator Dawes had not only become converted, he supplied what must have been by all odds the most fantastically optimistic statement offered in the entire course of the debate. It was a statement which brushed aside both fact and logic and assumed the tone of a threnody.

The occasion was the third annual Lake Mohonk conference in 1885. These annual meetings of the "Friends of the Indian" were initiated by Mr. A. K. Smiley, a member of the board of Indian commissioners, at his summer home.[9] Dawes had just returned from a visit to the Cherokees in Indian Territory, where he had been deeply impressed by the evidences of progress which came to his attention. He was wrong in saying that the Cherokees and others of the Five Civilized tribes had been "blanket Indians" when they left Georgia and Alabama. It was apparent, however, that after having been ripped out by the roots by Andrew Jackson's removal policy, the Cherokees had accomplished a thorough job of rehabilitation. He described what he saw:

"They have a principal chief and a written constitution, and a legislature elected once in four years; it is composed of a senate and a house. They have a supreme court, a county court, and a school system of which compulsory education is a feature . . . They have a high school for girls and one for boys, in buildings that would be respectable in Massachusetts . . . I heard Indian girls recite to an Indian teacher in moral philosophy . . .

"The head chief told us that there was not a family in that whole nation that had not a home of its own. There was not a pauper in that nation, and the nation did not owe a dollar. It built its own capitol, in which we had this examination, and it built its schools and its hospitals . . ."

All of that, in the fifty years since the Cherokees had been beaten out of Georgia. Yet Dawes was not satisfied. He told the friends of Indian civilization: "The defect of the system was apparent. They have gotten as far as they can go, because they own their land in common. It is Henry George's system, and under that there is no enterprise to make your home any better than that of your neighbor's. There is no selfishness, which is at the bottom of civilization. Till this people will consent to give up their lands, and divide them among their citizens, so that each can own the land he cultivates, they will not make much more progress."

So the bill was enacted into law as the Dawes Act of February 8, 1887, and then began the process which, in considerably less than the thirty years predicted by Senator Teller, would destroy everything that Dawes had witnessed in the Cherokee country, and much else besides.

The events which befell the Sisseton Indians—a branch of the great Sioux Nation—will illustrate for all the others the nature of the process which this act of Congress set in motion.

When the allotment law was adopted, the Sisseton Reservation in South Dakota consisted of 918,000 acres. Previously, in 1851, the tribe had ceded to the United States an area of close to 40,000 square miles in southwestern Minnesota—a land of lakes and pleasant meadows. Later still, in 1872, the tribe was persuaded to sell an area of 11,000,000 acres at ten cents an acre in the fertile Red River valley.[10]

The agent in charge of the Sisseton Reservation was persuaded as early as 1879 that his charges were anxious to learn the ways of the white man. "I find these people have a friendly feeling toward the government and also the whites, many of them expressing a willingness to live among them and to learn better how to manage their agricultural work."

As evidence, the agent reported in 1880: "One of these Indians has applied, under the treaty, for a patent to his land; and others are ready to do so."

Two years after the passage of the Allotment Act, the Indians agreed to cede to the United States all unallotted land, at a rate of $2.50 per acre. One of the provisions of the original Coke Bill allowed the government to purchase any land left over after selections had been made by each member of a tribe. Although Senator Teller had protested against this feature, it remained intact through all the discussions. At Sisseton, allotments were made to about 2000 Indians, accounting for 308,838 acres; while a much larger area, 574,678 acres, was sold to the United States. This area was then opened to white homesteaders.

By 1892 the allotments had been completed and the "surplus" area transferred to the United States. The agent wrote enthusiastically: "The Sisseton and Wahpetons no longer hold their land in common, having taken allotments in severalty, and on April 15 of the present year, this reservation was thrown open to settlement under the homestead law, and today the homes of white settlers dot the prairie in every direction . . . and the red and the white men will hereafter harvest their crops and herd their stock side by side."

This high promise was universally felt throughout the Indian Service, no less than in Congress itself. The Commissioner of Indian Affairs, T. J. Morgan, in his annual report for 1892, stated the basic thesis of the new policy: individualization of land, bestowal of citizenship upon the Indian people. In the commissioner's wording: "The essential element of the policy adopted by the government is

suggested in the one phrase—American citizenship . . .
Those who take their land in severalty, become citizens of
the United States, entitled to the protection of the courts
and all other privileges of citizenship, and are amenable to
the laws and under obligations for the performance of the
same duties as devolve upon their fellow citizens."

Enthusiasm by itself was not enough. The allotments
had scarcely been made before the dream began to dissipate.
The Indian agent reporting from Sisseton in 1894 offered
this observation: "The agency building, boys' dormitory,
and surroundings were in a dilapidated, neglected condition, everything having the appearance of a broken-down
business enterprise. Such a state of things, in my opinion, is
a great mistake since these Indian people are recognized as
more advanced in civilization than most western tribes, and
for that reason more care and judgment should be exercised in the management of affairs concerning them . . . It
has been clearly demonstrated this season, more than ever
before owing to the shortage of the hay crop all over the
state, that these Indian citizens must suffer petty offenses
committed by the unscrupulous white man who stands
ready to take advantage of the Indian whenever and wherever he can. The boundary lines of their lands cause much
trouble. In many instances the white man intrudes upon
the property of the Indian, disputing the lines and ownership of his land."

By 1899 the morale of the Sisseton Indians had disintegrated rather badly. Their agent in that year estimated
that only about one half of the tribe was interested in
working for its daily bread. The other half was shouting,
"Abolish the agency! Give us deeds to our land and what
money there is in the Treasury to our credit!" Those
belonging to this latter half, the agent reported, were
responsible for practically all of the crimes committed on
the reservation, to which he added this sad note: "I believe
that this has been caused by the large amount of money
paid to this class in the last few months and the insane
desire of rascally white men to get it away from them in the
shortest time possible."

Ten years later the Sisseton agent reported that out of
the 220 families living on the reservation, 174 were dependent on the allotment of either the husband or the wife, one
or the other having sold his or her land; 16 families had
sold all of their land and were living on inherited tracts.

Further, he observed: "The Indians who live farthest from towns are doing the best and make the most improvements."

Nothing remained in later years but to attempt to save some pieces. Of the better than 900,000 acres which the Sisseton Indians had in 1887, slightly more than 300,000 acres were retained for Indian use, the balance having been homesteaded by white men. Of the land which the Indians retained, almost 200,000 acres had been sold under patents-in-fee by 1933. By that time also, the original allottees were dying off and what land remained in Indian ownership was becoming divided into infinitesimal interests through heirship proceedings. Only 35,000 acres remained in the hands of the original allottees, while better than 80,000 acres had undergone heirship divisions and for most part were no longer in economically useful units.

The agency plant, which was reported to be old and dilapidated in 1894, was never rebuilt in any systematic fashion. With the government committed to liquidating the tribe at an early date, there was no point in modernizing a plant, the usefulness of which was at an end.

The condition of the Sisseton Indians was brought firsthand to the attention of Congress in 1946. In that year a subcommitte of the House committee on Indian affairs made a special investigation of Indian reservations. What the members of the subcommittee saw when they reached Sisseton agency in July shocked them. "One of the most disgraceful situations in America," a member reported. The Indians "were faced with a nasty, bad housing situation, living under impossible housing conditions." Or, as another member commented, "worse than the places in which we keep livestock."

The land had disappeared, but the Indians had remained, had even increased. This phenomenon had not been reckoned with by the framers of the Allotment Act. The 2,000 Indians who had received separate parcels of land at Sisseton had increased to better than 3,000 when the subcommittee visited the reservation in 1946. About 2,500 were trying to live where their fathers had lived.

An Indian witness explained to the visitors what had happened. He was Simon J. Kirk, big, deep-voiced, a retired Presbyterian missionary. "Our young people get married and have no place to go or no place to build a home. And so, supposing a certain relative was making his way pretty well, instead of the children going away and making their way, they go and double themselves up until the old man is finally broke.

"These Indians occupied a very good modest position in life back in 1910, and I sincerely believe if by some management pieces of land, such as forty or eighty acres, could be provided,. that would afford an opportunity for them to work on and to build homes . . ."

The process had run its full course, and at the end of it the Sisseton Indians were vainly hoping that they could regain only a small part of what they possessed at the beginning.

25

SECOND GROWTH

The Indian people survived, even increased in numbers, but their lands dwindled. For some bewildered tribes the land vanished entirely. In Michigan, Minnesota, Wisconsin, North Dakota, Montana, Nevada, and California, large groups lived as squatters on cutover forest areas, on public lands, on vacant city lots, on town dumps.

The National Resources Board after a survey in 1935 reported that perhaps as many as 100,000 Indians were without any land of their own. They were living like the Sissetons, by doubling up with relatives on a few acres. They had scant reason to believe that their lot would ever be any better.

Senator Ingalls in his sarcastic eulogy on the survival power of the Indian race was more nearly correct than he had reason to be. Certainly he meant no kindliness in his statement: "They have for centuries maintained a receding but insuperable barrier to the progress and advance of American civilization . . . In spite of diseases, wars, exposures, and migrations" they had not been exterminated.

The Indians survived. When Ingalls spoke in 1881 the Indian population was actually near its lowest point of decline—though such was the condition of Indian vital statistics then and for many years afterward it would have been difficult to make any safe prediction whether the Indian people would vanish or grow strong again.

Estimates of the Indian population, or of portions of it, have been compiled at intervals since Henry Knox in 1789 placed at 76,000 the number of Indians east of the Mississippi. He did not specify the names of the tribes included in his calculation, but it is presumed that he counted all the tribes with which the United States Government was in contact.[1]

The first attempt at an official estimate of the total Indian population within the boundaries of the United States was made by Jedediah Morse, appointed by the secretary of war in 1819 to investigate and report on the condition of the Indian tribes. This report was submitted in 1822, and while many of Morse's figures were admittedly based on plain conjecture, his subtotals for certain regions were probably not far wrong. His table showed:

Indians in:

New England	2,247
New York	5,184
Ohio	2,407
Michigan and Northwest Territory	28,380
Illinois and Indiana	17,006
southern states east of Mississippi	65,022
north of Missouri River	33,150
between Missouri and Red rivers	101,070
west of Rocky Mountains	171,200
between Red River and Rio Del Norte	45,370
Grand total	471,036

Later estimates fluctuated widely, according to the methods used, the definitions adopted, the area covered, and other factors.

Henry R. Schoolcraft, in preparing his compilation on the *Indian Tribes of the United States* (1851–57), was directed by Congress to undertake an actual enumeration of the Indian population. Analysis of the report issued by him in 1850, in which he showed 388,229 Indians, indicates that he relied almost entirely on estimates and second- and third-hand sources.

The report of the commissioner of Indian affairs for 1860 gave the number as 254,300.

The Census Bureau in 1870 attempted an actual enumeration, yet its published report indicates that more than 68 percent of its tally was based on estimates. It came up with 313,712 Indians in the United States and 70,000 in Alaska. The latter figure was more than double the number estimated by persons who had firsthand knowledge of the newly acquired territory.

The commissioner of Indian affairs and the Census Bureau define the term Indian each according to the requirements of an agency, and not surprisingly their differing estimates make for confusion. This was true in 1870, when the commissioner published his estimate of 287,640 Indians in the United States.

In spite of these conflicting estimates the general assumption is that the Indian population declined in numbers until about 1880 and the low point was probably close to the figure of 255,938 reported by the commissioner in that year (his report gave 240,136 Indians located on 68 reservations and 15,802 scattered in six states where no reservations existed).

The National Resources Board in 1935 concluded that "the rapid dying off of Indians, continuous for nearly three centuries, slackened late in the nineteenth century and terminated definitely about 1905."[2]

In an effort to determine Indian population trends, the authors of the section on population in this National Resources Board report compiled figures on 64 Indian agencies, reservations, or separate tribes. The census figures on each of the groups included were known to be reasonably accurate over a period of years. The 64 groups were located in nineteen states and had a total population in 1900 of 61,416. This was 22.7 percent of the whole Indian population reported for that year.

The period covered in the report was from 1900 to 1934, in which time the numbers grew from 61,416 to 78,139, an increase of 27.2 percent. The sampling further showed that the rate of increase accelerated toward the end of the period. In the first five-year period the rate of increase was 2.71 percent, while in the last five-year period the rate was 5.52 percent.

The most spectacular growth recorded by a single tribe was that made by the Navajo Indians. At two long intervals in time a fairly accurate census was made of the tribe. The first was in 1863, when Kit Carson drove the tribe to Fort Sumner in eastern New Mexico as prisoners of war and number tags were issued to each member.

Some few hundred are known to have evaded the army and never went to the prison camp. The total count of those rounded up was nearly 9,000, and that figure is generally accepted as coming close to the total for the tribe at that time.

During World War II effort was made to reach every family on the Navajo reservation in connection with registering for Selective Service or for the issuance of ration books. Again some errors may have occurred through omissions, duplications, or other deviations, but these could not have been great. The total of all Navajos in 1947 was reported to be about 61,000. In a period of about 80 years, the population had increased almost seven-fold. Net growth has continued, of course. The 1970 Census listed 97,000 Navajos, about 13 percent of the Indian population for that year.

In searching for the causes of this astonishing escape from doom, certain physical factors suggest themselves. First of these is the virility of the Indian people, a trait that survived years of hunger and displacement. The birthrate for the Indian population is in excess of 40 per 1,000, while the birthrate for the United States is 21.7 per 1,000. These Indian potentials are cut down severely by the accompanying death rates: 16 per 1,000 for the Navajo Indians, 13.3 per 1,000 for all Indians. The death rate for the United States is 10.5 per 1,000.

One other physical factor that has helped in reversing a trend that started 300 years ago is improved health care. "Whatever else reservation life did, its ultimate effect was to save and multiply Indian lives," the National Resources Board found in 1935. Settled life on reserved areas made possible the building and staffing of hospitals and the beginnings of public health work among the tribes. As medical work among Indians shifts from curative to preventive techniques—a shift that is taking place over the country—the rate of population increase may continue to accelerate.

The Indian people in 1970 numbered 763,594. In the very near future they could recapture 300 years of lost ground and return to the number estimated for the time of discovery. This could occur with even greater likelihood if certain nonphysical factors turn in favor of the Indians.

The status of the Indian tribe in the United States is almost universally misunderstood. By many it is assumed that Indians are imprisoned behind reservation walls, or that alternatively they have been racially segregated in rural ghettos. The truth is that the reservations are the private property of the Indians. Sometimes the title is a community title, shared by all members equally, as church property may be owned by the congregation or corporate property is owned by the shareholders. Some reservation land has been individualized and the title is held in the name of the Indian tribal member—but this fact of segregating the fee in an individual adds no odor of sanctity that was not present before. Property, whether corporately or individually owned, is guaranteed to the owner under United States law.

A closer look at the nature of Indian title in land, as the courts have viewed the subject through the years, should clarify the issue.

The apprehension which arose in the mind of the commissioner of Indian affairs in 1872 has long since been proven baseless. Congress had just voted to abandon its historic policy of treating the Indian tribes as if they were sovereign nations, and this worried the commissioner. He wrote in his annual report for that year: "This action of Congress . . . present[s] questions of considerable interest and of much difficulty, viz., what is to become of the rights of the Indians to the soil, over portions of territory which had not been covered by treaties at the time Congress put an end to the treaty system? . . . Confiscation, of course, would afford a very easy solution for all difficulties of title, but it may fairly be assumed that the United States Government will scarcely be disposed to proceed so summarily in the face of the unbroken practice of eighty-five years."

The Commissioner, Francis A. Walker, was correct in his view of the historic process, but he was quite wrong in assuming that officials of the United States would not attempt to accomplish confiscation under other guises. The final result was what concerned the Indians—and for that they could thank the white man's court.

Only the broader phases of the court record are here suggested:[3]

1. The administrative branch of the government may not ignore the rightful Indian owner in granting a lease on Indian land, even though the lease granted by the administrative branch be confirmed by a joint resolution of Congress. In this case (*Jones* v. *Meehan*), decided in 1899, a piece of land had descended from father (Moose Dung, *père*) to elder son (Moose Dung, *fils*) in accordance with Chippewa tribal custom. The secretary of the interior executed a lease in behalf of heirs having a lesser right by tribal custom and attempted to set aside the lease made by the elder

son. The court held that neither the secretary nor
Congress could divest the real owner of his rights.

2. In the earlier cases going back to Chief Justice
Marshall's time the Court was considering rights established or recognized by formal treaty. A more
difficult type of case was presented in *Cramer* v. *United
States* (1923), in which the Indian title was not based
on such firm ground. Here the United States (again
the Department of the Interior) attempted to issue a
patent covering certain lands to a railroad company,
on the assumption that no rights had lodged in the
Indians who were occupying the land without benefit
of treaty or statutory guarantees. The Court held
that "the fact that such right of occupancy finds no
recognition in any statute or other formal governmental action is not conclusive . . . To hold that . . .
they acquired no possessory rights to which the Government would accord protection, would be contrary
to the whole spirit of the traditional American policy
toward these dependent wards of the nation."

3. The base of this right of occupancy was greatly
broadened in *United States as Guardian of Hualapai*
v. *Santa Fe Railway Co.* In this case a reservation had
been set aside by presidential order for the "use and
occupancy" of the Hualapai Indians of Arizona in
1883. The territory involved was directly in the path
of the Santa Fe railroad, which, in 1866, had been
granted alternate sections of public land along its
right of way. The Indians knew nothing of this gift
until 1925, when Congress authorized the Department
of the Interior to arrange an exchange of lands between the Indians and the railroad company in order
to consolidate the holdings of each in solid blocks.
The Indians then protested, arguing that they had
been in the country before the railroad and the
company, in effect, had no land to exchange. The
Court was unanimous in its opinion (1941) that
"Indian occupancy, even though unrecognized by
treaty or act of Congress, established property rights
valid against non-Indian grantees such as the de-
fendent railroad." An area of 509,000 acres was consequently decreed to be the property of the Indians.

In summarizing the effect of the Court's decision in this case, Felix S. Cohen remarked that "aboriginal occupancy of an Indian tribe was here held to have survived a course of congressional action that had proceeded on the assumption that the area in question was unencumbered public land. The decision thus stands as a warning to purchasers of real property from the Federal Government, reminding them that not even the Government can give what it does not possess."

4. The quality of Indian ownership rights was examined in *United States* v. *Shoshone Tribe* (1938). Here the Department of Justice, defending the United States against claims presented by the Indians, argued that the Indians had only a right to the surface of the land—a right "limited to those uses incident to the cultivation of the land and the grazing of livestock," but excluding "the ownership of the timber and the mineral resources." The Court refused to entertain any such reasoning. "For all practical purposes, the tribe owned the land," it declared. "The Shoshone tribe had the right that has always been understood to belong to Indians, undisturbed possessors of the soil from time immemorial."

5. In a later decision, *United States* v. *Alcea Band of Tillamooks* (1946), the Court held that even the United States must pay if it takes lands from the Indians: ". . . the Indian's right of occupancy has always been held to be sacred; something not to be taken from him except by his consent, and then only upon such consideration as should be agreed upon."

Those who advocate the abolition of Indian reservations also argue, sometimes in the same breath, that Indian tribes should be dissolved. Our system cannot tolerate a nation within a nation, they declare, in disregard of the fact that politically our nation is a federation of sovereign states.

What John Marshall stated to be the settled doctrine in 1832 has not altered with the years: "A weaker power does not surrender its independence—its right to self-government —by associating with a stronger and taking its protection" (*Worcester* v. *Georgia*).

Indian tribes have rights under United States law and a

place in society as functioning units of political and social content. They cannot be destroyed without leaving a vacuum.

These rights to land and to local government are not the gifts of an indulgent nation. It would be more nearly correct to say that both the legislative and the executive branches of government, on different occasions, have attempted to destroy or to diminish the rights. Only the judicial branch has stood firm.

Two declarations of the Supreme Court will indicate how seriously the political right of self-rule is viewed.

In *Talton* v. *Mayes* (decided in 1896) the Court had to determine whether the Cherokee tribe had violated the Fifth Amendment to the Constitution by providing for a grand jury of only five members. The justices reasoned: "The case in this regard . . . depends upon whether the powers of local government exercised by the Cherokee nation are Federal powers created by and springing from the Constitution of the United States, and hence controlled by the Fifth Amendment to that Constitution . . . True it is that in many adjudications of this Court the fact has been fully recognized that . . . all such rights (of local government) are subject to the supreme legislative authority of the United States." Nevertheless, it was concluded: "The powers of local self-government enjoyed by the Cherokee Nation existed prior to the Constitution, they are not operated upon by the Fifth Amendment, which . . . had for its sole object to control the powers conferred by the Constitution on the National Government."

In an earlier case *Ex Parte Crow Dog* (1883), involving the murder of one Indian by another on an Indian reservation, the Court refused to admit that the United States courts had jurisdiction to try the murderer. This opinion was maintained in disregard of a treaty provision between the tribe and the United States by which it was agreed: "Congress shall, by appropriate legislation, secure to them an orderly government; they shall be subject to the laws of the United States, and each individual shall be protected in his right of property, person, and life."

The Court reasoned that the right of self-government was "the highest and best of all" the attributes of that orderly government which the United States undertook to secure to the Indians. In rejecting the argument for federal jurisdiction in criminal matters the Court refused to lend itself to what it considered an attempt to impose upon the Indians "the responsibilities of civil conduct, according to rules and penalties of which they could have no previous warning" and which judged them "by a standard made by others and not for them."

Such opinions never inspired any enthusiasm in Congress; they had a disquieting effect on minds accustomed to the use of power. For such minds it seemed an absurdity that a nation grown powerful could not control at will the affairs of some unreconstructed Indians. In the *Crow Dog* case the Congress within two years enacted legislation to extend federal jurisdiction over seven major crimes (later extended to thirteen). The legislation was not an indiscriminate extension of federal power, but was specific in limitation. This left unchanged the authority of the tribe to deal with offenses not included in federal law and to define offenses and related penalties.

The division of power between federal and tribal jurisdiction remained fairly stable through the years, with only occasional federal encroachment, but the notion persisted that the tribal component endured only by act of grace.

What the proponents of the use of power found most disturbing was the idea that tribal governments antedated the creation of the United States Constitution and were not subject to the restrictions imposed on the states and on Congress itself. This position, asserted repeatedly by the Supreme Court, was seen by assimilationists as a barrier standing in the way of Indian disappearance.

Some tribal members found themselves taking the position that their rights were not properly protected in tribal courts, and these complaints were made the occasion for congressional hearings in the 1960s. The upshot was a special Indian section in the Civil Rights Act of 1968—the most extensive intrusion into the area of tribal sovereignty ever legislated by Congress. Like other laws adopted in the field of Indian affairs, the so-called Indian Bill of Rights was intended to benefit the Indian people, but, by imposing concepts and practices arising from a different tradition of social control, it becomes a threat to Indian survival. In communities like the Pueblos of New Mexico and Arizona, where customary rather than written law prevails, the provisions of the 1968 legislation, if strictly enforced, could destroy social systems that have operated for centuries in comparative peace.[4]

26

THE COLLIER YEARS

At last that long century of shame had passed. The Native American survived, even grew in numbers, but the experience of living through the nineteenth century had reduced his humanity to stark statistics inscribed in the account books of countless government clerks.

Actually, the survival consisted of more than numbers, though government scribes under their green eyeshades concerned themselves only with items they could enumerate. Of the estimated 225 languages spoken north of Mexico in pre-Columbian times, more than half were extant at the end of the century. Embedded in the language and transmitted to each new generation were the legends, the stories of world beginnings, the chants and prayers of a people. Kinship systems and kin-related behavior oriented each tribal community. Custom and religious practices prevailed even when seriously impinged upon by government law and regulation. Respect for the individual extended to each least member of the community. To interrupt a speaker was a discourtesy. If there was food in a camp, nobody went hungry. This last trait was especially exasperating to latter-day welfare workers, who saw the custom of sharing as a way of encouraging the indolent and penalizing the thrifty.

The coming of the twentieth century brought no immediate improvement in the relationship between Indian and white man. For a while, conditions actually worsened, if that were possible.

A survey conducted by the Institute of Government Research (Brookings Institution) in 1926, under the direction of Lewis Meriam, was the first objective study of Indian life ever attempted. The opening statement of the survey report published in 1928 under the title *The Problem of Indian Administration* epitomized the situation:

"An overwhelming majority of the Indians are poor, even extremely poor, and they are not adjusted to the economic and social system of the dominant white civilization."[1]

While the findings were grim, it is notable that the poverty of the Indian people was discussed as a *problem of administration*. This implied that by reforming administration the people could be expected to adjust their lives to the "economic and social system" of the dominant culture and their impoverishment would somehow vanish. This is not to dismiss the Meriam report as unworthy, since it did focus public attention on what had become a national disgrace. It is evident, however, that the professional people who were responsible for the field investigations and for the recommendations that flowed from the data were reflecting some common assumptions about the Indian people, the basic one being that these victims of exploitation could restore their shattered lives by the simple device of accommodating themselves to the system. In this respect the Meriam report echoed what generations of administrators, educators, missionaries, and others had always presumed— that the Indian people would accept the white man's style of life, if properly encouraged. The problem according to this view could be reduced to details of law and management, assisted by fatherly coercion, as needed.

The report did at one point suggest an alternative policy course, as will be noted farther along.

Conditions, as described in the report, demeaned a nation grown rich and powerful. Indian health was wretched, with excessive death rates attributable to tuberculosis. Partial or total blindness afflicted thousands of individuals suffering with trachoma, a controllable infection. Inadequate and unbalanced diets, unsanitary housing, and contaminated water preordained early death. Family income was low. Schooling, where it was available, was conducted as an exercise in animal training. A pall of hopelessness overspread every Indian community.

Meriam and his associates looked for causes. They reported: "In justice to the Indians it should be said that many of them are living on lands from which a trained and experienced white man could scarcely wrest a reasonable living. In some instances land originally set apart for the Indian was of little value for agricultural operation other than grazing. In other instances part of the land was excellent but the Indians did not appreciate its value. Often when individual allotments were made, they chose for themselves the poorer parts, because those parts were near a domestic water supply or a source of fire wood, or because they furnished some native product important to the Indians in their primitive life. Frequently the better sections of land originally set apart for the Indians have fallen into the hands of whites, and the Indians have retreated to the poorer lands remote from markets."[2]

Elsewhere it was observed: "It almost seems as if the government assumed that some magic in individual ownership of property would in itself prove an educational civilizing factor, but unfortunately this policy has for the most part operated in the opposite direction. Individual ownership has in many instances permitted Indians to sell their allotment and to live for a time on the unearned income resulting from the sale."[3]

In spite of the staid language and cautious generalizations, the report managed to convey to the public a startling exposure of the mismanagement, callousness, wrongful assumptions, and petty tyrannies, which characterized the conduct of Indian affairs—and thus the report provided the seed ground for the era of reform that was to follow.

Since the focus was on the problems of administration, the references to native institutions are noticeably lacking or are cited as negative influences. In this respect the survey staff reflected another commonly held assumption: that native forms of social organization, if they existed at all, were but remnants of an aboriginal past on which no future community structure could be reared. The subject was largely disposed of in this passage:

"Forms of organized activity that are either indigenous or closely in harmony with primitive forms are clan organization, secret societies, the tribal council, and the Indian court. No less important in the lives of the people are the native ceremonies, such as celebrations, dances, games, and races. These forms of organization tend to disappear under the general influence of white culture, or to take on the form of a spectacle and become commercialized, thus losing much of their original significance in group life."[4]

The whole range of social organization was viewed as consisting of fun and games, thus: "Most Indians seem to cling longest to the recreational features of primitive group life and to appreciate recreational before other features of white community life. They cling to their dances and games long after they have abandoned distinctive Indian ways of dressing and living. They love celebrations and fairs and races, and in some places make Christmas, Easter, Decoration Day, Fourth of July, and other holidays of the whites occasions for going into camp and celebrating in their own way for a week or two at a time . . . Gambling is a part of most games and contests. Dancing is often so intense and protracted as to be injurious to the health. It is often accompanied by the giving of presents."[5]

The main thrust of the Meriam report was its insistence that administration be conducted as an educational process. The task of the Indian service, it urged, was "educational in the broadest sense of the word . . . devoting its main energies to the social and economic advancement of the Indians, so they may be absorbed into the prevailing civilization or be fitted to live in the presence of that civilization at least in accordance with a minimum standard of health and decency."[6]

The suggested policy alternative—the idea of "fitting" Indians to live in the presence of the dominant society without being destroyed—was such an alien concept in Indian affairs that it was not even challenged at the time. It became, in the years ahead, the central issue in and out of government. The fact that it became so, and that the first statement of such a possibility was set forth in the Meriam report, was the single most significant proposal offered by the team of investigators.

No effort to translate the recommendations of the Meriam report into action was made in the closing hours of Coolidge's administration. That austere Vermonter allowed himself to be photographed under a Sioux war bonnet, but that was the extent of his involvement in Indian affairs. President Hoover began promisingly by appointing as commissioner and assistant commissioner two Quakers of outstanding reputation and ability, Charles J. Rhoads, a Philadelphia banker, and J. Henry Scattergood, treasurer of Haverford and Bryn Mawr colleges. Good practical men with humanitarian preferences, they set about at once to improve education and health services. They succeeded in persuading Congress of the need of modernizing and expanding the school program, with the immediate result of increasing the annual appropriation for this single item from $3 million in 1929 to more than $12 million in 1932. Buried in the fiscal detail of this accomplishment was an increase in the allowance for feeding an Indian child in government boarding schools. With unbelievable reluctance, Congress agreed to an increase of from 11 cents to 30 cents per day to meet the nutritional requirements of growing children.

Of more far reaching consequence was the attack led by Rhoads and Scattergood on the boarding schools, which since the last years of the nineteenth century had perpetuated the bureau's educational philosophy. The boarding schools, located at points far removed from Indian country, had followed a deliberate policy of removing children from the home and alienating them from family and community. Vacation periods found the children farmed out to white families under an "outing" system, designed to widen the cultural gap between child and Indian parent.

The Rhoads-Scattergood administration succeeded in persuading Congress to close down a number of these off-reservation boarding schools and to transfer construction and operating funds to day schools located in Indian communities. Contracts with public school districts were substantially increased to provide local schooling where day schools were not available within the reservation.

Hoover's high-collared resistance to public demands for action in the deepening depression angered Congress and the country, and the Indian reform program quietly died.

The Meriam recommendations together with the Rhoads-Scattergood effort at publicizing the Indian situation set the stage for what followed. Passage of the Indian Reorganization Act, which President Roosevelt approved on June 18, 1934, was the culmination of several lines of endeavor. It was a compromise measure, which, in the process of enactment, sacrificed some features which later would prove costly, and it became saddled with several wholly incongruent provisions. The original measure offered the Indians a degree of control over the federal employees assigned to their reservations and it proposed a system of federal Indian courts. The failure to allow the Indians a voice in the selection and tenure of employees prolonged bureaucratic control, while the elimination of the federal court system encouraged the movement toward state jurisdiction over Indian reservations, as will be discussed in a later context.

Unrelated to the purpose of the act was a provision extending the mineral laws of the United States over the Papago reservation in Arizona, depriving the Papago tribe of the subsurface rights to their land. The concession was exacted by an Arizona representative in Congress, in return for a favorable vote. The Papago Indians were not parties to the compromise and only after some years of expense and effort were they able to regain full control of their tribal lands.

The only provision which after weeks of hearings and often clashing testimony remained unchanged was the prohibition against future allotment of tribal lands. The allotment law had failed in its avowed purpose of adapting the Indian people to white ways and dissolving the tribal relationship. It did succeed, however, in alienating enormous areas of Indian land—much of it rich in minerals, timber, and grass—but that had not been an avowed purpose. In spite of this total failing, it had taken exactly forty-seven years to enact the first article of the Indian Reorganization Act, declaring "Hereafter no land of any Indian reservation . . . shall be alloted in severalty to any Indian."

The central purpose of the new law was embodied in the provisions dealing with tribal government and property management. While the range of discretionary tribal action was greatly reduced from the original proposal submitted to Congress, what remained was tacit recognition of the tribe as a surviving political entity with definable inherent powers. The act referred specifically to "all powers vested in any Indian tribe or tribal council by existing law," and in addition recognized the right of a tribe to embody in a written constitution the power "to prevent the sale, disposition, lease, or encumbrance of tribal lands." Within this legal structure it became possible for an Indian tribe to function as a municipal body and to exert the common law rights of a property owner.

The legislation aroused expectations that were widely endorsed in liberal magazines and newspapers, but unfortunately the realization fell short for reasons which were complex and varied, as will be discussed farther along. Here it might be mentioned only that the way into the future had been marked, but time was needed to assure the certainty of an Indian future. That certainty was far from established in 1934, and in fact after two decades it could still be questioned whether the Indian people had a future.

The one person who envisioned the possibility of a restored Indian society capable of countervailing an industrialized urban world was John Collier, the commissioner of Indian affairs through the Roosevelt administration. For some years prior to his appointment in 1933, Collier had been a relentless and aggressive critic of the Indian Bureau. The investigations he conducted throughout the Indian country and his activities as a pamphleteer gave him a grasp of conditions such as no commissioner before him had brought to that office. Even more exceptional was his wide acquaintance among individual Indians, who knew him as a friend and champion long before he became their official advocate.

His involvement with social issues began as early as 1907 when, as a young man of twenty-five, he left his genteel Georgia-kin community and journeyed to New York City, where he joined the staff of the People's Institute. The Institute offered a program of political and social action designed to help recent immigrants and economically depressed city dwellers to form themselves into cooperating communities. The intensive life he lived during those New York years—witnessed by the writing and publishing of three small books of poetry—did not insulate him within the impersonalized city. He wrote of that experience later: "I had probed, with whatever resource I could command, the effects of machine technology and mass production and mass communication on the lives of people. I had studied industrial unionism and distributive cooperatives and had worked at adult education, public recreation, and racial relations." Of these efforts, he summarized: "I think I viewed accurately, back in those early years after the first World War, the sickness—not a passing one—of our age: its externalism and receptive sensualism, its hostility to human diversity, its fanatical devotion to downgrading standardization, its exploitative myopia, and that world fascism and home fascism which the boundless, all-haunting insecurity and the consequent lust for personal advantage were bringing to fatal power."[7]

From New York, the People's Institute program shattered by the exigencies of war, he moved to California and for a time served as director of community organization for the state. That experience did nothing to reassure him of western man's ability to avert ultimate disaster, and he resigned. As he wrote later, "I believed that I was done with public work, and I wanted to make the decision final." It was, then, as a troubled and disillusioned social theorist that Collier had his first encounter with Indians, and found his future.

He described that encounter: "We climbed to the Taos plateau [coming up from the canyon of the Rio Grande at Taos junction] in a blinding snow storm just before Christmas. Then while great snowflakes descended at twilight, we watched the Virgin and Child borne from the Christian church high along an avenue of fires to a vast chanting of pagan song. After two days the Red Deer Dance began, and the Sacred Mountain which haunts the sky northwestward from Taos shuddered and poured out a cold, flaming cloud to the sun and all the stars. It seemed that way."[8]

What came so unexpectedly was the discovery that the people of Taos Pueblo had retained something that had disappeared from the lives of the people he had encountered east and west. What he saw at Taos "were unsentimental men who could neither read nor write, poor men who lived by hard work, men who were told every day in all kinds of unsympathetic ways that all they believed in and cared for had to die, and who never answered back."

That Indian societies could survive in an environment so hostile to simple folk values could only astonish a mind as sophisticated as his. In spite of oppression, contumely, appropriation of their wealth, even threats of extermination through wars and pestilence, they had remained viable, keeping their languages, their religions, their kinship systems, and their view of self.

Reflecting on what he found at Taos and later in other tribal encounters, he remarked: "It is hard for us, citizens of an age of giant external power, to conceive that the human, psychic and social values . . . were not created by ourselves." For him, insight into Indian life gave access to "stupendous facts within tiny dimensions."

Commissioners of Indian affairs in times past had come to office sometimes as a step up to a larger political domain, more often perhaps as a temporary pause on the way out of public life. Collier came to office with a mission, conceived in terms of what he called "the Indian affirmative." He saw Indian society as "not fossilized, unadaptive, not sealed into the past, but plastic, adaptive, assimilative, while yet faithful to their ancient values." And he believed that the Indian record of survival against generations of despoilers carried a message to the world, witnessing that "through his society and only through his society, man experiences greatness."

Collier began his commissionership at a time when law and policy extending back 100 years had wrought incalculable damage to Indians, their property, and their societies. Tribes had been moved about like livestock until, in some cases, the original homeland was no more than a legend in the minds of old men and women. Children had been forcefully removed from the family and kept in close custody until they lost their mother language and all knowledge of who they were—while parents often did not know where the children had been taken or whether they even lived. Tribal religious practices when they were not proscribed outright were treated as obscenities. Land losses, as already related, were catastrophic, while the failure of government to provide economic tools and the training for proper land use left the land untenable or put out to white farmers and ranchers at starvation rates. The bureaucratic apparatus had penetrated the entire fabric of Indian life, usurping the tribal decision-making function, obtruding into the family, demeaning local leadership—and yet was totally oblivious of its inadequacies and its inhumanity.

All this has been cited above, but it is repeated here to indicate the nature and the dimensions of the task which the commissioner of Indian affairs encountered in 1933. Collier did not himself fully grasp the complexity of the problems he would face, and to the end of his twelve-year tenure some elements in the patchwork of administration escaped him. He never traveled to Alaska, for example, and he did little to clarify the hopelessly confused rights of the Natives in the lands they occupied. Issues such as the protection of water rights and treaty-guaranteed hunting and fishing rights, which later would come under heavy fire, probably received less study and tactical planning than they warranted. Most of the effort, especially during the first years of the administration, was directed at reversing the enertia of a hundred years of policy drift and meeting the emergencies spawned by the economic crisis of the period.

As the new commissioner, Collier who had attacked the bureau with vigor and often with shocking affect, first had to do a turn around and win the confidence of the Indian people as chief of the bureau he had vilified. It was an awkward situation to be in, and he never entirely succeeded in extricating himself.

One of his first acts was the issuance of an order declaring: "No interference with Indian religious life or expression will hereafter be tolerated. The cultural history of Indians is in all respects to be considered equal to that of any non-Indian group. And it is desirable that Indians be bilingual—fluent and literate in English, and fluent in their vital, beautiful and efficient native languages."[9]

Following close upon that, Collier brought about the repeal of twelve obsolete laws, some dating from as early as 1790, which collectively placed inordinate power over civil liberties in the hands of bureau officials. The vesting of absolute power in the bureau and its subordinates which the laws sanctioned was largely responsible for the hostility directed toward the bureau by the Indians, by members of Congress, and by the general public. Repeal of such laws was not enough, as later events proved, to place the bureau beyond the charge of authoritarianism. That stigma could only be removed by acts of contrition and the lapse of healing time.

In his first annual report, Collier expressed what was to constitute the central concern of his administration. He wrote: "If we can relieve the Indian of the unrealistic and fatal allotment system, if we can provide him with land and the means to work the land, if through group organization and tribal incorporation we can give him a real share in the management of his own affairs, he can develop normally in his own natural environment."[10]

What was not clearly apparent to Collier and his advisers—including the social scientists he appointed to a newly formed anthropological unit within the bureau—was the depth of the conflict between tribal traditionalism and the political and social reforms he proposed to introduce. Field studies of some tribes were carried out prior to the preparation of written constitution under the Indian Reorganization Act. These studies offered good ethnographic data without, however, attempting an assessment of the ability or the willingness of a tribe to make over its traditional institutions, however ineffective those may have become. There was at least an implied assumption, in which the social scientists of the period reflected attitudes prevalent in the dominant society, that tribal groups would accept change if they could see it as to their advantage. The administrator's problem was to demonstrate his own good will and to devise the strategies that would set the tribes on a course of change. In the first years of the administration optimism ran high, at least among those close to the new commissioner.

Collier's insight into Pueblo social structure prompted him not to attempt to substitute formalized constitutional government for customary law, although the Pueblos, with the exception of Jemez, voted to accept the Indian Reorganization Act. A modern critique has asserted that Collier mistakenly assumed, from his knowledge of Indians of the Southwest, "that Indians everywhere would wish to return to tribal, communal life, if given the opportunity."[11]

It would be more accurate to say that "Indians everywhere" were, in fact, more tribal and communal in outlook than administrators, missionaries, legislators, or social scientists of the period recognized. This condition was understood to be true of the Pueblos, hence the policy decision not to interfere with their internal management; but for tribes presumed to be more assimilated, as in Oklahoma, the Lake states, the Plains, the Northwest, the popular belief was that native custom no longer functioned, and therefore structures and institutions adapted to the white man's experience would be readily accepted by all such tribes. Substituting majority rule for a rule of consensus, elected representatives instead of heads of traditional societies or "respected elders," formal parliamentary procedure in place of long recitals of past history and moral harangues at council meetings—these seemed reasonable first steps by which Indians would take control of their affairs.

A more appropriate appraisal of this period would emphasize the failure to interpret the data already becoming available, in the works of Irving Hallowell and others, for example, suggesting some of the ways in which culturally wrought personality persists in societies that have been largely made over in outward form.[12] Indians might want to regain control of their affairs, as they indicated with increasing rancor, but only those individuals already outside of the Indian community were prepared to abandon behavior acceptable within the tribe.

Throughout his administration Collier searched for ways to make practical application of the field methods developed in the social sciences. After the anthropological unit was dismantled in 1937—the House Appropriations Committee balked at appropriating funds for anything so eso-teric—a special field investigating unit was established in collaboration with the Soil Conservation Service of the Department of Agriculture. This unit, known as Technical Cooperation-Bureau of Indian Affairs (TC-BIA) and com-posed of a variety of specialists, conducted human depen-dency and physical resource surveys on more than fifty reser-vations. The purpose of the surveys was to produce plans for the application of land use practices which would bring about full development and conservative management of reservation resources.

An even more searching inquiry was undertaken in 1941 in cooperation with the Committee on Human Develop-ment of the University of Chicago. The purpose of this effort, as described by Collier, was "to determine the extent to which Indian native autonomy in the United States has been affected by the many years of federal rule, which many observers believed all but destroyed the roots of Indian life. Essentially, the study will be directed toward Indian per-sonality at all the age levels as that personality moulds and is moulded by the community." Much of the field work was actually conducted by teachers and other field personnel, after a short orientation period, "without additional com-pensation," as Collier explained in a public statement. This element, he thought, "may have wide interest and possibly wide usefulness," among employees not normally engaged in abstract academic studies.

Elsewhere he stated: "We learned that social research of the cooperative, integrative, and layman-participating type can be helpful to government, even to a decisive extent."[13]

As fortune would have it, the project was launched just a few weeks before the catastrophe at Pearl Harbor, and many of the staff specialists as well as bureau personnel were swept into the war or war-related missions. While the project continued for two years, it was not able to mount the full-scale investigation that was intended. The pub-lished results appeared in the following volumes: *Warriors Without Weapons,* a study of the Pine Ridge Sioux by Gor-don Macgregor; *The Hopi Way,* by Laura Thompson and Alice Joseph; *The Navajo* and *Children of the People* by Clyde Kluckhohn and Dorothea Leighton; *The Desert People,* a study of the Papago Indians by Alice Joseph, Rosamond B. Spicer, and Jane Chesky; and *Culture in Crisis,* by Laura Thompson, a summarizing and generalizing analysis of the project, using Hopi material as a reference base.

The social and economic gains achieved during the first years of Collier's regime—expressed in the addition of almost four million acres to the land base and in a successful though limited revolving credit fund—came to an abrupt halt as the nation armed for war. The reversal is partly disclosed by the course taken by appropriations for administration. In Collier's first full year, 1934, at the bottom of the national depression, Congress appropriated slightly less than $19 million for the Indian Bureau, but the president ordered a 15 percent economy reduction in all federal appropriations, and this cut the Indian Bureau back to $16 million. During the next several years the annual funding increased each year, reaching a peak of $47 million in 1939, then receded each year until it came down to $25 million in 1943.

The record of appropriations for those years does not reveal the full impact of the retrenchment, however, for in addition to the appropriations in prewar years, the bureau had access to emergency program funds of other agencies. These supplementary sums made possible extensive public works and employment on Indian reservations. The loss of these programs in land management and conservation, livestock improvement, road construction, the furthering of irrigation works, and the rehousing of families, together with the in-service training which was part of some programs directly affected Indian life.

When Collier resigned in January 1945, the Indian service had been largely dismantled, its experienced personnel scattered, its planning and management units in shambles, its working capital reduced, its energy spent. What was worse, the Indians returning from the Armed Services and from wartime jobs found their reservation communities at the verge of disaster, the pre-war emergency employment had disappeared and social services were severely curtailed. Though it was not yet apparent, forces were building up which soon would challenge Collier's vision of the Indian developing "in his own natural environment."

Because he would not temper the quality of his conceptual grasp, Collier was sometimes dismissed as a visionary, an impractical intellectual. Whether writing letters to his field officers, addressing a meeting of DAR ladies, or preparing an editorial for the bureau's house organ, *Indians at*

Work, he wrote or talked in a prose style that often dazzled and confounded his audience. On one occasion, after he had spent several hours speaking eloquently on Indian values before a congressional committee, at the conclusion of which the committee members trooped out of the meeting room glassy-eyed, the clerk of the committee shook his head dejectedly. "What a pity," he remarked, "they didn't understand a word he said."

Because he expounded Indian worth, and more particularly, perhaps, because he insisted on extending religious and cultural freedom to Indian groups and proved to be politically astute in obtaining the enactment of such life-giving legislation as the Indian Reorganization Act, he was accused of turning the clock back on Indian development.

What troubled Collier's critics was not that he sometimes talked over their heads, but that he spoke out so plainly against those who would exploit Indian resources for their own profit. By vesting in the Indian tribe the power to make its own decisions, however imperfectly the decisions might be executed, he marked the way for Indians to move in the future.

When he resigned in 1945, then past his sixtieth birthday, he doubtless felt a certain weariness. He had traveled a long way, and yet, with the disastrous war sweeping away much that had been gained, he had not covered much ground. Others would have to put the future together again.

Along with his formal letter of resignation to President Roosevelt, Collier addressed "a particular word" to the Pueblos of New Mexico and Arizona, in which he acknowledged a long indebtedness: "For if it had not been for you, I probably would not have become Commissioner. If it had not been for you, I would never have started to wage my part of the battle for Indian rights and hopes which commenced in 1922. You are like my own people and my own home."

27

REPUDIATION

In less than ten years after John Collier stepped down from the commissionership, Indian lands were going on the block, access to production credit had been all but closed off, individuals and families were being hustled off into urban ghettos, schools and hospitals were being closed or allowed to deteriorate, reservation resource development had stopped dead, the states were being encouraged to step in and take control of the reservations, and, gravest blow of all, the United States was preparing to disavow all legal and moral responsibility for the people whose lands it had taken and whose institutions for social decision it had largely destroyed.

Any commissioner of Indian affairs has the burden of carrying the past on his back. He cannot disclaim it or otherwise evade what he inherited but did not create. He is the bureau incarnate, and he is the individual responsible for what happened and for what may happen in the future. In Collier's case, the irony was heightened by his own prior efforts in reporting on the wrongdoing of the bureau. Hence it happened that when he went before Indian gatherings to explain what was then called the Wheeler-Howard Bill and would later become the Indian Reorganization Act, he encountered suspicion and occasional outright anger. The dissidence within the Indian population was reflected by the seventy-seven tribes which voted to reject the act, in referenda which it authorized.

This dissidence did not disappear after the new law went into effect in 1934 but gathered fresh allies among the disaffected, and the American Indian Federation was soon formed to give battle. Hostility toward the bureau was not confined to Indians, however; among the general public and in Congress itself bitter criticism occurred. Senator Burton K. Wheeler of Montana, who with Congressman Edgar Howard of Nebraska had cosponsored the Indian Reorganization Act, became an implacable foe of Collier's program. Legislation to abolish the bureau and transfer its functions to other agencies of government was introduced and gave occasion for extensive and acrimonious testimony, but failed of passage. Later bills to repeal the Indian Reorganization Act or to exempt certain tribes from its application came to the same end, but again served as vehicles for noisy criticism.

While Collier and the bureau were the targets of these legislative attacks, the ideological base for the attacks ranged over a variety of personal grievances and animosities voiced by frustrated land grabbers, special-interest lobbyists, Indian "experts" of various shades of competence, and an occasional part-time Indian who had been discovered in some act of chicanery and ousted from a bureau or tribal position.

There was, nevertheless, a certain consistency in the attacks which would not be fully disclosed until the years immediately following Collier's resignation. What then came to the fore was the view that the time had come to deny the Indian his past. He must assimilate or be destroyed; that is, stripped of the treaty guarantees which assured the permanency of his economic base, his home, and his tribal community.

While Collier remained in office he managed to hold back the flood of anti-Indian sentiment gathering strength. With him gone, the assault quickened.

One of the first lines of attack was directed at the authority of the secretary of the interior to set aside lands used and occupied by the Natives of Alaska. This authority had been established by a 1936 amendment to the Indian Reorganization Act in fulfillment of promises made by Congress as early as 1884 to "define the terms" of Native land holdings. Secretary Ickes acted under this authority to set aside several small reservations in coastal areas. but when he created a large trapping and hunting reserve deep in the interior, where only Natives lived, he was accused of scheming to turn over to the Natives the major part of the Territory of Alaska. Ultimately legislation was introduced to rescind the secretary's authority. As a consequence, the status of Native rights was not determined until thirty years later—and the cost to the United States was considerably greater than it might have been under the 1936 formula. The Natives, of course, benefited by the long delay, but that was not what motivated those who opposed their rights of occupancy in the 1940s.[1]

Since the efforts to abolish the bureau outright had failed during the Collier years, a different strategy was devised beginning in 1947, and within the next few years became the main thrust of legislative and administrative action.

The movement began as an innocent-seeming effort to reduce the cost of government. World War II with its swollen budgets and enormously inflated national debt was followed by demands for retrenchment. Military forces and expenditures were drastically reduced, while civilian agencies found Congress hostile to "big" government and to the deficit financing that characterized the Roosevelt period. Even the Bureau of Indian Affairs, still suffering from the program dislocations of the war years, was not too small an enterprise to escape notice in the total federal household. In the course of hearings conducted in the Senate during the winter of 1947 the bureau was required to name specific tribes which could be released from trusteeship and the obligation of the federal treasury to finance services.

In that same (Eightieth) session of Congress legislation was introduced to remove restrictions against the alienation of Indian lands, to place the lands on state tax rolls (several states were insisting on the right to tax Indian lands), and to require the Indians of allotted reservations to make it on their own without federal assistance.

The bureau tried to respond to the congressional mandate by suggesting certain criteria by which a tribe's willingness or ability to remove itself from federal protection and financial aid might be measured. Four factors were suggested: (1) the degree of assimilation of a tribe, as indicating acceptance of white habits and acceptance of Indians by the white community; (2) economic condition of a tribe to indicate a reasonable possibility of gaining a livelihood through the use of available resources; (3) willingness of a tribe to dispense with federal aid and guidance; and (4) willingness and ability of states and communities to provide public services.

Commissioner William A. Brophy, in offering these criteria, commented that "only through such a procedure of measuring accomplishments and estimating needs can the federal government discharge its responsibility with any degree of satisfaction."[2]

Cooperating further with the Senate Committee, the commissioner provided a listing of tribes in three categories: (1) those for whom, at an early date, federal supervision could be eliminated; (2) those for whom a longer period of preparation was indicated; and (3) those for whom assistance would be required indefinitely, because of inadequate resources or other unfavorable circumstances. As it later developed, this listing of tribes, of the first category especially, was cited as justification for a determined drive within the Senate to terminate treaty obligations with all Indian tribes. The events leading up to that unilateral effort need to be recited in brief detail.

Not since the 1920s had there been a commissioner as badly informed about Indian society as was Dillon S. Myer, who succeeded to the office midway in President Truman's administration. The commissioner is a presidential appointee, subject to confirmation by the Senate. Myer's appointment was endorsed not in recognition of any competency in Indian matters, but because as former director of Japanese relocation centers he had displayed inflexible toughness in dealing with the displaced Japanese. That quality, it was hoped, would devise ways of dismantling the trust relationship and relieving the United States of responsibility.

Myer embarked at once upon a policy of curtailment of reservation services and reducing programs concerned with resource development. His reason for following such a course was explained at a church group meeting soon after he assumed the commissionership. The pertinent part of his statement ran: "Over the years governmental programs for the Indians have nearly always been framed in terms of basic land resources, and have had the effect of tieing the Indians to the land perhaps more closely than any other segment of our population. The government has tried in various ways to encourage the Indians to make productive use of their land resources and to acquire basic skills in agriculture, forestry, and other phases of land management . . . However, there are and always have been large numbers of the Indians who have no desire to be farmers or stockmen and who would much prefer some other type activity. Yet the ties holding the Indian to the land have been such that we have not had the kind of movement of the surplus population away from Indian areas that we have had over the past fifty years or so in most other rural areas."[3]

The statement contained questionable assumptions, such as might occur to a man of Myer's limited understanding of Indian values. The first such assumption was that land was valuable to the Indians only as an economic resource, and that their failure to use land to its fullest productive capacity reflected a misdirection of government effort. While the Native Americans had always relied on the land and its products for subsistence, land was not a material thing to be exploited; the people lived off the bounty of the land, but they did not demand that it yield more than its forests and streams and plant life were conditioned by their own nature to yield. Without land, a piece of the earth, moreover, people were nothing, for the two were interdependent. It followed that Indians were not tied to the land because of government policies and programs. That tie existed long before white men came upon the scene, and it remained as a force in Indian life even against the efforts of government to alienate tribes and individuals from the land or to alter their relationship with it.

Myer's assumption led to what was the most egregious miscalculation of his misdirected administration. The fact that Indians seemed to be fifty years behind the rest of the country in moving to the city stirred him to correct the balance. A survey of available resources in a selected group of reservations indicated to him that only 46 percent of the affected population could achieve "a minimum standard of subsistence," and it followed that "more than half of all Indians would have to seek their livelihood off-reservation."

A body of evidence had been accumulating since the Meriam survey of 1928, expanded and particularized by the National Resources Board in 1934 and by field studies carried out during Collier's administration, stressing the need for land for Indians made homeless by the devices of the General Allotment Act and for credit funds to develop the lands still owned by Indians. The amounts involved, both of land and of investment capital, were in staggering figures—millions of acres, millions of dollars. Only a very determined and sympathetic commissioner would have risked his political life by trying to rehabilitate Indians in their own communities. Expediency suggested that 50 percent of the Indian population would do better in the city, where other rural folk had already been lost, and Myer took the expedient course.

The relocation program initiated by Commissioner Myer did not gather much momentum during the three years he was in office (1950–52), but he provided the rationale and the program grew progressively each year until it constituted a major element of policy. A small but steady drift of the Indian population to urban areas had been noticeable over the years, but the process greatly accelerated under government pressure until, after more than a decade, half of the Indian population was living in the city at least part-time. Urban adjustment was rarely successful and many relocated families entered upon a pattern of camping in the city with relatives or other Indians, then returning to the home community.

Employment in the city was sporadic, since few of the relocatees had marketable skills. As itinerant residents, the families had difficulty in qualifying for welfare or health care, and children found their schooling interrupted. The return to the reservation did not improve matters, since development programs were not being funded, employment opportunities were lacking, and schools, health-care centers, and other service facilities were overburdened and often in need of repair. It is significant that toward the end of the 1950s the number of local so-called powwows, or social gatherings, noticeably increased throughout the Indian country. A pattern developed of individuals and families traveling from one to another of these affairs, during the summer months especially. Some ceremonies, such as the Sun Dance, which had lapsed or had been prohibited, were revived and attracted growing numbers of participants and spectators. These trends were symptoms of a mounting uneasiness and an apparent reaction to the hostility which government policy engendered. Indians of many tribes were drawing together and finding support in a common identity.

Finding it inexpedient to bring before Congress plans for massive rehabilitation of the Indian community, Myer allowed the office of commissioner to become the center for liquidating the federal trusteeship. Historically, that office had been the advocate of Indian interests; it now became, if not the antagonist, certainly the instrument by which Indian interests were subordinated to antagonistic political demands. The program-planning division Myer established in the bureau was not as its title suggested a unit for developing reservation economic opportunities, but a means of formulating "specific programs aimed at the ultimate objective of Bureau withdrawal from Indian affairs." He appeared to invite Indian participation in this endeavor, declaring, "This Bureau's ideal concept of its role in program development is that of a consultant to the Indian groups." But in case his concept was taken literally, he added: "As a practical matter, however, it is recognized that much of the initiative and responsibility for program formulation would have to be assumed, at least in the early stages, by Bureau representatives."[4]

It was highly unlikely that the tribes, in need of improved health care, greater educational opportunities, employment, and economic growth, would sit down with bureau officials and voluntarily plan their own extermination. Nevertheless, planning for the withdrawal of federal services and facilities gathered momentum under Myer, and when he left office in 1953 "consultations" leading toward withdrawal plans had been initiated with the Osage tribe of Oklahoma, the scattered Indian communities in California, the Indians of western Oregon, the Klamath tribe of Oregon, the Menominees of Wisconsin, the seven Sioux tribes of North and South Dakota, the Sauk and Fox Indians of Iowa, small bands in Michigan and Kansas, the Ute bands of Utah and Colorado, the Jicarilla Apaches of New Mexico, the Red Lake band of Chippewas of Minnesota, the Colville and Spokane tribes of Washington, the Flathead tribe of Montana, and scattered groups in Oklahoma, Nevada, Nebraska, and western Washington.

Almost no tribes were overlooked in the drive to extricate government from its historic and constitutionally imposed responsibility in Indian affairs. This set the stage for the massive assault on the treaty guarantees and civil rights of Indians which characterized President Eisenhower's administration.

Senator Arthur V. Watkins of Utah, writing in 1957, expressed the view that prevailed in Congress through most of the 1950s. In this view, Congress was seen as the friendly ally, the compassionate benefactor. Watkins wrote: "Historically . . . the Congress, although perhaps more or less ineffectively until recent years, has sought in the nineteenth and early twentieth centuries to free the Indian . . .

"Unfortunately, the major and continuing Congressional movement toward full freedom was delayed for a time by the Indian Reorganization Act of 1934, the Wheeler-Howard Act. Amid the deep social concern of the depression years, Congress deviated from its accustomed policy under the concept of promoting the general welfare. In the post-depression years Congress—realizing this change of policy —sought to return to the historic principles of much earlier decades."[5]

Such a view obscured the congressional role in compelling the removal of the eastern tribes, in arbitrarily abolishing the treaty-making power of Indian tribes, in destroying the territorial integrity of tribal land holdings, and opening the way to crippling land losses. The only "historic principles" to which there could be a return, prior to the Indian Reorganization Act, was the long process of diminishing the political substance and the material wealth of the Indian tribes. It was this process of diminution which was resumed in the Eisenhower years, set in motion by the forceful drive of Senator Watkins and like-minded lawmakers.

Two pieces of legislation, both adopted in the first session of the Eighty-third Congress (1953), provided the machinery for grinding up what was left of tribal autonomy and tribal resources.

Control over Indian country—the right to legislate with respect to it—had always been shared by the Indian tribes and the national government. Indeed, one of the bitterest debates during the formation of the nation involved the question of centralizing this authority and withholding it from the several states. Under the Articles of Confederation, the states had forced a compromise protecting their right to legislate on matters within their territorial boundaries, but this compromise was not carried over into the Federal Constitution, which gave the Congress exclusive jurisdiction, except that the tribes retained the right to govern in internal matters. The federal primacy was later reinforced when territories seeking membership in the union were required to incorporate in their constitutions a permanent disclaimer to any right or title in Indian lands within their boundaries.

Beginning with Georgia's open defiance of the superior power of the national government in Indian affairs, states have never been entirely reconciled to a hands-off policy. An area of particular concern was the denial of the right to tax Indian land or other property held in trust. Repeatedly over the years states have challenged the denial, and repeatedly they have lost in court.

Against this historic background the enactment by Congress in August 1953 of Public Law 280, an act to allow states to extend their laws over Indian reservations, was a disquieting invasion of tribal home rule. A few tribes, lacking resources of their own and obtaining no relief from the bureau, had requested federal legislation authorizing the states to assume jurisdiction in civil and criminal matters. The Eighty-third Congress was willing to comply, so willing that it not only granted jurisdiction to the five states in which the petitioning tribes were located but broadened the law to allow any state, by its own action and without consulting the tribes within its boundaries, to extend its court system to Indian reservations. President Eisenhower signed the legislation with misgivings and urged an amendment to provide for tribal concurrence. The presidential advice went unheeded. Eisenhower did not press the matter, and Public Law 280 became in the next few years a principal source of Indian distress and anger.

More disquieting, and more immediately destructive of the legal committments by which the United States bound itself to respect Indian property rights and rights of self-rule, was the adoption in the same session of Congress of House Concurrent Resolution 108. The declared purpose of the resolution was to abolish "as rapidly as possible" the special status accorded Indian tribes and "grant them all the rights and prerogatives pertaining to American citizenship." This was intended to beguile the uninformed by giving a good appearance to an otherwise unworthy design, since in fact Indians had "enjoyed" full citizenship since 1924. Their problem all along had been the lack of education, the good health, and the economic means to exercise the rights of citizenship.

To accomplish the congressional purpose, the resolution provided that all tribes as well as individual Indians in the states of California, Florida, New York, and Texas, and certain named tribes in Montana, Oregon, Wisconsin, Kansas, Nebraska, and North Dakota "should be freed from federal supervision and control"; and all bureau offices and facilities serving the indicated states and tribes should be abolished. Looking ahead to future possibilities of spoliation, the secretary of interior was directed to examine all existing legislation and treaties and recommend appropriate action for the further nullification of the safeguards to which the United States had pledged itself. It was to be a complete renunciation of any honorable dealings which the nation might have been party to in the past.

Indians at first could not believe that Congress would pursue its declared purpose, but all doubt disappeared when in 1954 legislation was introduced to terminate trusteeship and compel the liquidation and distribution of the assets of the Alabama and Coushatta tribes of Texas, the Klamath tribe of Oregon, the tribes of western Oregon, the Menominee tribe of Wisconsin, the Ute and Paiute tribes of Utah, and like legislation was proposed for a dozen other tribes plus all the Indians of California. In referring to the introduced legislation, Senator Watkins remarked: "Approximately 10,000 Indians were thus set on the road to complete citizenship rights and responsibilities."[6]

The so-called termination policy failed to accomplish the complete negation of national morality in Indian affairs, although it moved in that direction. It did, however, precipitate almost a decade of agitation, bitterness, and mounting anger. The Klamath tribe, rich in forest wealth, was dismantled and its assets distributed. Smaller tribes were cut loose from a trusteeship that had not benefited them except to hold their lands intact. But the experience of the Menominee tribe demonstrated the futility of the policy as well as the damaging consequences that could flow from it.

The Menominees of Wisconsin, like the Klamaths, possessed a valuable forest of pine and hardwoods. The timber was harvested on a sustained-yield basis, and since 1910 the tribe had operated its own sawmill. Members of the tribe were employed in the woods as well as in the mill, an arrangement that made for family stability and well-being. The field staff of the Meriam survey, after visiting the Menominee reservation, reported: "One got the impression that the Indians there were doing more work and prospering more than was the case on other reservations, and for this situation the policy of employing Indians in the timber and mill operation was apparently responsible." Profits derived from the operations were not as great as they might have been from a mill of comparable size operated strictly for profit. The survey found: "The tendency is to give the Indian who applies for work a job, whether he is actually needed at the moment or not, because the welfare of the Indians is placed ahead of the immediate interests of the balance sheet." And on this it commented, "Even if the profits are not what they might be with a white staff, the undertaking is well worthwhile because of the training and economic opportunities it affords the Indians."[7]

All of this was to change. Because the Menominee tribe was relatively wealthy, in Indian terms, and was able to pay most of the costs of administering its affairs, the Eighty-third Congress, at the insistence of Senator Watkins, enacted legislation to terminate trusteeship. The legislation was complex, but essentially it allowed the tribe five years in which to adopt a management plan and relieve the United States of responsibility, while the state of Wisconsin was required to enact legislation accepting civil and criminal jurisdiction over the reservation, including the cost.

To maintain control over its resources, the tribe created a corporation, Menominee Enterprises, Incorporated, to which the tribal property was transferred. Management of the corporation was in a nine-man board of directors. This board, however, was not elected directly by the tribal members but by an intermediate body called a "voting trust," representing the individual shares of the members. The effect of this, as it turned out, was to shift into the hands of outsiders power over the tribal assets, and the Menominee people found themselves removed from the decision-making process. In a specific situation, the Menominee mill, which had provided jobs, sometimes at the cost of profit-taking, was mechanized for greater efficiency, "excess" jobs were eliminated, and the ranks of welfare recipients spiraled upward.

Rather than have the reservation territory broken up and attached to adjoining counties, the people asked that the reservation be admitted as a separate county within the state of Wisconsin. This was accomplished, whereupon a new set of problems emerged. The taxable base of the new county was not capable of providing the revenue required to meet expenses, and moreover nontribal residents of the county now had a voice in determining public policy. To meet the crisis of fiscal shortage, Menominee Enterprises,

Inc., resorted to a policy of liquidating assets—selling to outsiders choice building sites along the streams and lakes in what had been a setting of great natural charm. Construction of roads and domestic water and sewage lines to service the sites threatened to destroy the natural environment.

As the disastrous effect of termination began to make itself felt and seen, the Menominee people found themselves frustrated in their efforts to take countering action. With their traditional methods of reaching group decisions, based on open discussions in public meetings, replaced by impersonal corporate procedures they struggled among themselves to achieve consensus.

By proclamation of the secretary of interior in May 1961, the Menominee tribe was legally terminated, but the people did not feel any less tribally affiliated, even though they were finding it difficult to act in concert. Before the end of the decade, however, a coalition began to form among emerging younger intellectuals and the more traditional older leaders. They found sympathetic listeners, among other Indians first of all, but also among professional people—lawyers, church leaders, social scientists—and even in Congress itself. With encouragement from the outside and with their internal gathering of force, the Menominee people began a campaign to regain tribal status. They received unexpected support from a decision of the United States Supreme Court in 1968, the court holding that the hunting and fishing rights guaranteed to the tribe by the Wolf River treaty of 1854 had not been abrogated by the Menominee Termination Act of 1954. This brought about the anomalous situation in which the tribe had ceased to exist for the purpose of holding property, and yet remained a legal entity with respect to hunting and fishing. While Congress can renounce a treaty, the courts have always held that renunciation must be specifically intended and not indirectly inferred. In this Menominee case, the court ruled that the termination act was not to be construed "as a backhanded way of abrogating the hunting and fishing rights of Indians."[8]

The court decision was important not for the small economic advantage it restored to the tribe, but for the encouragement the people could take from it. It led to legal action challenging the termination act itself.

In December 1973, twelve years after the secretary's proclamation, Congress repealed the Menominee Termination Act and tribal status was restored.

The final chapter in the Menominee debacle will not be written until, at some future time, a fair assessment can be made of the effect of the law on the people. The loss of some land and timber, if not recoverable, will be severe in itself, but more damaging would be the loss of a sense of community, if that should occur.

The "freedom" which Senator Watkins professed to cherish for the Indian people turned out to be no more than an updated version of the General Allotment Act of 1887, a pious but legal device for relieving the Indians of land and other valued possessions.

28

THE INDIAN WAR THAT NEVER ENDS

After 1953, as pressure was building up in Congress and in the Interior Department to dismantle tribes and give access to trust property for private exploitation, Indian attitudes changed, and these changes had consequences.

The economic and political promises contained in the Indian Reorganization Act were only partially fulfilled before war and a hostile Congress cut them short, but they encouraged expectations which persisted even when rebuffed. Congress might refuse to appropriate money for land purchase, but tribes bought land with their own limited funds. The Interior Department might concentrate on the relocation of Indians to urban centers, but tribes went forward with plans to bring small industries to their reservations and expand employment opportunities. Tribal councils gained experience in using the political apparatus created by the written constitutions adopted in the 1930s, and a new dimension was added when regional intertribal organizations appeared. Tribal alliances had not been a common occurrence in native America, but they grew in number and in effectiveness as reservation councils matured.

The creation of the National Congress of American Indians in 1944, after a wavering beginning, repudiated the often repeated assertion that Indians could not agree among themselves sufficiently to form a common bond. The importance of these associations, whether or not they promoted agreement, was the learning experience they provided. Tribal representatives coming together from opposite ends of the country, and from a diversity of cultural traditions, found that they had common problems and a shared concern for tribal survival. The sense of being Indian and a people apart from those who administered their affairs, or operated the reservation trading posts, or exhorted them to Christianity, was expressed in various ways. It was significant that beginning in the 1950s, or even earlier, the peyote religious movement had a rapid growth and neglected or proscribed tribal ceremonies were revived and drew increasing numbers of participants.

Veterans returning from World War II and the Korean War and war workers released by industrial shutdowns did not always react in expected ways when they arrived in their home communities. Administrators and others concerned with Indian affairs generally assumed that exposure to the general society and travel to foreign lands would stimulate the veteran and the ex-war worker to seek employment away from the reservation, especially in view of the economic depression that prevailed in most reservations. The former servicemen and industrial workers had in many cases learned skills, including greater familiarity with the English language, if that had been a handicap before, which presumably prepared them for the job market. It was further assumed that contact with non-Indians and non-Indian society would hasten the process of assimilation and that the Indians who experienced these contacts would no longer be content with reservation life.

The actuality turned out to be more complex than bureau planners, legislators, and others anticipated. Evon Vogt's study of Navajo veterans revealed a wide range of adjustment, accommodation, deviation, and disorientation as an aftermath of the wartime experiences.[1]

For some individuals, at least, the foreign experience, the chance to observe other societies, the sharing of a comrade-in-arms relationship with servicemen and wage earners of other ethnic and cultural origins, had an awakening affect; it brought into sharp relief the disparities between reservation conditions and life elsewhere. The anger which often followed upon the awakening was not directed at the reservation world of kin relationships, but at the institutions, the officials, the laws and regulations which impoverished Indian life. The tragedy of Ira Hayes, the Pima Indian hero of Iwo Jima, who tried unsuccessfully to reconcile the disparities, demonstrated how grossly the administrators had miscalculated in assuming that Indians would find answers outside of the Indian community.[2]

Citizenship had not been requested by Indians, and although great numbers were enfranchised under a provision of the General Allotment Act, few individuals exercised the privilege of voting. Even after Congress in 1924 extended citizenship to all Indians born in the United States the ballot was seldom used in elections outside of the tribe, except by assimilated Indians in a few states. Citizenship was not seen as an advantage, and indeed in traditional Indian communities enfranchisement was viewed with suspicion; it suggested encroachment by outsiders into the internal affairs of the community. It also posed the possibility that states would want to levy a tax on Indian lands in exchange for the voting privilege; it was better not to get involved.

But then attitudes changed. Returning veterans and the generation that came to maturity after World War II reacted more pragmatically. Confrontations, often bitterly contested, occurred within the Indian communities over the voting issue, but confrontations also occurred between individual Indians and state election officials who barred Indians on technical grounds of residence or other legalisms. Two states in particular, Arizona and New Mexico, had been defiant in this matter. War veterans brought the states into court in 1948, and were easy victors. Within a few years various tribal leaders were urging their members to go to the polls, and politicians at state and national levels were made conscious of a new electorate. In several instances, in fact, office seekers were able to determine that victory in a closely contested election was accounted for by the Indian vote.[3]

Part of the drive for mobilizing the political potential of the Indian people came from a new force in the field—the growing number of high school- and college-trained young people. The motivation for greater participation in political action and for tribal involvement was not stimulated by educational institutions, however. Secondary-level schools were concerned only with directing the student away from the Indian community, while the colleges were unaware of the presence of Indians in the student body. It was rather a feeling shared by younger Indians that conditions had to change; this was not verbalized in any precise way, but a mood of anger was in the making. Young veterans made use of GI educational benefits to return to school and the Bureau of Indian Affairs provided some minimal scholarship assistance and student loans. By the mid-1950s Indians in college courses numbered in the hundreds—a figure that would later grow into thousands.

Only rarely had Indians continued in school beyond the secondary level, at which point the alienating effect of the school experience raised critical problems for the young adult.

The change of attitude came about, not just because educational assistance became available in various forms, but more directly as a reaction to the policy of treaty repudiation and tribal liquidation sanctioned by the Eisenhower administration. There had been many occasions in the past for protest against government policy and action, but the leaders in earlier generations, once the Indian wars brought defeat, found themselves without real power. For many older Indians in the 1950s the congressional threat of terminating federal responsibility brought anguish but no clear perception of a countering strategy. Their collective experience with the general society of white America was too limited to provide the insight for effective action. The leaders of tribes not immediately threatened by termination legislation preferred to remain quiet, in the hope that the danger would not touch them.

Younger Indians moved into the leadership vacuum. Those who were in college and many who had dropped out discovered that education gave them knowledge and literacy skills which could be used to protect or advance Indian interests. They talked about "education for Indian purposes"; more important, they realized that they could not be self-appointed leaders. Their constituency was the Indian community and they were deliberate in affirming Indian identity.

This in itself was something new. The "returned students" of boarding-school days often presumed to leadership because of their knowledge of English and their acquaintance with the white man's ways, only to find themselves rebuffed at home. The boarding schools had, in fact, alienated them from their communities, forbidding them to speak their tribal language, and in various ways fostering contempt for tribal life.

This affirmation of Indianness, after a quiet initial growth, came into the open in the summer of 1961. The occasion was the American Indian Chicago Conference held on the campus of the University of Chicago during June 13–20, 1961.

What emerged as the notable achievement of the conference was not the wording of agreements, often painfully deliberated, but the realization evidently shared by many that new leadership was needed. One expression of this was the formation of an ad hoc group of young Indian college students that later became the National Indian Youth Council. In the months that followed this insurgent group contrived to make apparent a condition of crisis, which older leaders had ignored or kept to themselves.

Feeling themselves challenged, the older men were sharply critical of the younger for joining in civil rights demonstrations, such as the Poor People's March on Washington. The young, however, did not think of themselves as abandoning the Indian community and its traditional ways. Rather, they were intent on asserting the right of survival for community and tradition. This was the testimony offered by Melvin Thom, a member of the Walker River, Nevada, Paiute tribe, speaking as president of the National Indian Youth Council. The occasion was the American Indian Capital Conference On Poverty held in Washington, D. C., in May 1964, at which he declared: "We must recognize and point out to others that we do want to live under better conditions, but we want to remember that we are Indians. We want to remain Indian people."[4]

Protest mounted in volume and vehemence during the 1960s, perhaps stimulated by the civil rights protests sweeping across the nation, but in no sense imitative of those essentially urban movements. Civil rights were involved, but they were more properly equities and moralities arising out of treaty relations. They were peculiarly Indian issues, understood and asserted only by Indians.

A particular issue that came to national attention during this period was the longstanding, court-ridden controversy over fishing rights in the waters of the Pacific Northwest. Treaties entered into by the United States in 1855 with tribes from Montana to Puget Sound contained almost identical language guaranteeing the right of taking fish "at all usual and accustomed grounds and stations . . . in common with all citizens of the [Washington] Territory." The phrasing of the latter part of that article came to have disastrous consequences for the tribes whose traditions and continuing existence depended on the fish runs in the streams and tidal waters of the area. The signatory tribes had agreed to the conditioning language at a time when "all citizens of the territory" were but shadows on the horizon, and the headmen who touched the pen and gave their consent were willing to share the bounty of the waters with the strangers who would come among them. Rules of hospitality required that the stranger be fed.

The time of peaceful sharing ended when fisheries became a profitable commercial enterprise and Indians found strangers crowding in on the "usual and accustomed" fishing places. The encroachment was seemingly halted by a Supreme Court decision in 1942 (*Tulee* v. *Washington*), which held that "treaty takes precedence over state law and state conservation laws are void and ineffective insofar as their application would infringe on rights secured by treaty." The court test came about as a result of an effort by the state of Washington to regulate the amount and the manner of the fish taken by Indians.[5]

In spite of that decision the state persisted in narrowing these treaty rights, even as it acknowledged that it could not exercise its police power within the exterior boundaries of an Indian reservation where federal and tribal law prevailed. A state court tried in one instance to overcome this inconvenience by ruling that the Puyullap tribe and Puyullap reservation no longer existed. The ruling was denied when it reached the U. S. Supreme Court on appeal.

Finding itself blocked in the effort to regulate fishing within reservation boundaries, the state of Washington through its Game and Fish Department concentrated on off-reservation fishing, and here the ambiguity of the wording "in common with all citizens of the territory" soon transformed itself into an instrument for severely reducing Indian livelihood. And here, too, the courts muddied the issue further by issuing contradictory or inconclusive decisions.

The challenge by state power was not a recent development, but Indians in earlier years offered no organized resistance as they watched their subsistence base eroded away by the construction of dams, which destroyed fish runs, by conservation measures, which presumed to save fish, and by the growing demands of sports fishermen to reduce the Indian fish take. They protested, but their patience outlasted their anger.

All this changed in the 1950s, as moods changed all through Indian country in reaction to the termination policy in Washington. Termination of trust responsibility in the Northwest conveyed a special threat, since the abolishment of reservations would destroy the only remaining defense against state encroachment. The determined effort in Congress and in the Interior Department to put an end to the special status of Indians doubtless gave encouragement to state officials to increase the harassment of Indian fishermen, and this resulted in a surge of arrests, physical beatings of Indian fishermen, seizure and destruction of fishing gear, court enjoinments, and a general heating up of emotions.

Toward the end of 1963 and early in 1964 two rivers in the southern Puget Sound area on which the Indians were heavily dependent were closed to them by state courts. When the federal trustee did nothing to protect these "usual and accustomed" places, the Indians were driven at last to act in their own defense. They conducted the first, demonstration "fish in" on the Nisqually River, one of the streams closed to them by court order. The act of defiance not only won enthusiastic support among Indians beyond Puget Sound, it attracted national attention and to their considerable surprise the Northwestern tribes found themselves sharing their fish-in demonstrations with Marlon Brando, the actor, and Dick Gregory, the comedian-turned-civil-rights activist. Both men were arrested and Gregory served an abbreviated term in jail.

The controversy remains only partly settled, and it is likely to remain in that condition so long as the states in which Indian tribes have treaty-guaranteed rights insist on diminishing those rights to accommodate the commercial and sport-fishing interests of their non-Indian constituents. The Indians, having asserted themselves, can be expected to persist in their effort to live the manner of life to which they are adapted, whatever the harassment.[6]

At the end of a trial in which six Indians who had been arrested for fishing at a closed area on the Nisqually River were acquitted, Janet McCloud, one of the participants, wrote an account of the incident, concluding: "The history books are wrong when they talk about 'the last Indian wars.' They have never stopped!"

So it must seem to Indians who try to hold fast to whatever rights of property or custom they still possess.

Sentiments of this order prompted a small group of displaced Indians living in the San Francisco Bay area to occupy the abandoned federal prison on Alcatraz Island in November 1969. With a certain grim satisfaction, the group justified the action by citing a section of the General Allotment Act, which allowed Indians "not residing on a reservation" to acquire allotments on unoccupied public lands by following certain formal procedures. The group ignored the procedures, but still maintained the right to establish themselves on the vacant land.

The Alcatraz incident, occurring at the height of the fisheries controversy in the Northwest, sharpened national awareness of Indian existence in a manner not experienced since the close of the Indian wars and gave color of credibility to the statement that those wars had never ended. The seizure was at first regarded as something of a stunt whose only purpose was to attract attention and embarrass some public officials. But very quickly Indians all across the country were voicing their support and caravans of battered motor cars were on the road to San Francisco. The Indians on the island formed themselves into a loose confederation called Indians of All Tribes and sent out word of their intention to build a cultural center for their children to be trained in traditional ways. Newspapers began regular coverage of the island occupation. A variety of church and citizen groups expressed sympathy. Money and old clothes were contributed. The Indians in the middle of San Francisco Bay became a tourist attraction.

After nineteen months, with sympathy for the Indians building up all the while, the General Services Administration, which has control of federal surplus property, decided it had endured enough embarrassment. The Coast Guard discovered that the island was a navigation hazard. The Department of the Interior announced a plan to create a national park on the island, which would include a permanent Indian exhibit. The upshot of all this government concern was a predawn landing party of United States marshals, who packed up the Indians and ferried them across to the mainland, warning them not to return. To enforce the warning, armed guards were posted on the island and Coast Guard boats patrolled the offshore water.

The Alcatraz incident sparked a succession of protest actions: The evicted Indians seized an abandoned missile site near San Francisco; in New York City Indians defaced an equestrian statue of President Theodore Roosevelt posed to express white supremacy; in South Dakota Indians demonstrated at Mount Rushmore, where the heads of four presidents are carved in the living granite.

These and a score of similar local incidents were but the beginnings of a spreading wave of contentious behavior that seemed uncharacteristic of Indian ways. It was anger without focus, anger that showed itself in a hundred guises but left no clear image of aim or purpose.

It seemed for a while in the summer of 1970 that Indian protests had been heard and would result in a new era of responsive public policy. The threat of terminating federal trusteeship would finally be laid to rest. The occasion for the brief excursion into euphoria was the message delivered to Congress by President Nixon on July 8, 1970.

The message repudiated the termination policy of the Eisenhower years (in which Nixon served as vice-president); it urged legislation authorizing Indian tribes to administer federally funded reservation programs; it promised improved education and health services; it proposed additional funds and discretionary tribal authority for reservation economic development; it recommended the creation of an independent Indian Trust Council Authority to assume responsibility for the protection of Indian land and water rights. "We must begin to act," the message declared, "on the basis of what the Indians themselves have long been telling us." The goal must be "to strengthen the Indian's sense of autonomy without threatening his sense of community . . . Indians can become independent of federal control without being cut off from federal concern and federal support."[7]

It was a handsome declaration, coming from the president of the United States, and it seemed to take cognizance of all the frustrations against which Indians had battled for a decade and a half. It offered hope in what had become a dismal outlook.

But much of what was promised depended upon a Congress committed to a revision of attitudes and a willingness to restore a measure of tribal autonomy. It depended equally on a Bureau of Indian Affairs prepared to give leadership in drafting legislation and in formulating administrative procedures for bringing Indian communities into the planning process. None of these conditions prevailed. Legislation was introduced in behalf of the administration, but it failed to find support in Congress. The bureau attempted to reform some of its operating practices, but became entangled in its own web of bureaucratic prerogatives and was stymied.

The consequence was a deepening frustration—a sense of being put off with fair words. At an earlier time this might have been accepted. The long history of government-Indian relations was but a long record of unfulfilled promises and misplaced trust. Indians in other years complained; they wrote letters and received ambiguous responses; they collected pennies within the community and sent delegations to Washington, and the delegations returned in greater confusion than when they left. That was the accustomed pattern of protest.

Now it was different. The changed attitudes that brought about the challenges over the voting issue in Arizona and New Mexico and resulted in defiance of state fishery regulations in the Northwest were not likely to tolerate the "brush off" treatment of other days. Protests mounted, were more sharply phrased. Moreover, another change, attracting small notice at first, became a force in shaping events. This was the spread of Indian newspapers, some directed to a local tribal population, others aimed at a national readership; some cranked out on a malfunctioning mimeograph machine in the editor's kitchen, others had the benefit of modern printing. However poorly written and assembled, the message was clear. Indians wanted control of their affairs; they wanted the white man in whatever form—government agent, missionary, school teacher—to get out of the way and allow Indian choices to determine the course of Indian life. And the Indian publications spread the word.

While the leaders of protest admitted to no kinship with the university students who occupied and defaced campus buildings or with black militants who rioted and put the torch to ghetto districts, they were aware of the spreading social unrest during the 1960s and the tactics they adopted were strikingly similar. A Bureau of Indian Affairs field office in Littleton, Colorado, was noisily occupied. Demonstrations against exploitation were staged in Gallup, New Mexico. An attempt was made to land on unoccupied Ellis Island in New York harbor. The Pit River Indians in northern California rejected a court decreed money settlement for lands illegally taken by whites in 1853. The court offered to pay the Indians 43 cents per acre for lands that had brought wealth to many Californians. The Indians answered by moving on lands in a national park and on other lands held by the Pacific Gas and Electric Company, all part of the original tribal domain. University museums and anthropology departments were invaded and the associated scientists were charged with grave robbing and callously displaying the bones of honored ancestors. The Field Museum in Chicago not only returned skeletal material for reinterment in a tribal burial ground, but assumed responsibility for trying to bring about improved understanding between Indians and the scientists who study man.

A collision between established authority and this emerging consciousness was inevitable. The confrontation was brought about not only because the Indians were finding voice and acquiring the techniques of protest; it resulted equally from the failure of government officials to read the danger signs and to offer remedial action.

An incident forewarning what was to come occurred in Washington, D. C., in September 1971, when a small but determined group of Indians attempted to carry out a "citizen arrest" on the deputy commissioner of Indian affairs, himself part Indian, who it was thought was opposed to the policy of self-determination enunciated in the president's message of July 1970. When security guards moved in to block the way, the protesting Indians refused to back down and some scuffling occurred. A riot squad of the Washington Police Department was called, and after more scuffling twenty-four Indians were placed under arrest. The deputy commissioner refused to make himself available, and, in fact, no one in authority met with the group until the Indians were released from police custody, when Louis R. Bruce, the commissioner, also an Indian, heard their complaints.

It was a small incident, but it gave clear indication that the temper of protest was hardening. Even with that warning the Department of the Interior and the Bureau of Indian Affairs seemed unable to resolve their internal policy differences and the grievances of the Indians were unanswered.

The succeeding months brought a steady deterioration in government-Indian relationships. Some Indian leaders in their exasperation recommended that the bureau be taken out of Interior, which administered public lands, irrigation projects, national parks, fish and wildlife, and mining development, as well as Indian affairs, and frequently these agencies pursued policies in direct conflict with Indian interests in land and water. This recommendation coming from Indians was an extraordinary deviation from the past, since tribal leaders had consistently opposed the breakup of the bureau or its transfer to other federal agencies. It indicated a continuing loss of confidence in the government hierarchy.

The failure of Congress to enact legislation implementing the proposals contained in the president's message added further to a growing cynicism. As issues involving the protection of Indian water rights became critical throughout the West, the reluctance of Congress to establish an independent Trust Council Authority was especially resented. When the bureau attempted to remove one of its own employees who had been critical of the government's performance in water matters, tribal leaders protested so effectively that the order transferring the employee was withdrawn.

Late in the fall of 1971, a young Indian executive, Leon F. Cook, resigned from the bureau. He had been recruited only a year earlier, with others, to give administrative effect to the policy of self-determination. His letter of resignation contained a bitter denunciation of the bureau and the department for being "grossly negligent in years past and even at the present" in not advocating "the protection of [Indian] resources." He distributed his letter widely throughout the Indian country.[8]

These events built toward the inevitable clash of forces that climaxed in Washington at the beginning of November 1972, just before the national election, when the administration would be sensitive to public opinion.

At local meetings during the summer of 1972 strategies for political action were discussed. Tribal leaders and their constituents were becoming convinced that the promised legislative and policy reforms would not be accomplished without strong words and demonstrations.

By October the summer of talk resulted in a plan to assemble a massive caravan made up of contingents from the principal Indian centers around the country, urban and tribal, to carry the message to Washington. Eight different Indian organizations meeting in Denver, Colorado, agreed jointly to sponsor the action, to which they gave the resounding name Trail of Broken Treaties—Pan-American Native Quest for Justice. At St. Paul, Minnesota, the caravan paused for a week late in October and prepared a position paper stating the purposes of the demonstration. The twenty items comprising the statement dealt with a broad assortment of legal, economic, and social conditions of Indian life.

When the caravan arrived in Washington on October 30 the Bureau of Indian Affairs locked its doors, later agreeing to a limited use of the building facilities. On November 2, some five hundred or more Indians crowded into the building. Police were called, but were held back from mounting an assault. Bureau employees closed their desks and went home.

Having gained entrance to the building, the caravan members decided to remain inside. With a threatening police force outside, doors were barricaded and the occupiers fashioned defensive weapons out of broom handles and pieces of broken furniture. The building remained in control of caravan members until November 8, and during that time considerable damage occurred. Official files were ransacked and an unknown number of documents were sequestered for later removal.

As early as the first week of October, officials in Washington knew of the massive delegation. A letter to President Nixon requesting a meeting had been dispatched on October 4. Later in the month the National Park Service was queried about permitting an encampment in one of the Washington parks. On October 30, Indians representing the caravan held a press conference in the bureau's auditorium.

Officials at the White House, in the Department of the Interior, and in the bureau knew that the Indians had prepared a twenty-point position paper as a basis for discussion and negotiation. But not until November 6, after a week of temporizing and repeated threats of forceful removal, were the Indians accorded a formal audience with persons in authority. Damage to the building and its contents reflected the anger sparked by the failure to give serious and prompt attention to the Indians' petition.

The bureau was forced to cease operations for a month. The commissioner, the deputy commissioner, and an assistant secretary of the interior were removed from office. Documents relating to important tribal matters disappeared into the countryside. The national Indian community was deeply divided between those who supported the Trail of Broken Treaties movement and those who condemned the wanton destruction of property and records. The outburst of violent anger was something never before displayed. During Commissioner Collier's administration, Indians had protested against what they considered bureaucratic interference in their lives, but the protests were within reason, however forcefully stated.

The retreat from Washington—at government expense, incidentally—did nothing to lessen the tensions that had been building up in Indian society. The change of mood that became noticeable after the return of veterans from World War II and the Korean War, embittered further by the disastrous years presided over by Senator Watkins and other terminationists in the Eisenhower administration, increased in range and in vehemence. Without doubt the spreading violence of the civil rights protests during the 1960s contributed to the rise in temper of the Indian protest, but Indians were speaking for themselves out of their own history of defeat and humiliation.

The nature of the relationship between a bureaucracy and the people who must look to it for services or, as in the Indian situation, for permission to exercise local power, inevitably creates problems in communication. When those problems go unresolved, the relationship collapses. What the national administration and the lawmakers in Washington had failed to realize was the changing Indian attitude. The wars that closed out the nineteenth century brought defeat to all the major tribes and the policies followed by government were those of an occupying force. The reservations were occupied territories and no one thought it necessary to consult the people whose lives were under control. The first break with that absolutism occurred in the 1930s, when tentative steps were taken to restore a measure of local autonomy. The move was not generally understood by Indian people, and for that matter the bureaucracy of the period, still fettered to the past, was not free to allow a return to effective local self-government.

Even that incomplete effort was denounced by those who still thought of reservations as occupied territory under absolutist control. This led to the countermove of the 1950s to demolish what remained of tribal land holdings and tribal political power.

In all those interactions the failure of communication was the critical factor. It embittered every relationship whether the intention was altruistic or something less. In assessing what happened at Washington and the events that followed, these antecedents have to be kept in mind.

The Indians coming back from the twentieth-century wars, finding their reservation communities in ruins and their personal liberties diminished, were not willing to accept the immobilized status forced upon their defeated ancestors. Some individuals of the postwar generation allowed their frustrations to betray them, as happened to Ira Hayes, when they realized that their participation in the concerns of the larger society had not enlarged their freedom to act in their own communities. But generally the reaction was positive, not clearly directed at first, but finding direction and gaining force through the months that saw the occupation of Alcatraz Island, the fisheries protests in the Northwest, and the literally dozens of challenges in local situations involving discrimination or an assertion of civil rights.

The publication in 1969 by Vine Deloria, Jr., of the caustic manifesto, *Custer Died for Your Sins,* appeared at a time when the ferment of Indian unrest was approaching some as yet undefined resolution. The book, with its pungent characterizations of the ineptness of government, missionaries, social scientists, and an assortment of exploiting groups, brought clarity to many issues under discussion. Himself an Indian, member of the Standing Rock Sioux Tribe of North Dakota, Deloria gave articulation to what many Indians were groping to say, and moreover he not only reached a wide non-Indian audience but drew from segments of the white world exclamations of injured feelings.[9]

National attention was again attracted to the Indian presence in contemporary America by N. Scott Momaday, a Kiowa Indian, whose novel *House Made of Dawn* achieved the Pulitzer Prize for fiction in 1969. By winning the prize, Momaday gave convincing proof that an Indian could write about his own people and the rest of America would accept the writing as a statement about the quality of American life. Indians could be seen not as people living beyond their time, burdened by the wrongs they had endured, but a contemporary people making their own way within a system they had not created.[10]

In such affirmations was the genesis of the angry demonstrations in Washington and the militant occupation of the village of Wounded Knee, South Dakota, in February

1973. The activists in these movements, all young, many of them reared in urban centers, affirmed their identity as Indians and insisted that as Indians they had a proper place in American society. They would no longer accept the status of colonial subjects managed by absentee overlords, and neither would they abandon traditional lifeways in order to gain polite acceptance among white men. They proclaimed the right to be Native Americans and to be free of assimilationist pressures. In this, they had traveled a long and tortured journey from the closing years of the nineteenth century.

The happening at Wounded Knee began as a factional quarrel among the Oglala Sioux on the Pine Ridge Reservation and exploded in news columns across the country. It brought together in one angry outburst many cankering grievances. Within the space of a few years Indians in South Dakota, Nebraska, Washington, California, and Pennsylvania had been physically beaten and murdered, in some instances by law officers seemingly with impunity. Power and flood control dams had swallowed up large acres of living space in reservations already severely diminished, in spite of tribal pleas and in violation of treaty guarantees. Promised economic assistance had foundered in congressional committees. Unemployment in Indian reservations ran ten times higher than unemployment in the nation. Reservation housing was an abomination, breeding disease and social disorder. Indians died fifteen or twenty years earlier than other Americans. An inordinate percentage of Indian infants failed to survive the first years of birth.

These calamities were in the minds of the Indians who came to Wounded Knee—where in 1890 disarmed Sioux men, women, and children were slaughtered by soldiers of the 7th Calvary, Custer's humiliated troop. For reasons they failed to make clear, the Indians at Wounded Knee in February 1973 stated their grievances in generalized terms relating to treaty right and tribal sovereignty, not in the particulars of the conditions destroying their lives. As a consequence of this strategy, the public at large watched in bewilderment and dismay as armed Indians took over the hamlet, occupied a church, a trading post, and sundry buildings, which they looted and barricaded to form an armed camp. A potentially sympathetic public read news stories prepared by correspondents who treated the episode as a kind of seriocomic Wild West tale of Indians on the warpath, and learned nothing of the basic grievances motivating the action.

The occupation continued into the month of May, the insurgent Indians ringed by armed troops and armored vehicles, with each side firing in the general direction of the opposing side. Two Indians were killed and one federal officer wounded. Fortunately, no attempt was made to mount an assault. The tragedy of Wounded Knee was not reenacted.

No massacre occurred in 1973, but it could be questioned whether, after eighty-three years, the opposing parties had come any closer to an accommodation. The nature of the contact had changed, at least the brutal aspect of the original Wounded Knee encounter was lacking—perhaps that was net gain.

On the Indian side, a certain sophistication was apparent; the leaders managed to render the overpowering government force impotent, unable to use force without discrediting its mission. Whether this was calculated maneuvering or the unforeseen advantage of being in public view would be difficult to determine. The 1890 tribesmen faced an army that did not have to concern itself with headlines in the morning newspapers; the corpsmen of that day could shoot unarmed victims and expect to be awarded citations. The difference between the two eras was one of degree, not of quality.

The forces of law and order surrounding the Indian encampment saw their role in simple status-quo terms; they had to maintain what then and there existed. Some other body, at some other time and place, would decide whether the Indians had a justifiable complaint and what to do about it. That was standard operating procedure, but in fact no channels existed for directing the grievances of the Indians to a proper forum of adjudication. Deployed behind the forces of law and order lay a greater army of clerks, supervisors, field directors, branch chiefs, commissioners, cabinet officers, and presidential assistants, and none of these knew what issues were at stake. Each within his limited domain had administered Indian affairs over intervals of years, without discovering the nature of Indian society, except that it seemed never to change. Such a premise offered small opportunity, and even less impulse, to search for causes.

Indian society had changed; it had been changing since the first Spaniards rounded up the "loving" Arawaks and forced them to labor in mines and plantations. Change, however, could only be calculated as a departure from the norms of native life, not as an approximation of the values, beliefs, and rules of behavior prevailing within the intruding European society. Indians changed under the impact of new tools, new materials, and a modified or depleted subsistence base—as they had changed before the arrival of Europeans in response to population growth, environmental shifts, and the acquisition of new technologies or social systems. These were natural processes, such as shape the habits of men everywhere, in all times. The incoming Europeans observed changing Indian life and concluded that, given time, that which was Indian would disappear and be replaced by Europeanisms. All policy, all action, all legal and administrative procedures came to be founded on that premise. When Indian society, with seeming perversity, continued to be Indian, albeit modified in various dimensions and forms, the premise proved itself to be a fallacy—but no one in that encircling army at Wounded Knee realized that he was beating a dead horse.

It was to this verity that the Hopi village leader spoke all through one warm summer afternoon long ago. Why to you ask us to follow rules that are not of our own making? Why do you punish us for being what we are? "How do you explain that?" his refrain ran—and he received no proper answer.

Thirty years have passed since that afternoon in the sun, and the answer has yet to be discovered.

29

RETROSPECT

The conflict between Indian and white and the complications of law and public policy growing out of the conflict could have been avoided at the outset if the aboriginal population had been exterminated. At critical moments in the relationship such a policy was practiced, though not legally sanctioned.

It was impractical in the first days, of course; the territory of the Americas was vast and no one knew where to find the Indians or how many there were. Other considerations prevailed as well. A labor force was needed by the early Spanish settlers, and while Indians proved not to be good in the mines or the plantations, since they either died or ran away, still they represented a labor potential and expediency argued for their preservation.

When the American government was being formed another consideration obtruded at an inconvenient moment. The new nationalists, many of them still exasperated because Indians had tried to protect their homelands while the Revolutionary War swirled around their heads, urged a policy of extermination as the quickest way of determining who owned the land. But Henry Knox, secretary of war and the first federal officer in charge of Indian matters, had moral scruples. A nation, he insisted, should establish its character "on the broad basis of justice." President Washington agreed, and the moment passed.

Expediency and a practical morality combined to ensure the preservation of the Native Americans, and to project into the future the problem of what to do with them. This was not an Indian problem, as common reference would have it, but a white man's problem. The Indians knew what they wanted, which was to be left alone within the boundaries of their ancestral lands. The white man could not allow that, since he wanted the land for himself. This left him with the burden of discovering ways in which the taking of Indian land could be defended as an altruistic act. The burden has remained with him.

Extermination never became a sanctioned national policy for a reason that derived neither from expediency nor from public morality. It was believed from quite early times that the red race quickly degenerated when civilization caught up with it; it was incapable of adapting to civilized ways and could only follow certain major fauna, like the buffalo, into extinction.

Men in the fur trade were the first Europeans to penetrate into the interior of the continent and to observe Indian societies become debauched by trade rum and diverted from traditional skills and competencies. A modern student of the fur trade offers this assessment; "Fur trade opinion held that the few admirable qualities the red man possessed were inherent in the wilderness circumstances. Tampering with these circumstances robbed the Indian of his happiness."[1]

The fur traders knew from observation what happened when men of differing values and technological levels met, but direct observation was not a necessary basis for an opinion in the matter. Europeans were convinced of their innate superiority, and they never doubted that destiny was on their side. Imbued with such inner satisfaction, no one felt compelled to inquire into the nature of Indian society. The consequence of this initial attitude reached into modern times. The government bureau created to administer Indian affairs never found it necessary to study tribal customs or forms of organization, and personnel selected for employment were not required to be informed about such matters.

Another consequence was the shaping of a national policy of deracination, to which the euphemistic term assimilation was applied. If the red race could not be exterminated, it could be allowed to atrophy by reducing the subsistence base and by withholding economic assistance, health protection, educational advantages, and access to sources of power in the larger society. Under such a policy trusteeship became a static holding operation against the day when the estate could be conveniently liquidated.

The course of history invalidated the policy and the

assumptions underlying the policy. By the middle of the twentieth century accumulating evidence derived from field studies refuted the view that Indian societies could not survive in an industrialized world. De Tocqueville's woeful comment—"the Indians have been ruined by a competition which they had not the means of sustaining"—spoke only a limited truth. Jackson's removal policy inflicted suffering; it did not destroy the will of the people to reconstitute their lives.[2]

In the space of a short generation the Indian community seemed to appear out of the shadows, much as ancestral Indians materialized out of rocks and trees to confront an astonished invader. The modern Indian abandoned the tactic of surprise in favor of publicizing his presence, his needs, and his outraged feelings. Those who purported to speak and act for the community were rejected. Special vehemence was aimed at the public officials who by law and practice made decisions affecting the welfare of the Indian community without Indian concurrence.

The turnabout was so sudden and so complete, the agencies and the men charged with administering Indian affairs were taken unawares and carried on as if nothing had changed. The notion that Indians were institutional wards was deeply ingrained, even though the better informed legal scholars had insisted over the years that the relationship of guardian to ward was not properly descriptive of the government-Indian relationship. Trusteeship over property, these students averred, did not sanction the abridgement of civil rights. The public officials who confronted the protesting Indians in Washington and later at Wounded Knee were not prepared to abandon the idea that they were dealing with people in tutelage to whom they did not have to explain themselves.

Through a long history of contact between Indian and white, the Indian was by turns coerced and coaxed to cross over from a traditional society and accept a diminished role, most likely as an unskilled worker, in the dominant society. But Indians would not allow themselves to become a labor-force statistic isolated from the tribe. The civil rights riots of the 1960s and the symptomatic violence that continued to erupt even after comparative quiet was restored made it clear that the world created by the white man was not a safe place. It was a world in the process of destroying itself. The tribal traditional world, with its web of kinfolk and its calendar round of duties and expectations, was a world of tranquility by comparision, even allowing for days of hunger. So long as individuals or families could move between an urban center and a viable reservation community it was possible to survive, knowing that they were not alienating themselves from their own kind. They could even gather around a drum in a city ghetto and share a sense of belonging. The city in this way became an extension of the Indian community— and in a remote way a part of native America.

The words of the Hopi village spokesman had not been lost during those years. Every time some high official or some committee in Congress issued an edict or otherwise prescribed how things were to be, the voice was there in the summer twilight.

"Why do you come into our country uninvited and tell us what we must do? Why do you punish us for being what we are?"

With the passing of the years the voice became more insistent, and in fact it became the voice of all Indians, everywhere.

The speaker questioned the validity of decision by force, and his challenge went to the roots of Indian-white relations in the New World. Power had come to the white man, and with it the idea of intrinsic merit. The combination of power and righteousness made it possible to frame the limits within which Indians could live their lives, and call it altruism.

The quality was not in the voice alone, but was expressed as attitude, in the way the speaker coming from his cornfield seemed to carry the field with him, in the curve of his brown fingers, in the slight dip of his knees, as of a man under a burden. He stood squarely planted, asking a white man to justify his power and his presumptions.

And the quality was not alone in this one man of flesh and a living voice. He was mortal, a man of measured days, but he was the carrier and the agent of human process. He spoke for the thousand generations who lived before him to make his world habitable.

The words grew in clarity and depth of consequence as the events of these later years brought to crisis the latent threat of power. Indian society lived under sentence of death from the first landings of an alien race. The sentence had not been pronounced in any formal proceeding and no grand strategy ever emerged. At intervals humane concern even characterized the acts of governing bodies. But the nature of the relationship was always that of executioner and victim, poised in suspense.

In the nation's early growth obstructing tribes were simply pushed aside, the action sometimes slowed by an inconvenient border war. The method proved cumbersome, involving treaty bargaining and at least limited compensation. After a while more direct measures were devised—the treaty process was denounced; the General Allotment Act allowed for massive land transfers. But even these refinements proved inadequate. After the tribes had been pushed away from main lines of expansion and princely territories had passed from their domain, they were still in possession of prime water rights, their remaining lands grew valuable timber and grass, they even owned oil and mineral deposits. Great wealth was still under Indian control, and all of it in short supply in a nation striving for supremacy as a world power.

Here, all calculations and forecasts went astray. The drive to bring an end to national trusteeship and treaty guarantees collapsed. The repeal of the Menominee Termination Act was a rejection of nineteenth-century power methods.

The miscalculation went deeper and revealed the fallacy of the basic assumption on which national policy had been predicated—the assumption that the native Americans would eventually disappear. The judgment seemed self-fulfilling, as Indians succumbed to European diseases and as their cultural adaptations crumbled under the impact of a more heavily laden material culture.

What was not anticipated, even by early social scientists, was the tendency of human societies to regenerate themselves, keeping what is useful from the past, and fitting the new into old patterns, sometimes incongruously, to make a working system. Indian societies did not disappear by assimilating to the dominant white culture, as predicted, but assimilated to themselves bits and pieces of the surrounding cultural environment. And they remained indubitably Indian, whether their constituents lived in a tight Indian community or commuted between the community and an urban job market.

National policy might still have employed forceful methods to accomplish its objective of liquidating the

Indian presence, but the time for that had passed. Two determinants had emerged, one world wide, one domestic, that made the use of force an unacceptable choice.

The colonialism that had stifled self-choice among native peoples around the world and transformed them into dependencies of the major European powers, disintegrated with astonishing momentum, like a spreading contagion. The expansion of member nations making up the General Assembly of the United Nations reflected the break up of colonial empires. In a twenty-five-year period (1945–1970) that number had grown from 51 to 126, and most of that increase could be accounted for by the conversion of political dependencies into new independent states.

The effect of post-World War II power realignments was to bring into play a strong, often vehement, anti-colonial attitude, even within those countries which had profited from overseas territorial holdings. The emerging new nations might not achieve instant equality or improve living standards for their emancipated citizens, but except for the racist policies supported in countries like South Africa and Rhodesia, world opinion was on the side of self-determination for all people. When tribes in the United States claimed self-determination for themselves and insisted that the national government honor its treaty commitments, they found sympathy, even when understanding was lacking.

The second determining factor originated in this wider context. Indians saw their history extending beyond tribal limits and sharing the world experience of other native peoples subjected to colonial domination. They wanted an end to the condition which had placed their liberties in the hands of absentee decision-makers and their properties under the management of bureaucrats. To have met this demand by marching out a troop of cavalry would have reminded the nation of an unsavory past and made heroes of some Indians.

The time had come to show faith in the democratic process which the nation avowedly practiced. The Hopi speaker gave practical meaning to that avowal: Let him pray for the rain that would bring grass and save his sheep. If the white man wanted to count the sheep, that was his concern: the Hopi had a world to keep in order and counting sheep interfered with what he had to do.

If the nation is ever to demonstrate the moral strength

of the democratic process, it must find it possible to allow the Hopi villager to make his own adjustments within a changing world society. Men born out of Europe came to power by insisting on just such a course for themselves.

The possibility of such an accommodation is within reach, at remarkably little cost, and even with some gain in honor and self-respect.

The Congress in 1871, in a moment of pique brought about by the conduct of Indian affairs of the time, declared that the United States would no longer treat with Indian tribes as independent political entities. Thus it yielded to President Andrew Jackson's choleric demand "to do away with the farce of treating with Indian tribes." Treaty-making became a farce only when the United States ceased to bargain in good faith and, after the Removal Act of 1930, used the treaty process as a cynical device for expropriating Indian land.

The Jackson era has passed. The nation has no need now to express contempt for the people whose accomplishments in the New World is told briefly in these pages. The decision was made long ago not to exterminate that people. Let the decision now be made to respect their right to survive in their own lights.

The years since 1871 demonstrated the folly of legislatively determining how Indians should live. Their histories show a remarkable talent for determining such matters for themselves. Return the right of decision to the tribes—restore their power to hold the dominant society at arm's length, and to bargain again in peace and friendship. Only by possessing such power can the tribes make useful choices within the social environment encompassing them.

With such power, shared with all other tribesmen in the United States, the Hopi villager can tend to his corn and his sheep with that quietness of mind all men require. The answer will be with him.

NOTES

1. A FABULOUS LAND

1. Tribal names are taken from Frederick W. Hodge, ed., *Handbook of American Indians North of Mexico*, Bureau of American Ethnology Bulletin 30 (Washington, D. C., 1907–1910). The names cited are those of the Arapaho, Biloxi, Caddo, and Navajo.

2. An excellent summary of early man discoveries in Africa is given in Wilfred E. LeGros Clark, *Man-Apes or Ape-Men: The Story of Discoveries in Africa* (New York: Holt, Rinehart & Winston, 1967). A more technical discussion is in Phillip V. Tobias, "Early Man in East Africa," *Science* 149, no. 3679 (1965): 22–33.

2. ICE TELLS THE TIME

1. Creation myths cited are from Matthew W. Sterling, *Origin Myth of Acoma and Other Records*, Bureau of American Ethnology Bulletin 39 (Washington, D. C., John R. Swanton, *Tlingit Myths and Texts*, Bureau of American ,Ethnology Bulletin 39 (Washington, D. C. 1909); Elsie Clews Parsons, *Kiowa Tales*, American Folklore Society (1929) ; Ruth L. Bunzel, "Zuñi Origin Myths," Forty-seventh Annual Report, Bureau of American Ethnology (Washington, D. C., 1932) .

2. The early literature is reviewed in Lee Eldridge Huddleston, *Origins of the American Indians: European Concepts, 1492–1729* (Austin and London: The University of Texas Press, 1967). A more critical review is in Edwin N.

Wilmsen, "An Outline of Early Man Studies in the United States," *American Antiquity* 31 (1965): 172–92.

3. The subject is extensively reported in David M. Hopkins, ed., *The Bering Land Bridge* (Stanford: Stanford University Press, 1967). See also J. L. Giddings, "The Archaeology of Bering Strait," *Current Anthropology* 1, no. 2 (1960): 121–38.

4. Quoted from W. S. Laughlin, "Human Migration and Permanent Occupation in the Bering Sea Area," in Hopkins, *The Bering Land Bridge*, pp. 409–50.

3. FLINT AND FIRE

1. These early discoveries are described in H. M. Wormington, *Ancient Man in North America*, rev. ed. (Denver: Museum of Natural History, 1957).

2. The dating of prehistoric sites is reviewed in Gordon R. Willey, *An Introduction to American Archaeology*, vol. 1 (Englewood Cliffs, N.J.: Prentice-Hall, 1966).

3. For summary of information about this early period, referred to as "pre-projectile," see Alex. D. Krieger, "Early Man in the New World" in Jesse D. Jennings and Edward Norbeck, eds., *Prehistoric Man in the New World* (Chicago: University of Chicago Press, 1964), pp. 23–81.

4. The evidence is discussed in P. S. Martin and H. E. Wright, eds., *Pleistocene Extinctions* (New Haven: Yale University Press, 1967).

4. FLESH AND BONE

1. For discussion of these linguistic relationships see Morris Swadesh, "Linguistic Relations Across Bering Strait," *American Anthropologist* 64, no. 6 (1962): 1262–91. A generalized summary is given in Wendell H. Oswalt, *Alaskan Eskimos* (San Francisco: Chandler Publishing Co., 1967), pp. 31–36.

2. See S. L. Washburn, "A Study of Race," *American Anthropologist* 65, no. 3 (1963) : 521–31. For further discussion of the term see Frank B. Livingstone, "On the Non-Existence of Human Races," *Current Anthropology* 3, no. 3 (1962): 279–81. A useful summary of physical traits is

given in T. Dale Stewart, "A Physical Anthropologist's View of the Peopling of the New World," *Southwestern Journal of Anthropology* 16, no. 3 (1960): 259–70.

5. *AND STRANGE TONGUES*

1. For early attempts to correlate linguistic data and New World migrations, see Franz Boas, *Race, Language and Culture* (New York: Macmillan, 1940); and Edward Sapir, "Time Perspective in Aboriginal American Culture, A Study in Method," *Geological Survey Memoir 90* (Canadian Department of Mines, 1916).

2. Morris Swadesh, "Linguistic Overview," in Jennings and Norbeck, eds., *Prehistoric Man in the New World* (see chapter 3, note 3), pp. 527–56, for discussion of developments in language classification. Appraisals of language chronologies are suggested in the symposium, Morris Swadesh et al., "Time Depths of American Linguistic Groupings," *American Anthropologist* 56, no. 3 (1954): 361–77.

3. For language classification see: J. W. Powell, "Indian Linguistic Families of America North of Mexico," Seventh Annual Report, Bureau of American Ethnology (Washington, D. C., 1891); Encyclopaedia Britannica, 14th ed., s. v. Edward Sapir, "Central and North American Languages"; Harry Hoijer, "Methods in the Classification of American Indian Languages," in *Language, Culture, and Personality, Essays in Memory of Edward Sapir* (Menasha, Wis.: George Banta Co., 1941).

4. The migration sequence is suggested in C. F. Voegelin, "Relative Chronology of North American Linguistic Types," *American Anthropologist* 47, no. 2 (1945): 232–34.

5. Ales Hrdlicka, *Handbook of American Indians North of Mexico*, Bureau of American Ethnology Bulletin 30, vol. 1 (Washington, D. C., 1910) pp, 540–41.

6. Population estimates: James Mooney, revised by John R. Swanton, "The Aboriginal Population of America North of Mexico," Smithsonian Miscellaneous Collections, vol. 80, Washington, D. C., 1928; A. L. Kroeber, *Cultural and Natural Areas of Native North America* (Berkeley: University of California Press, 1939).

7. Henry F. Dodyns, "Estimating Aboriginal American

Population," *Current Anthropology* 7, no. 4 (1966): 395–416.

6. NEW WORLD PERSPECTIVES

1. One of the first attempts at a general survey is Clark Wissler, *The Relation of Nature to Man in Aboriginal America* (New York: Oxford University Press, 1926). A more elaborate and better documented effort is offered by A. L. Kroeber, *Cultural and Natural Areas* (see chapter 5, note 6).

2. The developments discussed in this section are based on Ronald J. Mason, "The Paleo-Indian Tradition in Eastern North America," *Current Anthropology* 3, no. 3 (1962): 227–78; Joseph R. Caldwell, "Trend and Tradition in the Prehistory of the Eastern United States," *American Anthropological Association Memoir* no. 88 (1958); James P. Griffin, "The Northeast Woodlands Area," in Jennings and Norbeck, eds., *Prehistoric Man in the New World*, pp. 223–58 (see chapter 3, note 3); William H. Sears, "The Southeastern United States," in the same volume, pp. 259–87; Waldo R. Wedel, *Prehistoric Man on the Great Plains* (Norman: University of Oklahoma Press, 1964).

These regional developments are summarized in Gordon R. Willey, *An Introduction to American Archaeology*, vol. 1 (see chapter 3, note 2), and Jesse D. Jennings, *Prehistory of North America* (New York: McGraw-Hill, 1968).

The Southwest

3. Jesse D. Jennings, ed., "The American Southwest: A Problem in Cultural Isolation," *Seminars in Archaeology: 1955*, Memoirs of the Society for American Archaeology no. 11 (1956).

Joe Ben Wheat, "Mogollon Culture Prior to A.D. 1000," *American Anthropological Association Memoir* no. 82 (1955).

Harold S. Gladwin, Nora Gladwin, Emil W. Haury, E. B. Sayles, "Excavations at Snaketown," *Medallion Papers*, nos. 25 and 26, Gila Pueblo, Globe, Arizona.

Emil W. Haury, *The Stratigraphy and Archaeology of*

Ventana Cave, Arizona (Tucson: University of Arizona Press, 1950).

Alfred Vincent Kidder, *An Introduction to the Study of Southwestern Archaeology*, rev. ed. with a summary of southwestern archaeology by Irving Rouse (New Haven and London: Yale University Press, 1962).

Alfonso Ortiz, ed., *New Perspectives on the Pueblos* (Albuquerque: University of New Mexico Press, 1972).

The Great Basin

4. Jesse Jennings and Edward Norbeck, "Great Basin Prehistory: A Review," *American Antiquity* 21, no. 1 (1955): 1–11.

Jesse D. Jennings, "Danger Cave," Memoirs of the Society for American Archaeology no. 14 (Menasha, Wis., 1957).

Julian H. Steward, "Native Cultures of the Inter-Montane (Great Basin) Area," Smithsonian Miscellaneous Collections, vol. 100, Washington, 1940, pp. 445–502.

California

5. Robert F. Heizer, "The Western Coast of North America," in Jennings and Norbeck, eds., *Prehistoric Man in the New World* (see chapter 3, note 3), pp. 117–48.

Alfred L. Kroeber, "History of Native Culture in California," Publications in American Archaeology and Ethnology, vol. 20 (Berkeley: University of California, 1923).

The Arctic North

6. Richard S. MacNeish, "Men Out of Asia, As Seen from the Northwest Yukon," Anthropological Papers, vol. 7, no. 2, University of Alaska, 1959.

Henry B. Collins, "The Arctic and Subarctic," in Jennings and Norbeck, eds., *Prehistoric Man in the New World* (see chapter 3, note 3), pp. 85–144.

Wendell H. Oswalt, *Alaskan Eskimos* (see chapter 4, note 1), pp. 36–60 for summary of cultural origins.

Gordon R. Willey, *An Introduction to American Archaeology*, vol. 1 (see chapter 3, note 2), pp. 446–49.

7. THE NOBLE GRASS

1. J. H. Kempton, "Maize: Our Heritage from the Indians," Annual Report, Smithsonian Institution (Washington, D. C., 1937), p. 385.

2. Paul C. Mangelsdorf and Robert G. Reeves, "The Origin of Corn," five papers published in Botanical Museum Leaflets vol. 18, nos. 7–10 (Boston: Harvard University, 1959).

In the same series, E. S. Barghoorn, M. K. Wolfe, and K. H. Clisby, "Fossil Remains from the Valley of Mexico," vol. 16 (1954), pp. 229–40.

3. Herbert W. Dick, "Bat Cave," Monograph no. 27, School of American Research, Santa Fe, 1965.

4. Richard S. MacNeish, "The Origins of New World Civilization," Scientific American 211, no. 5 (1964): 29–37.

5. Paul C. Mangelsdorf, Richard S. MacNeish, and Walton C. Galinat, "Domestication of Corn," Science 143 (1964): 538–45.

6. G. W. Beadle, "Teosinte and the Origin of Maize," Journal of Heredity 30 (1939): 245–47. A later paper by the same author, "The Mystery of Maize," Field Museum of Natural History Bulletin 43, no. 10 (1972).

7. Robert J. Braidwood, "The Agricultural Revolution, Scientific American (reprint, San Francisco: W. H. Freeman Co., 1960). See also Emil W. Haury, "The Greater American Southwest" in Robert J. Braidwood and Gordon Willey, eds., Courses Toward Urban Life, Viking Fund Publications in Anthropology, no. 32 (1962): 106–31.

8. OF LAW SYSTEMS

1. William Seagle, The Quest for Law (New York: Alfred A. Knopf, 1941). For an anthropologist's exploration of the problem of definition, see Morton H. Fried, The Evolution of Political Society (New York: Random House, 1967).

2. Franz Boas, Race, Language, and Culture (New York: Macmillan, 1940).

3. Jane Richardson, "Law and Status Among the Kiowa Indians," Monographs I (New York: American Ethnological Society, 1940).

4. K. N. Llewellyn and E. Adamson. Hoebel, *The Cheyenne Way* (Norman: University of Oklahoma Press, 1941). For another tribal study see Watson Smith and John M. Roberts, "Zuñi Law: A Field of Values," Papers of the Peabody Museum, Cambridge, Harvard University, 1954.

5. The Pueblo material is from a manuscript report in the files of the Bureau of Indian Affairs, Department of the Interior.

6. The Hopi incident is drawn from Mischa Titiev, "Old Oraibi," Papers of the Peabody Museum, Cambridge, Harvard University, 1944.

9. THE TOOL THAT SHAPES ITSELF

1. For descriptive material on Navajo language see Robert W. Young and William Morgan, "The Navaho Language," Education Division, U. S. Office of Indian Affairs (Washington, D. C., 1943).

2. Clyde Kluckhohn and Dorothea Leighton, *The Navaho* (Cambridge: Harvard University Press, 1946).

3. Francis H. Elmore, "Ethnobotany of the Navajo" (Monograph of the University of New Mexico and the School of American Research, Albuquerque, 1944).

4. The Hopi language is analyzed by B. L. Whorf, "The Relation of Habitual Thought and Behavior to Language," in *Language, Culture and Personality, Essays in Memory of Edward Sapir* (Menasha, Wis., 1941). Whorf's views are discussed in "The Sapir-Whorf Hypothesis," and other articles in *Language in Culture,* Harry Hoijer, ed., American Anthropological Association Memoir no. 79 (1954).

5. Dorothy Lee, *Freedom and Culture* (New York: Prentice-Hall, 1959).

10. THE INNER WORLD

1. For general descriptive materials see Frederick H. Douglas and Rene d'Harnoncourt, *Indian Art in the United States* (New York: Museum of Modern Art, 1941). Frederick J. Dockstader, *Indian Art in America* (Greenwich, Conn.: New York Graphic Society, 1960). Other volumes in the same series by Dockstader: *Indian Art in Middle America* (1964) and *Indian Art in South America* (1967).

2. John Adair, *The Navajo and Pueblo Silversmiths* (Norman: University of Oklahoma Press, 1944). See also Charles Avery Amsden, *Navaho Weaving* (Santa Ana, Calif.: The Fine Arts Press, 1934), and Alice Mariott, *Maria: The Potter of San Ildefonso* (Norman: University of Oklahoma Press, 1948).

3. George I. Emmons, "The Chilkat Blanket," *Memoirs III* (New York: American Museum of Natural History, 1929), p. 135.

4. Helen H. Roberts, "Basketry of the San Carlos Apache," Anthropological Papers 31, American Museum of Natural History, New York, 1929, p. 135.

5. Carl Lumholtz, "Decorative Arts of the Huichol Indians," *Memoirs III* (New York: American Museum of Natural History, 1929).

6. Ruth Underhill, *Singing for Power* (Berkeley: University of California Press, 1938), p. 5.

7. May G. Evans and Bessie Evans, *American Indian Dance Steps* (New York: A. S. Barnes, 1931), p. 7.

8. Ruth L. Bunzel, "Introduction to Zuñi Ceremonialism" and "Zuñi Ritual Poetry," Forty-seventh Annual Report, Bureau of American Ethnology (Washington, D. C., 1932).

11. THE CURTAIN RISES

1. The voyages and settlements between the time of Columbus and the American Revolution are compiled in Herbert E. Bolton and Thomas M. Marshall, *The Colonization of North America, 1492–1783* (New York: Macmillan, 1920). See also Franklin T. McCann, *English Discovery of America to 1585* (New York: King's Crown Press, 1952); Charles Norman, *Discoverers of America* (New York: Thomas Crowell Co., 1968); and John Bakeless, *The Eyes of Discovery* (New York: Dover Publications, 1961).

2. The Norse voyages and literature that has grown up around them are reviewed in John R. Swanton, "The Wineland Voyages," Smithsonian Miscellaneous Collections, vol. 107, Washington, D. C., 1947. See also G. M. Gathorne-Hardy, *The Norse Discoverers of America* (New York: Oxford University Press, 1921).

3. Spanish failures to establish themselves north of

Mexico are recounted in John R. Swanton, "The Indians of the Southeastern United States," Bureau of American Ethnology, Bulletin 137 (Washington, D. C., 1946).

Exploration and settlement in New Mexico and California are narrated from original sources in G. P. Winship, ed., "The Coronado Expedition, 1540–42," Fourteenth Annual Report, Part 1, Bureau of American Ethnology (Washington, D.C., 1896) and Herbert E. Bolton, ed., *Spanish Exploration in the Southwest, 1542–1706* (New York: Scribner's, 1916).

4. The overland trade route was traced by Carl O. Sauer in *The Road to Cibola* (Berkeley: University of California Press, 1932). A later period in the Southwest is covered in Herbert E. Bolton, ed., *Athanase de Mezieres and the Louisiana-Texas Frontier, 1768–1780* (Cleveland: Arthur H. Clark, 1914).

5. Early voyages to the northeast coast and settlement along the St. Lawrence are related in Herbert P. Biggar, "The Voyage of Jacques Cartier," Publication no. 11, Public Archives of Canada, 1924, and W. J. Eccles, *The Canadian Frontier, 1534–1760* (New York: Holt, Rinehart & Winston, 1969). Numerous references to French settlement are found in Reuben Gold Thwaites, ed., *The Jesuit Relations and Allied Documents . . . 1610–1791*, 73 vols. (Cleveland, 1896–1901). Indian materials were selected out and published by Edna Kenton, ed., in *The Indians of North America*, 2 vols. (New York: Burrows Brothers Guardian Co., 1927).

6. Russian exploration in Alaska is reported in Frank A. Golder, *Russian Expansion on the Pacific, 1641–1850* (Cleveland: Arthur H. Clark, 1914).

12. THE GOLDEN MYTH

1. Columbus's letters are quoted from Paul L. Ford, ed., *Writings of Christopher Columbus* (New York, 1892), quotations from pp. 52 ff., 163, 165. The royal proclamation is given in this volume, p. 155.

2. Hoxie N. Fairchild, *The Noble Savage* (New York: Columbia University Press, 1928), and Benjamin Bissell, "The American Indian in English Literature of the 18th Century," Yale Studies in English, 68 (New Haven, 1925).

3. Jesuit accounts are quoted from Kenton, *The Indians of North America* (see chapter 11, note 5), pp. 137, 141, 138, 10–11, in that order.

4. John Lawson, "History of North Carolina," ed. Frances Latham Harriss (reprint ed., Richmond: North Carolina Society of the Colonial Dames of America, 1937), p. 25 quoted.

5. Daniel W. Harmon, *A Journal of Voyages and Travels in the Interior of North America* (reprint ed., New York: Allerton Book Co., 1922), pp. 61, 64.

6. Sir William Francis Butler, *The Wild Northland* (New York: Allerton Book Co., 1922), quotation from p. 70.

13. THE WORLD IN FLUX

1. Annie Heloise Abel, ed., *Tabeau's Narrative of Loisel's Expedition to the Upper Missouri* (Norman: University of Oklahoma Press, 1939), quotation from p. 135.

2. The spread of the horse from the Spanish settlements is the subject of two articles by Francis Haines, "Where Did the Plains Indians Get Their Horses?" and "The Northward Spread of Horses Among the Plains Indians," *American Anthropologist* 40, nos. 1 and 3 (1938), p. 430 quoted.

3. The probable movement of tribes into the Great Plains is sketched in Waldo R. Wedel, "Culture Sequence in the Central Great Plains," Smithsonian Miscellaneous Collections, vol. 100, Washington, 1940; in same volume, William D. Strong, "From History to Prehistory in the Northern Great Plains." For close look at one of the great Plains tribes, see Gene Weltfish, *The Lost Universe* (New York: Basic Books, 1965). For still another study of Plains culture, see Frank Raymond Secoy, "Changing Military Patterns on the Great Plains," *Monographs of the American Ethnological Society* (New York: J. J. Augustin, 1953).

4. The spread of trade from the Iroquois country is suggested in George T. Hunt, *The Wars of the Iroquois, A Study in Intertribal Trade Relations* (Madison: University of Wisconsin Press, 1940). For later view, see William N. Fenton, "The Iroquois in History," in *North American Indians in Historical Perspective*, Eleanor Burke Leacock

and Nancy Oestreich Lurie, eds. (New York: Random House, 1971), pp. 129–68.

5. Culture change in the Blackfeet tribe was investigated by Oscar Lewis, "The Effects of White Contact Upon Blackfoot Culture," Centenary Publication, American Ethnological Society (1942). A later and better balanced review of some of the same materials is given in John C. Ewers, *The Horse in Blackfeet Culture*, Bureau of American Ethnology Bulletin 159 (Washington, D. C., 1955).

14. SYSTEMATIZING THE CONQUEST

1. The substance for this chapter is drawn from two studies by Lesley B. Simpson, *The Encomienda in New Spain, Forced Native Labor in the Spanish Colonies, 1492–1550* (Berkeley: University of California Press, 1929), pp. 23, 19, 27, 28–29, 49, 68, 148–50, 188 quoted, in that order, and *Studies in the Administration of the Indians in New Spain* (Berkeley: University of California Press, 1934), p. 31 quoted. Henry Stevens and Fred W. Lucas, eds., *The New Laws of the Indies for Good Treatment and Preservation of the Indians, Promulgated by the Emperor Charles V, 1542–43*, a facsimile reprint of the original Spanish edition, with a literal translation into the English language (London, 1893). For a later study of the impact of Spain on the New World, see Edward H. Spicer, *Cycles of Conquest, the Impact of Spain, Mexico, and the United States on the Indians of the Southwest, 1533–1960* (Tucson: University of Arizona Press, 1962); and Charles Gibson, *The Spanish Tradition in America* (New York: Harper & Row, 1968).

2. For studies of Las Casas see Sir Arthur Helps, *The Life of Las Casas, the Apostle of the Indies* (London, 1896), and Lewis Hanke, *The Spanish Struggle for Justice in the Conquest of America* (Philadelphia: University of Pennsylvania Press, 1949), and by the same author, *Bartolome de Las Casas, Historian* (Gainesville: University of Florida Press, 1952).

3. Silvio Zavala, "The Frontiers of Hispanic Spain," in Walker D. Wyman and Clifton B. Kroeber, eds., *The Frontier in Perspective* (Madison: University of Wisconsin Press, 1957).

15. THE POLITICS OF TRADE

1. The record of French royal grants is given in William B. Munro, "The Seigniorial System in Canada, A Study in French Colonial Policy," Harvard Historical Studies, 13, New York, 1907. Colonial administration is discussed in Norman W. Caldwell, "The French in the Mississippi Valley, 1740–1750," University of Illinois Studies in the Social Sciences, 26, Urbana, 1911.

2. Contrasts between English and French policies are described in the introductory essay by Charles H. McIlwain to his edition of Peter Wraxall's *An Abridgement of the Indian Affairs . . . Transacted in the Colony of New York, from the Year 1678 to the Year 1751* (Cambridge: Harvard, 1915); p. xliii quoted. The subject is also treated in Mason Wade, "The French and the Indians," in Howard Peckham and Charles Gibson, eds., *Attitudes of Colonial Powers Toward the American Indians* (Salt Lake City: University of Utah Press, 1969), also in W. J. Eccles, *The Canadian Frontier: 1534–1760* (see chapter 11, note 5).

3. Dutch colonial experience is treated in Allen W. Trelease, *Indian Affairs in Colonial New York: The Seventeenth Century* (Ithaca: Cornell University Press, 1960).

4. William N. Fenton, "The Iroquois in History," in Leacock and Lurie, eds., *North American Indians in Historical Perspective* (see chapter 13, note 4).

16. THE ROYAL WILL AND PLEASURE

1. The introduction by Cyrus Thomas to C. C. Royce, "Indian Land Cessions in the United States," Eighteenth Annual Report, Part 2, Bureau of American Ethnology (Washington, D. C., 1902), contains excerpts from the laws of the several colonies on Indian relations. Governor Winslow's letter is quoted from p. 601. See also James A. James, *English Institutions and the American Indian* (Baltimore: Johns Hopkins University Press, 1894).

2. Excellent material is to be found in George L. Beer, *British Colonial Policy, 1754–1765* (New York: Macmillan, 1907), and Helen L. Shaw, "British Administration of the Southern Indians, 1765–1783" (Ph.D. diss., Bryn Mawr College, 1931).

3. John R. Alden, "The Albany Congress and the Creation of the Indian Superintendencies," *Mississippi Valley Historical Review* 27 (1940): 193–210.

4. Wilbur R. Jacobs, ed., *Indians of the Southern Colonial Frontier: The Edmund Atkin Report and Plan of 1755* (Columbia: University of South Carolina Press, 1954). See also John R. Alden, *John Stuart and the Southern Colonial Frontier: A Study of Indian Relations, War, Trade, and Land Problems in the Southern Wilderness, 1754–1775* (Ann Arbor: University of Michigan Press, 1944).

5. For these critical developments in British policy, see Clarence W. Alvord, *The Mississippi Valley in British Politics* (Cleveland: Arthur H. Clark, 1917), and by the same author, "The Genesis of the Proclamation of 1763," Michigan Pioneer and Historical Society Collection, 36, Lansing, 1908. A later study, revising Alvord in some respects, is R. A. Humphreys, "Lord Shelburne and the Proclamation of 1763," *English Historical Review* 49 (1934): 241–64.

6. On Pontiac, see Francis Parkman, *History of the Conspiracy of Pontiac* (Boston, 1857); Charles Moore, "The Gladwin Manuscripts, together with an Introduction and an Historical Sketch of the Conspiracy of Pontiac," Michigan Pioneer and Historical Society Collection, 17, Lansing, 1897; Howard H. Peckham, *Pontiac and the Indian Uprising* (Princeton: Princeton University Press, 1947).

17. COLONIALISM ENDS

1. Principal sources are Helen L. Shaw, "Administration of the Southern Indians" (see chapter 16, note 2) and Walter H. Mohr, *Federal Indian Relations, 1774–1788* (Philadelphia: University of Pennsylvania Press, 1933).

2. Max Farrand, "The Indian Boundary Line," *American Historical Review* 10 (1905): 782–91.

3. James H. O'Donnell III, *Southern Indians in the American Revolution* (Knoxville: University of Tennessee Press, 1973).

18. NATIONALISM BEGINS

1. *Journals of the Continental Congress*, Worthington C. Ford, Gaillard Hunt, J. C. Fitzpatrick, and R. R. Hill,

eds., Washington, 1904–1937, for entries: June 16, 1775, see vol. II, p. 93. Committee report, vol. II, p. 174. Letter to Six Nations, vol. II, pp. 177–83. Treaty of August 1775, vol. II, p. 365. Repudiation of Walton and Taylor, vol. VII, p. 166. Instructions to Col. Brodhead, vol. XV, p. 1249. Discussion of land policy, vol. XV, pp. 1320–23. Instructions to Virginia, Sept. 14, 1786, vol. XXXI, pp. 656–58. Proclamation of Sept. 22, 1783, vol. XXV, p. 602. Ordinance of Aug. 7, 1786, vol. XXXI, pp. 490–93. Northwest Ordinance, July 13, 1787, vol. XXXII, p. 334–43.

2. Efforts of the British to control settlement, the rate at which settlement occurred, and the intrigues between the Iroquois leaders and the British are discussed in Walter H. Mohr, *Federal Indian Relations, 1774–1788* (see chapter 17, note 1).

3. The letter prepared by the Indians meeting on the Detroit River is published in *American State Papers*, vol. I, pp. 8–9. Instructions to the governor of the Northwest Territory and his report are found in vol. I, pp. 9 ff.

4. The article on General St. Clair in the *Dictionary of American Biography* gives the details of his encounter with Little Turtle, November 4, 1791.

19. BASIC TENETS

1. Reports and recommendations of Henry Knox are in *American State Papers*, vol. 1, pp. 12 ff. See *Dictionary of American Biography*, article on Knox; and Noah Brooks, *Henry Knox* (New York, 1900).

2. A good summary of the tribal situation is given in Edward H. Spicer, *A Short History of the Indians of the United States* (New York: Van Nostrand, Reinhold Co., 1969), pp. 52–57.

3. Washington's letter to Duane from W. C. Ford, ed., *The Writings of George Washington*, vol. 10 (New York, 1891), pp. 300–12.

4. Patrick Henry's statements are from William W. Henry, *Patrick Henry: Life, Correspondence, and Speeches*, vol. 3 (New York, 1891), pp. 263, 292–94, 350.

5. Jefferson's opinion in the Yazoo matter is in P. L. Ford, ed., *The Writings of Thomas Jefferson*, vol. 5 (New York, 1892–99), pp. 166–67; the statement on ultimate objective is from vol. 8, p. 214.

20. THE LAWGIVER

1. For characterization of Marshall's last years, see V. L. Parrington, *Main Currents in American Thought*, vol. 2 (New York: Harcourt, Brace & Co., 1927), chapter 3.

2. The Marshall quotation from the 1828 campaign is in A. J. Beveridge, *The Life of John Marshall*, vol. 4 (Boston: Houghton Mifflin Co., 1919), p. 463.

3. The three opinions cited are: *Johnson* v. *MacIntosh*, 8 Wheaton 543 (1823); *Cherokee Nation* v. *Georgia*, 5 Peters 1 (1831); and *Worcester* v. *Georgia*, 6 Peters 515 (1832).

4. The relationship between the Indian tribes and the national government is discussed in W. G. Rice, "The Position of the American Indian in the Law of the United States," *Journal of Comparative Legislation and International Law*, 3 ser. 16 (1934): 78–95. Also Felix S. Cohen, *Handbook of Federal Indian Law* (Washington, D. C.: Government Printing Office, 1941).

21. THE FRONTIER SWALLOWS THE LAW

1. Charles and Mary R. Beard, *The Rise of American Civilization* (New York: Macmillan, 1933), pp. 507, 524–25 quoted.

2. Francis Baily, *Journal of a Tour in Unsettled Parts of North America in 1796 and 1797* (London, 1856), pp. 214, 218, 220, 234 quoted.

3. V. L. Parrington, *Main Currents in American Thought* (see chapter 20, note 1), p. 62.

4. The course pursued by Georgia is discussed in U. B. Phillips, "Georgia and State Rights," *Annual Report*, American Historical Association, vol. 2 (Washington, D.C., 1901). The earlier period is covered in V. W. Crane, *The Southern Frontier, 1670–1732* (Durham: University of North Carolina Press, 1929).

5. For Creek political organization, see William C. Sturtevant, "Creek into Seminole," in Leacock and Lurie, eds., *North American Indians in Historical Perspective* (see chapter 13, note 4).

6. William Bartram's letter appears at pp. 481–83 of his *Travels . . .* (1792).

7. Ralph H. Gabriel, *Elias Boudinot, Cherokee, and His America* (Norman: University of Oklahoma Press, 1941), pp. 77, 107 quoted.

8. The letter to the Richmond *Family Visitor* was quoted by Thomas L. McKenney in a report to the secretary of war, December 13, 1825, *American State Papers,* Class 2, Indian Affairs, vol. 2 (1825), p. 651.

22. BEYOND THE GREAT RIVER

1. Jackson's statements on treaty rights, in correspondence with Dinsmore and others, are from *Niles Register,* 34, March–April, 1828, pp. 110 ff. His letter to Monroe is from J. S. Bassett, ed., *Correspondence of Andrew Jackson,* vol. 2 (Washington, D.C.: Carnegie Institution, 1926–35), pp. 277 ff. Letter to Calhoun from same edition, vol. 3, pp. 31–32. First inaugural address from J. D. Richardson, ed., *Messages and Papers of the Presidents,* vol. 3, pp. 1001 ff; draft of the first annual message from Bassett's *Correspondence,* vol. 4, pp. 97–104, and the final text in *Messages and Papers,* vol. 3, pp. 1019–22.

2. Jefferson's letter to Benjamin Hawkins in P. L. Ford, ed., *The Writings of Thomas Jefferson* (see chapter 19, note 5), vol. 3, p. 214; proposed constitutional amendment, vol. 8, p. 241.

3. The history of removal is told in great detail in Annie H. Abel, "The History of Events Resulting in Indian Consolidation West of the Mississippi," Annual Report, American Historical Association (Washington, D. C., 1906), reprinted as House Document no. 986, Sixtieth Congress, first session, 1908. Jackson's instructions to his agents and the reply of the Choctaw are found at pp. 372 ff.

4. For developments in the Choctaw country see Angie Debo, *The Rise and Fall of the Choctaw Republic* (Norman: University of Oklahoma Press, 1934); also her, *And Still the Waters Run* (Princeton: Princeton University Press, 1940).

5. Events in Georgia are from Phillips, "Georgia and States Rights" (see chapter 21, note 4). A sympathetic analysis of Jackson's position is given in Francis Paul Prucha, *American Indian Policy in the Formative Years* (Cambridge: Harvard University Press, 1962), pp. 233–49.

6. Senator Frelinghuysen's speech is in Thomas H.

Benton, ed., *Abridgements of the Debates in Congress, 1789–1856*, vol. 10 (Washington, D.C., 1859), pp. 519–26. See also the editorial in *Niles Register*, 38, March 20, 1830, p. 67.

7. The de Tocqueville quotation is from Henry Reeves, trans., *Democracy in America*, vol. 1 (New York, 1898), pp. 435–36, 448.

23. WESTWARD THE COURSE

1. The events resulting in the opening of a corridor to the Pacific are recounted in Roy Gittinger, "The Separation of Nebraska and Kansas from the Indian Territory," *Mississippi Valley Historical Review*, III (1917): 442–61.

2. Various proposals were offered in Congress for the creation of a separate Indian territory. On this, see Annie H. Abel, "Proposals for an Indian State: 1778–1878," Annual Report, American Historical Association, vol. 1 (Washington, D. C., 1908), pp. 87–104.

3. The statement by Bear Rib and the Red Cloud incident are summarized from Ralph H. Case, *The Sioux Tribe of Indians* vs. *the United States* brief presented to the Court of Claims, case no. c-531 (7), Black Hills, 1927.

4. The Annual Report of the commissioner of Indian affairs for 1868 contains an account of the events leading to the creation of the Peace Commission, the instructions to the commissioners, and other information.

5. The debates in Congress over the issues raised by these treaties are found in *Congressional Globe*, Forty-first Congress, first Session, 1869, and third Session, 1871. The legislative history is further summarized in Lawrence F. Schmeckebier, "Office of Indian Affairs," Institute of Government Research (Baltimore: Johns Hopkins Press, 1927).

24. SOLUTION BY LAW

1. Felix S. Cohen, *Handbook of Federal Indian Law*, Government Printing Office (first printing, Washington D. C., 1941). Government lawyers during the Eisenhower administration revised and somewhat restricted the text, which was published as *Federal Indian Law*, Government Printing Office (Washington, D. C., 1958). The original text has since been reissued.

2. The Dominican is quoted in Lesley B. Simpson, *The Encomienda in New Spain* (see chapter 14, note 1), p. 169. Father Biard's observation is from Kenton, *The Indians of North America* (see chapter 11, note 5), p. 42.

3. The correspondence between the Countess Huntington and Patrick Henry is given in W. W. Henry, *Patrick Henry*, vol. 3 (see chapter 19, note 4), pp. 253–61.

4. Henry Knox in *American State Papers*, vol. 1 (see chapter 19, note 1), pp. 53–54.

5. Report of the secretary of war to United States Senate, March 13, 1816, *American State Papers*, vol. 2, p. 27.

6. The 1609 statement of Virginia policy is quoted in J. A. James, *English Institutions and the American Indian* (see chapter 16, note 1), where notice is also taken of early reservation experiments.

7. A full account of the motives leading to the adoption of the allotment law, its legislative history, and the consequences of the law are given in D. S. Otis, "History of the Allotment Policy," published in *Hearings Before the Committee on Indian Affairs*, House of Representatives, 73rd Congress, 2nd Sess., on H. R. 7902, 1934. This obscure congressional document has been edited and retitled *The Dawes Act and the Allotment of Indian Lands*, Francis Paul Prucha (Norman: University of Oklahoma Press, 1973).

8. Debates on the Coke Bill, an antecedent of the Dawes Allotment Act, are contained in *Congressional Record*, 46th Congress, 3rd Sess., vol. 11, 1881. The petition of the Five Tribes is contained in part 1, p. 781.

9. See *Americanizing the American Indian*, a representative collection of articles and speeches delivered at Lake Mohonk conferences, compiled by Francis Paul Prucha, Harvard University Press, 1973.

10. The Sisseton reservation allotment record is summarized in D'Arcy McNickle, "Rescuing Sisseton," *The American Indian*, published by the Association on American Indian Affairs, 3, no. 2, 1946.

25. SECOND GROWTH

1. For general discussion see J. Nixon Hadley, "The Demography of the American Indian," *The Annals*, Ameri-

can Academy of Political and Social Science (May 1957), pp. 23–30.

2. National Resources Board, *Indian Land Tenure, Economic Status, and Population Trends*, part X of the Supplementary Report of the Land Planning Committee, Washington, 1935. The population estimates are taken either from this report or from the annual reports of the commissioners of Indian affairs for the years mentioned.

3. The court cases are reviewed in Felix S. Cohen, "Original Indian Title," *Minnesota Law Review*, Journal of the State Bar Association 32 (1947) : 28–59.

4. The Civil Rights Act of 1968 and its application to Indian tribes is discussed in Monroe E. Price, *Law and the American Indian* (Indianapolis: The Bobbs-Merrill Co., 1973) pp. 742–78.

26. THE COLLIER YEARS

1. Lewis Meriam et al., *The Problem of Indian Administration*, Institute for Government Research (Baltimore: Johns Hopkins University Press, 1928).

2. Ibid., p. 5.

3. Ibid., p. 7.

4. Ibid., p. 629.

5. Ibid., p. 630.

6. Ibid., p. 86.

7. John Collier, *The Indians of the Americas* (New York: Norton and Co., 1947), pp. 17–18.

8. Ibid., p. 19 passim.

9. Office of Indian Affairs circular no. 2970 (January 1934).

10. Annual Report, secretary of the interior (1953), p. 109.

11. Lawrence C. Kelly, "John Collier and the Indian New Deal" (Paper presented at National Archives Conference on Research in the History of Indian-White Relations, Washington, D. C., June 1972).

12. A. Irving Hallowell, *Culture and Experience* (Philadelphia: University of Pennsylvania Press, 1955) contains research findings in culture and personality published in the 1930s and 1940s.

13. Laura Thompson, *Culture in Crisis*, foreword by John Collier (New York: Harper & Bros., 1950), p. xiii.

27. REPUDIATION

1. This settlement is summarized in D'Arcy McNickle, *Native American Tribalism* (New York: Oxford University Press, 1973), pp. 151–59.

2. Annual Report, secretary of the interior (1947), pp. 348–49.

3. Speech before National Council of Churches, Buck Hill Falls, Pennsylvania, December 1951.

4. Annual Report, secretary of the interior (1952), p. 393.

5. Arthur V. Watkins, "Termination of Federal Supervision," *The Annals*, American Academy of Political and Social Science (May 1957): 47–55.

6. Ibid., p. 51.

7. Lewis Meriam, *The Problem of Indian Administration* (see chapter 26, note 1).

8. Monroe E. Price, *Law and the American Indian* (see chapter 25, note 4).

28. THE INDIAN WAR THAT NEVER ENDS

1. Evon Z. Vogt, "Navaho Veterans: A Study of Changing Values," Papers of the Peabody Museum, Harvard University, vol. 41, no. 1, 1951.

2. The Ira Hayes story is told briefly in Harold E. Fey and D'Arcy McNickle, *Indians and Other Americans* (New York: Harper & Row, 1970 edition), pp. 37–48.

3. Reviewed in Helen L. Peterson, "American Indian Political Participation," *The Annals*, pp. 116–26.

4. Quoted in Alvin M. Josephy, Jr., *Red Power: The American Indians' Fight for Freedom* (New York: American Heritage Press, 1971), pp. 65–69.

5. The contested issues are reviewed in "Uncommon Controversy" (Report prepared for the American Friends Service Committee, Seattle, University of Washington Press, 1970).

6. The legal issues are discussed in Monroe E. Price, *Law and the American Indian* (see chapter 25, note 4), pp. 294–309.

7. Message from the president of the United States,

House of Representatives document no. 91–363, Ninety-first Congress, second Session, July 8, 1970.

8. Reported in *Akwesasne Notes* 3, no. 8 (Autumn 1971): 5.

9. Vine Deloria, Jr., *Custer Died for Your Sins* (New York: Macmillan, 1969).

10. N. Scott Momaday, *House Made of Dawn* (New York: Harper & Row, 1968).

29. RETROSPECT

1. Lewis O. Saum, *The Fur Trader and the Indian* (Seattle: University of Washington Press, 1965).

2. See, for example, John Provinse, ed., "The American Indian in Transition," Wenner-Gren Foundation Supper Conference, *American Anthropologist* 56, no. 3 (1954): 387–94.

ACKNOWLEDGMENTS

I take this occasion to express my gratitude to the tolerant teachers I have had as co-workers in the Bureau of Indian Affairs—workers who labor incredibly hard at a task they understand better than any one else, for negligible rewards.

I am particularly indebted to former Commissioner John Collier for suggesting that I do the Indian volume in "The Peoples of America Series," and to his successor, William A. Brophy, and to Acting Commissioner William Zimmerman, Jr., for administrative arrangements by which it was possible for me to take leave from a hard-pressed office.

I would acknowledge the helpfulness of the Library of Congress in making available the Library's excellent facilities for research and writing; the Archivist of the United States in allowing full access to the search rooms of the National Archives; Miss Barbara Ethier in preparing the manuscript; Miss Ayako Honda in compiling bibliography; and Alexander and Dorothea Leighton in making possible the summer in Nova Scotia, where the final writing took place.

And let it not go unsaid that I owe a special debt to my wife, Roma, for her labors in checking sources, preparing the Notes, and general editorial drudgery.

The following authors and publishers were kind enough to grant permission to quote from their publications:

Mrs. I. H. Alvord, *The Mississippi Valley in British Politics,* by Clarence W. Alvord, Arthur H. Clark Company, Cleveland, 1917.

Appleton-Century-Crofts, Inc., *Democracy in America,* by Alexis de Tocqueville, translated by Henry Reeves, 1898.

J. J. Augustin, Incorporated, *Law and Status among the Kiowa Indians,* Monograph I, 1940, American Ethnological Society.

A. S. Barnes and Company, *American Indian Dance Steps*, by Bessie and May G. Evans, 1931.

Brookings Institution, *The Problem of Indian Administration*, by Lewis Meriam and Associates, 1928.

Burrows Brothers Guardian Co., *The Indians of North America*, Edna Kenton, editor, 1927.

Carnegie Institution of Washington, *Correspondence of Andrew Jackson*, John S. Bassett, editor, 1926–35.

Harcourt, Brace and Company, Inc., *Main Currents in American Thought*, by Vernon Louis Parrington, 1927.

Harvard University Press, *The Navaho*, by Clyde Kluckhohn and Dorothea C. Leighton, 1946; *An Abridgment of the Indian Affairs Transacted in the Colony of New York, 1678–1751*, by Peter Wraxall, Charles H. McIlwain, editor, 1915.

Melville J. Herskovits, editor, *The American Anthropologist*, "Where Did the Plains Indians Get Their Horses?" by Francis Haines, 1938; "The Nature of the Potlatch," by H. G. Barnett, 1938; "American Culture History," by Robert H. Lowie, 1940.

Houghton Mifflin Company, *The Life of John Marshall*, by A. J. Beveridge, 1919.

Alfred A. Knopf, Inc., *The Quest for Law*, by William Seagle, 1941.

The Macmillan Company, *Race, Language, and Culture*, by Franz Boas, 1940; *The Rise of American Civilization*, by Charles and Mary Beard, 1927, 1930, 1933; *British Colonial Policy, 1754–1765*, by George Louis Beer, 1907.

University of California Press, *Cultural and Natural Areas of Native North America*, by Alfred L. Kroeber, 1939; *The Road to Cibola*, by Carl O. Sauer, 1932; "Origins of American Agriculture," by Carl O. Sauer, in *Essays in Anthropology in Honor of Alfred Louis Kroeber*, 1936; *Singing for Power*, by Ruth Underhill, 1938; *The Encomienda in New Spain*, by Lesley Byrd Simpson, 1929.

University of Oklahoma Press, *Tabeau's Narrative of Loisel's Expedition to the Upper Missouri*, Annie Heloise Abel, editor, 1939; *McGillivray of the Creeks*, by John Walton Caughey, 1938; *Elias Boudinot, Cherokee, and His America*, by Ralph Henry Gabriel, 1941; *The Cheyenne Way*, by K. N. Llewellyn and E. Adamson Hoebel, 1941.

Yale University Press, *The Agricultural and Hunting Methods of the Navaho Indians*, by W. W. Hill, 1938.